What Happened
to the Hippies?

D0613421

What Happened to the Hippies?

Voices and Perspectives

EDITED BY Stewart L. Rogers

McFarland & Company, Inc., Publishers
Jefferson, North Carolina

LIBRARY OF CONGRESS CATALOGUING-IN-PUBLICATION DATA

Names: Rogers, Stewart L., editor.
Title: What happened to the hippies? : voices and perspectives / edited
by Stewart L. Rogers.
Description: Jefferson, N.C. : McFarland & Company, Inc., Publishers,
2019. | Includes index.
Identifiers: LCCN 2019036439 | ISBN 9781476678955 (paperback) ∞
ISBN 9781476637716 (ebook)
Subjects: LCSH: Hippies—United States—History. | Hippies—United
States—Interviews. | Social history—1960–1970. | Social history—
1970– | United States—Social conditions—1960–1980.
Classification: LCC HQ799.7 W47 2019 | DDC 305.5/680973—dc23
LC record available at https://lccn.loc.gov/2019036439

BRITISH LIBRARY CATALOGUING DATA ARE AVAILABLE

ISBN (print) 978-1-4766-7895-5
ISBN (ebook) 978-1-4766-3771-6

Front cover: *from top* A female demonstrator offers a flower to
military police, October 21, 1967 (National Archives); poster image
for United Women's Contingent demonstration, 1971 (Library of
Congress); a scene from the documentary *Woodstock*, 1970 (Warner
Brothers Pictures/Photofest)

Printed in the United States of America

McFarland & Company, Inc., Publishers
Box 611, Jefferson, North Carolina 28640
www.mcfarlandpub.com

This book is dedicated to my beautiful sister who joined the Spirit in the Sky last year.

She was the hippie I wish to be, creative, strong, and loving to all. She lived a simple life with few possessions and did what she could to make this world a better place. Despite being tortured by mental demons most of her life, she never lashed out at anyone and found some degree of peace in her solitude.

I will always remember her sitting on the steps outside her small apartment on a cloudless summer day in 1970 strumming her guitar as a cool breeze caressed her long blonde hair. She was pure and innocent, flesh-and-blood proof that goodness can survive in a world too often filled with greed and anger.

I miss her. But I know that her love is still alive in this world.

Thanks "B!"

STEWART

Acknowledgments

I wish to extend my deepest appreciation to assistant editors Lucille Rogers and Tim Mata for their exhaustive research and meticulous proofreading. I am also particularly grateful to the insightful, honest writers who contributed their recollections to this book.

Table of Contents

Preface

For me, 1970 was the beginning of something profound and beautiful. It was the first step on that "long and winding road" to love, peace, and freedom. It was the year I took Timothy Leary's advice to "turn on, tune in, and drop out." It was the year I became a self-proclaimed "hippie."

True, I was a latecomer to the party. After all, the Summer of Love was in '67; Led Zeppelin was formed in '68; and Woodstock was in '69. Still, you get there when you get there.

Nineteen seventy was the year I turned 20 and transferred from a small religious college to a huge coed university. That was the year I first made love, smoked a bowl, dropped a tab, rocked to Santana, grew long hair, and marched on Washington. That was the year I read Malcolm X, discovered existentialism, and meditated to Ravi Shankar. That was the year I dismantled my old identity and began the slow painful journey of replacing it with a new one.

In 1970, I was tired of following rules that didn't make sense and pleasing people I couldn't respect. I was tired of chasing goals that didn't really matter and squeezing myself into smaller and smaller boxes. I was tired of observing life. I was ready to live it. I longed to feel without intellectualizing, to know without thinking, and to act without fear.

I saw myself as an authentic pioneer of a new world built on love and understanding, a world where the generous outnumber the greedy, where opportunities belong to the many, and people resolve their differences without killing each other. With all my heart, I believed that such a world was not simply possible, but inevitable.

I wasn't alone. My brothers and sisters were everywhere. Some organized demonstrations, shut-down universities, and periodically wound up in jail for their beliefs. The rest of us were followers, faces in the crowd, content to speak out when the price wasn't too high or too inconvenient. Still, we all drank the Kool-Aid (thanks Ken), sang to the choir, and immersed ourselves emotionally, if not physically, in the movement to save the world.

It's ironic that I would think of myself as a hippie. After all, labels are against my religion—I rarely use the term to describe myself. In fact, the name has most commonly been used as an insult by close-minded, reactionary folks trying to degrade those with longer hair and more liberal views than their own. And yet, when I saw my peers celebrating life and challenging the moral evils back in the day, I wanted to belong. I wanted to be part of something honest and true, something morally good and spiritually fulfilling. I was an instant believer in a magical, indefinable hippie nirvana.

Of course, no one really knows what being a "hippie" means. In fact, I'm not even sure where the word came from. The story I like best is that Malcolm X invented the term to describe white dudes trying to act "hip," but never quite making it.

There's no hippie bible; no pledge to recite; no membership card to sign. You don't have to dress, talk, or act in any particular way. That's the beauty of it! It is what you think it is. You're in when you say you are.

And yet, in my opinion, hippies were—and still are—united by a set of common values. We believe that love is the most powerful force in the universe, that peace is our highest purpose, that freedom of thought and action belongs to all, and that the accumulation of money is a dead-end.

We believe in making love not war, giving power to the people, getting back to the land, opening the doors of perception, feeding our heads, giving peace a chance, and doing our own thing. We believe in rock and roll, free speech, and free love. We believe in flower power, Black Power, civil rights, women's lib, gay liberation, and being part of the solution. We believe in love-ins, be-ins, and teach-ins. We believe that no nukes are good nukes, money can't buy happiness, and that love is all you need.

Exhilarated with hope, giddy with freedom, turned on with idealism, the years of 1970–1973 were by far the best time of my life! To this day, I've never laughed so hard, thought so deeply, loved so passionately, or acted so authentically as I did in that luscious sliver of time.

Tragically for me, the magic of those years too quickly dissolved into marital chaos and the relentless struggle for money. By 1974, without realizing it, I began descending deeper and deeper into a financial and moral pit from which I did not surface for another 30 years.

I had rejected war but couldn't find peace of mind. I had rejected greed but couldn't pay my bills. I had rejected racism but couldn't accept myself. I had rejected religion but felt spiritually empty. I had rejected sexual norms but couldn't find real love. I had rejected traditional careers but couldn't find my place in the working world. I had rejected my parents but couldn't stop wanting their approval. I had rejected sobriety but couldn't enjoy the high. I had rejected the old answers but couldn't find the new ones.

Finally, after suffocating years of dead-end streets and never-ending hangovers, I found myself lying in a metaphorical open grave, looking up into the cold black sky. It was the moment I had secretly prayed for. One more swig, one more hit, one more failure, and I knew that I'd be on that peace train at last, forever free of a hypocritical world that had promised so much but delivered so little. The choice was mine. It had always been mine, starting way back in 1970.

Thankfully, I stopped using and started climbing. When I finally crawled out of the hole and onto solid ground, I realized that my old hippie values hadn't abandoned me. I just couldn't see them in the dark.

Possessed with the clarity that only sobriety and peaceful living can bestow, I began remembering the past with a new perspective, reexamining the slogans, people, music, and events that had defined me then and deciding what they mean to me now. Slowly, I began to fuse my old values with my real-world experiences to create a 21st century version of myself who is happier than he's ever been.

So, what happened to my brother and sisters, the ones who shared my hippie values back in the day?

I am reminded of a story I learned in elementary school about the "Lost Colony," one of the earliest British settlements in the New World, that mysteriously disappeared from Roanoke Island, NC, between 1587 and 1590. A hundred colonists vanished without a trace. Perhaps they were killed by the native people or assimilated by them. No one knows for sure.

In its prime, the Hippie Nation was a powerful, moral force for a more peaceful world and a more open society. We were counted in the millions—east and west, black and white, rich and poor, gay and straight, young and old. We lived everywhere and nowhere. We shared a common passion for love, peace, and freedom that bound us together without membership cards or name tags.

Then, without warning, it seems that the Hippie Nation quietly, almost imperceptibly, disappeared without a trace. Perhaps it was killed by the Establishment or assimilated by it.

No one knows for sure. In the summer of 2018, I began looking for survivors and recording their stories. This book is the result.

This volume is a collection of memoirs written by 50-plus individuals who considered themselves hippies in the 1960s and early '70s and who responded to my request for "Old Hippie Writers" in Craigslist ads across the country. Each memoir compares what the writer did or believed in the hippie era to what he/she does and believes today. My personal comments begin each chapter. Compilations of important events and quotes illuminating the hippie movement conclude the book.

With a handful of exceptions, this book includes every article that I received. I have made no attempt to censure or manipulate anyone's point of view. I have no interest in formulating broad sociological conclusions or speculating whether the contributors to this book represent a scientific cross-section of the long-lost Hippie Nation. Instead, I've assembled a collage of self-identified hippies from which you can draw your own conclusions

I am deeply grateful to everyone who contributed to this book. Their honesty, energy, and insight have opened doors long closed over the decades. To each, I send my love and my thanks for showing me that the Hippie Nation, and the immutable values for which it stands, still lives.

If you have a "then and now" hippie observation that you'd like to share or a comment about this book, please contact me at: Stewart@ WhatHappenedtothehippies.com.

Each chapter in this book leads off with italicized prefatory remarks from me, signed *S.L.R.*

About the Contributors

Carrie B: Nearly 50 years after driving from the Midwest to San Francisco in the late 1960s, I still live in the City and work part-time as a litigator for a small historic law firm in the San Francisco Bay Area. I'm a widow, after a 30-year marriage, with one son living in Southern California. My passion is flying my small airplane on the weekends. On weeknights, I play pool in leagues. Like Peter Pan, I resolve to never grow up.

Henrietta B: I am 67 and live in Colorado. I have settled in a place where I can continue with some of my "hippie" ways … gardening, meditating, trusting the process of peace and love in these "troubled" times. I still love listening to the music of my times and still find that so many of the words in those songs are very relevant to myself and the world. I am an artist and think creativity is one way to change the world enabling us to learn more about ourselves and even to heal. I am teaching intuitive art classes for well-being/healing/and self-expression.

Tara B: Born in Casper, Wyoming, I am an elder hippie, artist, activist, educator and counselor currently living near Eureka in Humboldt County in northern California. I worked for nearly two decades as a broadcaster, DJ, and voiceover artist for commercial and public radio as well as a graphic designer and professional sign painter. Having performed since childhood: I am a dancer, musician, and professional singer of several genres.

Jack Besser: I'm 65, living in Hilo, HI. I am president of Antevasin, a 501(c3) nonprofit designed to develop innovative food solutions within a sustainable community, uniting different cultures and belief systems and offering a model for eliminating homelessness.

Ashley Kent Carrithers: I am 72, married, and living in the Argentine

Patagonia with two of my children where I practice "Creation Enjoyment" on a daily basis. Over the years, I helped to start an alternative school in northern California and created several successful businesses including one that recently replaced all of the windows in the Empire State Building. I've also authored six books, established a nonprofit for Earth Rescue initiatives, and created UPNOW University.

Noa Daniels: I grew up with a desire to understand the hearts and souls of people. My life's work is to share the discovery and exploration of life's experiences. Through simple poetry, I show the emotions and reactions, the highs and lows, of what we, as people, hold in common. *The Common Ground* is my first e-book of poetry in a series of three. Living in South Carolina, I am a contributor to several Southern publications including "His Mother," a collection of stories about mothers-in-law written by women.

Rick Denney: Originally from Portland, Oregon, I graduated from high school in 1967, giving me a front row seat to the magical times of the '60s. Starting in the summer of 1968, I began making occasional trips to San Francisco, the melting pot for the hippie generation. My writing style is a personal reflection of my experiences, challenges, triumphs, and disappointments growing up in that era. I've been married to my wife Lorena for 36 years and have a daughter, Monica, and two grandchildren. Today, I live in Seattle and enjoy doing volunteer work for various faith-based organizations and writing occasional articles sharing my faith and experiences.

Steve Dickson: I currently live in Port Orchard, Washington, with my lovely wife. I'm 64 and have been a U.S. merchant mariner for the past 27 years. I was a wandering hippie in my youth and still believe in peace and love.

Judah Freed: I'm a seasoned, award-winning, journalist and author from Colorado who's now living on Kauai in Hawaii. My forthcoming book is *Making Global Sense*, grounded in hope for the 21st century, inspired by Thomas Paine's *Common Sense*.

Steve Gifford: I'm 68 and live in Florida, next door to the love of my life. My bipolar disorder condition is stable with medication. I lead a quiet life, writing prayer poems and spending time with my lady. My principal website is kindnesspoems.blogspot.com.

Stuart Glascock: Since about 1985, I have worked as a staff writer for daily newspapers in Colorado, California and Washington state. For about the last 10 years, I've been a freelance magazine writer, a role that has given me more freedom of expression but less consistent assignments. I'm 58 and live with my family in Seattle where I walk my dog, go to yoga and practice kindness as often as possible.

Raina Greenwood: I've been writing since I was eight years old and have changed from a California girl into a 68-year-old writer and teacher in Seattle. I'm currently working on a book of urban fairy tales and a trilogy set in the 1950s.

Wanda H: I'm 72 and living in Los Angeles. A native New Englander, I infiltrated Los Angeles 20 years ago. It's a marvelous city for old hippies, as anyone can find a welcome here. I've spent my working life on the fringes of the Establishment but always as a bit of a rebel. Now blessedly retired, my passions include my hippie-ish musician son, my hippie-ish dramatist granddaughter, my 16-year-old pup Casey, documenting my family's history, books, and figuring out life as I go along.

Sue Hanauer: I'm an artist and writer living in New Mexico in my retirement years after raising and home-educating five children. Now widowed, I spend my spare time enjoying my 15 grandchildren and four great-grands.

Susan Hawke: I am a writer and teacher in Washington State. I actively participate in wildlife conservation efforts across the U.S. and work with birds of prey. I also perform, record, and publish poetry for local and national audiences.

CeliaSue Hecht: At age 69, I am a published writer, editor, blogger and doggie mama who loves cats, too. Originally from NYC, now living in Monterey, CA, I have a substantial background in print media as a newspaper reporter, editor and newsletter editor. I've been published in newspapers, magazines, and online. I've worked with international CEOs, bestselling authors, health care professionals, artists, and nonprofits serving in roles such as Public Relations Director, Writer and Newsletter Editor. I've also co-authored five romantic travel guides, traveled worldwide, and written blogs for the last 10 years. I am currently working with anti-trafficking Liberty Asia.

Lew Jones: I was born in Denver, Colorado, in 1951 during a huge snowstorm. I grew up blue-collar with a mom from Washington/West Virginia and a father from Arkansas/Oklahoma. I went to public schools, played some sports, learned to play guitar, and flew falcons and hawks before I started dating girls. I went to college to keep out of the Vietnam War after being warned not to join by a friend who had just came back. Today at 67, I work as a professional musician, a professional painter, and a teacher of music at three community colleges. My own music can be found online under "Lew Jones," "The Lew Jones Act" and "The Lew Jones Band."

Stack K: I was born in 1951 in New Rochelle, New York, and have been bouncing around the eastern United States since 1969. Inexplicably, I've found myself working at times as a chef, mud-man, and Head Start playmate, among other roles, on what seems to be an ever-changing path in this crazy country of ours. I currently live in Asheville, North Carolina, spending my time weaving, playing music, gardening, cooking and loving. My passions include peace, justice, the ocean, the mountains, and cilantro.

Kahish: I'm 65, living on the Northern California coast and concentrating on my passions for organic gardening, songwriting and visual arts. I continue to be an activist of peace through those mediums of expression. I've owned/operated three restaurants and manage vacation rentals where I hang my art and feed my guests. In Harmony.

Janice L: I currently live in Los Angeles where I went to high school and college. Prior to my return in 2015, I spent six years living in Peru, where I was born. I am now 65. I worked in education, both public and private. I have one grown son and two grandchildren, both under the age of five. I spend joyful time with them, write and read a great deal, do artwork, cook, walk, swim, visit with friends, both local and far, and am currently mentoring a high school student.

Patricia Lapidus: I am 76, living now in the northwestern hills of Connecticut after growing up on a farm in Maine and setting out to see the world. I lived on "The Farm," founded by Stephen Gaskin and his students, in Tennessee and in New York. My memoir about these hippie days is *The Farm That Tried to Feed the World.* I am still enough of a hippie not to care about money or fame, but I do love readers and I love to discuss our many adventures and what they mean. I've discovered more than I ever thought I would about our planet and the roots of our troubles. We are elders now and happy to share what we learned.

J Laurence: I was born in New York, but think of myself as a pure Californian; surfer, rebel and "hummingbird." Today at 62, I look back on an ever-winding career path ranging from drug smuggling to technology, I prefer bucking authority, while living life on my own terms. I focus on contributions in their many forms while remaining present, awake and truthful. Passion runs high. Humor is essential. While currently working on creative projects, I'll continue exploring the planet, people and life until my final breath. I'm happy, healthy, energized and ready for the next chapter.

Wayne Lee: I grew up in Bellingham, Washington, as a good Methodist. But after I graduated from high school, the "Summer of Love" turned me into a heathen after discovering the virtues of cannabis, free love, peace marches, macrobiotic food, psychedelics, Buddhism and communes. One of my friends used to call me an "elegant hippie" because I had beautiful, long hair and bathed daily. I also held actual jobs, graduated from college, and drove a big, orange International Travelall named Lucille. I still consider myself a hippie, although most of my long hair fell out decades ago.

Larry M: I was born in Los Angeles and lived just outside of Hollywood in the shadow of Paramount Studios. Education was highly valued in my family, and I have a BA degree in history and an AA in photography. I was introduced to the "hippy culture" through friends and participated in its politics, music, and drugs. This was a huge influence in what I was and what I became. I made my living as a photographer in Los Angeles. Today at 73, I live in Olympia, Washington, work part-time, and keep a close watch on the political activities of our nation.

Ocean M: I'm a freelance writer who divides his time between Northern California and South America. I write the "EarthRx" environmental column for "Paste Magazine." I'm also co-editing the anthology *Infinite Perception: The Role of Psychedelics in Global Evolution*.

Risha Linda Mateos: I was born in 1955 and currently reside in South Florida with my husband and our dachshund, Zeppo. My background includes traveling to many countries and throughout the U.S., helping the Dalai Lama and traveling Tibetan monks with promotion plus working as a photojournalist and operations manager at a local magazine. I am certified third degree in Reiki practice with continued studies in energy therapies, consciousness, herbal medicine, chi development and meditation. I live a simple lifestyle and love to cook healthy, organic, vegetarian and vegan meals.

Cathy Matters: I'm 63 and happily reside in the beautiful Northwest state of Washington. I have a degree in early childhood education and love teaching young children, especially those at risk. I'm a serious advocate for animals, children, and literacy with a passion for preserving the Earth. My love of the arts is visible in my missives, paintings, drawings, and thespian endeavors. I wonder what my next adventure in life will be and look forward to retirement so I can focus more on my creative writing.

Gordon Muir: I have lived a somewhat conflicted life as I have always been a martial artist and a dedicated hippie at the same time. As I approached 30, my issues with finances came to a head; and I decided to actually get a job, not just an education. So, I went to college, became a computer programmer, and joined the suited crowd—not really, but it was corporate anyway. I hated that world. Today, I'm semi-retired, making things that were useful and doing what I love.

Robert O: Better known to most as Bo, I was born in Pennsylvania and compelled to write fiction from the age of six. Many short stories followed, but the distractions of life led me down other paths personally and professionally. I wrote a sports column for several newspapers in my younger days, tried my hand at being a musician and songwriter, and collaborated on some teleplays, screenplays and radio plays. But I always wanted to write a full-length novel, a goal I finally achieved in 2013. Since then, I've published another. My wonderful wife and I have raised two children. I'm now 69.

Tea R. Peronto: At 56, I'm a retired homemaker who's spent most of her life working in customer service and raising three kids. From my home in southern Oregon, I now enjoy playing with my grandchildren and crafting, both with a variety of arts and with words. My writings can be found at lovethelittlestuff.com.

Sal Polcino: I was born in Philadelphia and was lucky enough to see many major bands from the 60s with my older brother who was a staff photographer for a newspaper in Trenton, New Jersey. Our concert jaunt ended with the granddaddy of them all, Woodstock. A few years later, I followed my brother to Seattle and spent 13 years there before finally moving to southern California. Today, I'm a professional jazz guitarist as well as a writer who at one time blogged for the great Joe Zawinul and Wayne Shorter of Weather Report. I now play in a local trio called Uncle Sal's Band.

Eric Proteau: I am 70 and live in San Rafael, California. I play pool, write poetry and love my kids and grandkids. I guess I am still a hippie in my own style, which to me means you follow the Golden Rule with people and do your best to be a good shepherd for our planet.

Nancy Pruitt: I'm 68 and a resident of Florence on the central Oregon coast. Having graduated from San Diego State University in Dance and from the New York Institute of Photography, I have taught dance exercise and served as a public speaker about health and nutrition, while enjoying photography, yoga, music and dance, scratch cooking, writing, being in nature, shell sculptures, drawing and oil painting. I volunteer as a photographer for local events like Vision Quest, kite festivals, and animal shelter programs. Future activities? All of the above, especially growing my photography post-process skills, learning video editing, and enjoying my grandchildren.

Linda R: The hippie movement was already in full bloom when I turned 15 in 1968. Having been raised in a small town, west of Ann Arbor, Michigan, I was barely aware of the cultural changes taking place, including those at the University of Michigan. After a friend bought me The Beatles' Sgt. Pepper album, I became extremely idealistic, taking a stand against racism, the Vietnam War, and corrupt government. Disillusioned, I joined a Jesus Revolution commune which took me to 10 different countries. Years later, I discovered that religious organizations can be as corrupt as governments. At 55, trained as a Montessori teacher, divorced with three grown children, six grandchildren, and one great-grandchild, I went back to the University to obtain a BA in Management.

Ron R: Raised in South Dakota, I'm a 68-year-old emerald dealer living in California with a second home in Bogotá, Colombia. I'm also the founder of "Clayhands" (clayhands.org), a nonprofit organization that increases employment and sustainability for rural Colombians by promoting earth-based construction using adobe, pressed wood, and bamboo.

Beth Richards: I'm 68, having traveled for many years as a wandering hippie, living on communes, in teepees, and in an old International Scout. My husband Shine and I spent those years climbing mountains around the country, birthing four babies, going to Rainbow Gatherings, making a living at numerous types of jobs from picking fruit to janitorial work to breeding laboratory rats, and exploring human consciousness before finally settling in mid-coastal Maine. I'm retired from teaching laboratory classes at Bowdoin College and serving as a volunteer firefighter/EMT for 17 years. Currently, Shine and I spend our days playing music with a Celtic/American roots band called the Montsweagers, traveling extensively in and out of the U.S., riding motorcycles, and operating ham radios.

Larry Roszkowiak: I was born in 1948 in New Jersey—Exit Four. The U.S. Navy sent me to electronics and radio schools. I've made a living doing that kind of work ever since. I now live and write in Weed, California.

Mari S: I'm 70 and live in the Pacific Northwest, having retired after careers in Association Management and Real Estate Appraisal services. My daughter, son-in-law, and four grandchildren live nearby. I sing in a bluegrass band that has performed for the past 10 years in senior centers and retirement facilities. Travel, making art, friends and attending Burning Man (14-year attendee) are my favorite interests. My friends and I still talk of moving into some sort of shared co-housing arrangement just like we talked about back in the day.

Tom S: I'm a retired educator living in the Cascade foothills. I still write some, but mostly just enjoy this Magical Mystery Tour called life.

Richard Schoebrun: I was born in the Bronx, New York, in 1944, raised until the age of 14 over my father's bakery in the Catskills. My family then relocated to Los Angeles, where I graduated from high school and joined the National Guard. My first son was delivered by a midwife on Mt. Tamalpais in 1970, and my other two children were delivered by midwives on The Farm in Tennessee in 1972 and '74. Their mother is buried on The Farm. I've lived my entire adult life in either California or Tennessee. Although I no longer use them, nor do I espouse them, I feel that my lifestyle choices stem from the psychedelics I experienced in my youth.

Carol Seaton: I was born in Seattle, Washington, grew up in Southern California, then spent most of my adult life in Oregon. My children, grandchildren, and great-grandchildren were all born in Oregon, a state with a history of standing against war and in favor of protecting the environment. I am devoted to my family and have done a lot of volunteer work revolving around them. As I look back on life at age 73, there are things that I wish had gone differently; but I am very proud of my family members who take stands on issues that really matter and who prepare their children to do the same. We aren't rich, but we do stand for important things. To me, that is what being a hippie is about, human values and making the world a better place.

Marty Skiles: Born in Richmond, Missouri, in 1957, I'm now retired and still married to my wife Angie after 33 years. (It only seems like 15 minutes ... under water, that is.) We've raised two girls and a boy (without eating any of them). Today, I'm a singer, songwriter, and cover guitar player who loves to make people laugh and has managed to remain vertical and breathing, although there are probably sometimes that wish I wasn't. That's all I can tell ya! Any more, and I'd have to kill ya!

Perry Sobolik: I was born July 14 (Bastille Day), 1953, in Grafton, North Dakota. My family moved to Seattle in 1963, and my life was influenced thereafter by torrents of winter rain rather than blizzards of snow. My career as a journalist began in junior high school and continued after a BA in Communications from Washington State University. I wrote professionally for various newspapers and enjoyed a career in college radio. This tie-dyed-in-the-wool hippie is the proud father of two boys and has been in love for 35 years with their mother, Sherry. Since I am a modern-day Luddite and eschew technology, credit for transcribing and proofreading goes to my son, Alynn, without whose invaluable assistance you would not be reading my words.

Barry Sommer: I was born in Los Angeles in 1954 and raised on the Sunset Strip. Middle class family, Democrats and proud of it. Ran away from home in 1969, went to Woodstock and upon returning followed in my dad's retail shoes. Left LA after the quake in 1994 and went to Oregon. Spent 25 years in Eugene redefining myself within a very liberal social order. Finally retired to Westlake on the Oregon coast where I now volunteer, work part time and write for the local paper. The quiet life is what my life has led me to, my politics now less strident and more introspective. I love my neighbors and the new friends. The simple life suits me.

Douglas Stevenson: I have been on the cutting edge of alternative lifestyle and technology for many years, working also as a writer, with over 1000 published articles. Although my work has taken me around the world, home base is a log cabin out in the woods, surrounded by nature. I am the media interface and principal spokesperson for "The Farm," once the world's largest hippie commune, now the most famous intentional community in the world, a living example and model for a sustainable lifestyle, and have authored two books about the community's history and evolution: *Out to Change the World: The Evolution of The Farm Community* and *The Farm Then and Now*. My interviews have appeared in newspaper and magazine articles, documentaries and TV news programs.

Dan T: I'm 62 and live in Shrub Oak, New York. I've mowed lawns, worked on a railroad track gang, repaired barns, packed health food, bound books, painted houses, fixed cars, and built boats. These days, I still fix cars and build boats. I am also a cooperative observer for the National Weather Service (NOAA). My wife and I have two daughters and a grandson. We enjoy the time spent with our hippie alumni family. Much good music and laughs.

Jean T: Originally from New Mexico, I spent time in Montana before moving to Seattle, Washington, where I worked as a licensed massage practitioner for 15 years. Currently retired, I reside in Carrizozo, a small artist community in central New Mexico. I enjoy writing, traveling, dancing, and serving on the board of the local library. Divorced with two grown children, I'm 66 years old.

Edwin Thomasson: I spent years working as a critical care/emergency nurse and helping draft the first certification exams for nurses in Pediatric and Neonatal ICU competencies. I have volunteered in free clinics and in the Peace Corps. Now retired in Texas, I restore rare books, paint, and enjoy motorcycling through the twisties with my beloved wife Tyger. It turns out that The Moody Blues were right: "Just what you want to be, you'll be in the end."

Steve Trinward: I'm 69, a lifelong libertarian and liberty activist, now living in Nashville, Tennessee. I'm a semi-retired professional book editor with over 100 works in publication, a long-time test-scoring Reader, and an educational consultant. I currently serve on the Board of the Nashville Sudbury School, a no grades, no classes, no teachers model for open education.

Rose V: I'm 64 and currently living in Austin, Texas. I am originally from North Carolina but decided to move to Austin in my early twenties to follow my dream of designing landscapes. Austin was full of hippies and cowboys in the 1970s, all trying to follow their dreams too. In many ways, it remains that way today. I own a landscape design and construction company and am fortunate enough to have found many creative clients and friends that are all about supporting the arts. Retire? Not a chance. I am still following my dream.

Jack Jacobi Verde: I'm 67, retired, living in San Antonio, Texas. I do odd jobs around the city and fish the local streams when I'm not doing anything else. I'm also working on a musical play entitled *Young Jesus*, the story of Jesus as a teenager and the relationship he had with his family.

Ray York: I am 75 and married. I spend my time writing and traveling in America and around the world visiting my children and grandchildren. I live in Alameda, California.

Age of Aquarius

When I was a kid, I loved to climb the big tree in our front yard and look out at the far horizon like a wide-eyed sailor in the crow's nest of a tall ship. I would stare out into the great beyond from the highest branches knowing that I was destined to discover an incredible new world lying just over the horizon. The 1960s and early 70s brought that new world into view.

Many of us saw those times as the beginning of the "Age of Aquarius," a magical era of "harmony and understanding, sympathy and trust abiding, and the mind's true liberation," or at least that's what the Fifth Dimension said. We were certain that the very appearance of our generation had brought about a Golden Age. We saw ourselves as the source of a spiritual and political transformation unprecedented in the history of the world.

Whether we aligned the planets or the planets aligned us was unimportant. We were here, beaming with inexhaustible love, determined to enlighten the dark corners and scare away the monsters who had so corrupted this paradise called Earth. "We are stardust. We are golden," Joni Mitchell told us. We believed it.—S.L.R.

Perry Sobolik: The Times They Are a-Changin'

Tumult. War. Drugs. Civil rights. Environmental concerns. Gay rights. Women's rights. All churning and tumbling like wet clothes in the giant dryer of our brains. These daily topics clashed and clanged throughout our lives (and many still do) as we tried to sort out the significance of each.

Everything from bisexuality to biracial dating confronted us at every corner. The hippies had been born into an evolving morass of new views that challenged the very culture from which it sprang. As with previous generations, we struggled to juggle our newfound freedoms with the expectations of our forefathers and ourselves.

As we navigated the convoluted corridors of our culture and ever-changing world, we began to succeed at newfound ways of life. Many did not make it. Some still struggle. A few emerged intact and continue to this day. It was terrific, terrifying and tumultuous.

"Pot." "Weed." "Smoke." "Boo." "Herb." "MJ." "Dope." "Joints." "Sticks." "Doobies." "J's." "Squares." Marijuana! The binding social characteristic of the shared use of this mild psychotropic plant cannot be understated. The Doobie Brothers named their band after it.

Smoking "pot" was always a social endeavor. Unlike alcohol, where one *could* share a bottle or glass with others, marijuana was *always* passed around (still is) if more than one person was present. One good joint could stone five or six people. Try *that* with one beer.

We were cautious (A cop on every corner. A narc in every bush. Just because you're paranoid doesn't mean they're not out to get you!) The fervent prayer that our unholy communion with the "Devil's Weed" might somehow be legally consecrated seemed unattainable in our lifetime. Not everyone smoked pot, but that didn't matter. You were still a part of the group. "Pot" was not exclusionary. In fact, I've smoked weed with doctors, lawyers and Indian chiefs (literally). Even cops.

We understood the medicinal properties of marijuana long before it was accepted by mainstream medical practitioners. Pot didn't make people crazy. It helped keep us *sane,* particularly during the uncertain political environment of racial upheaval, environmental activism and anti-war protesting. More "stoners" returned from Vietnam than were sent there.

Once thriving multi-acre farms were a dwindling resource in the 1970s. Most had been carved into smaller five or 10-acre plots with many falling into the hands of developers. In the post–World War II era, large-scale corporate farming became a more efficient way to feed the "baby boomers." It was these same "boomers" who yearned for a life closer to Mother Earth.

Classes in animal husbandry, companion planting and natural fertilization and pest control were sprouting like spuds at colleges and community halls. Self-sustaining slices of "hippie heaven" evolved into full-blown communes (not unlike the Israeli "Kibbutz") and organic farming techniques were rediscovered. Herbal medicine reemerged.

Old McDonald had a farm, and so do a lot of hippies who sought a simpler (not always easier) life outside the boundaries of modern American cityscapes. The reversion to the satisfaction of dirt under your fingernails was ultimately another form of rebellion against the norms of their parents. Hippies are darn good at rebellion.

Rock-n-Roll. Blues. Acid Rock. Psychedelic Rock. Southern Rock. Pop Rock. R&B. Motown Sound. British Invasion! The sounds that bound "My Generation" came from every point on the compass, every country on the planet, bring incredibly diverse backgrounds of cultures and intellects.

The Beatles. The Rolling Stones. The Doors. Jimi Hendrix. Pink Floyd. Santana. Young Rascals. Strawberry Alarm Clock. The Grateful Dead. Creedence Clearwater Revival. The Allman Brothers Band. Jefferson Airplane. Janis Joplin. The Who. Jethro Tull. Led Zeppelin. Smokey Robinson. Canned Heat. Moby Grape. The Animals. Steppenwolf. Aretha Franklin. The Supremes. Stevie Wonder. *All* nurtured by Chuck Berry, Elvis, Sam Cooke, Buddy Holly, Little Richard and every Delta blues master to ever record a riff.

We listened to *every*thing, because all of it was co-mingled on pop music stations (many of them occupying the AM broadcast band) and the few scattered "Underground FM" stations that might play the most eclectic recordings from across the global music spectrum. We talked music. Shared it. Memorized it. Mimicked it (who *didn't* play air guitar like Clapton). We experienced it live—$6.00 to see Long John Baldry, Fleetwood Mac, and Savoy Brown in the same show!

Woodstock was the granddaddy of Rock festivals, but only the beginning. In Washington State, the Sky River Rock Festivals preceded the last (and only legally permitted) one—the Satsop River Fair and Tin Cup Races in 1971. We danced, partied and sang away the rain.

They were all just kids. Kids with a dream. After all, if four "Lads from Liverpool" could somehow become the most recognizable faces on the planet just by playing music, why couldn't *any*body! Young men and women with musical talent and ambition were always everywhere; but *now*, it seemed, they swarmed out of basements and garages like locusts hungry to feed on the psyche of our time.

The new-found freedom of the hippie era brought together neighborhood playmates in a different manner than baseball teams, pick-up sandlot football scrums, or Saturday afternoon "frozen tag" games. These new "teams" maybe, just maybe, could become—famous! Like the "Fab Four," they started as school buddies, forming, deforming, reforming, and morphing into new configurations trying to cover the top pop hits of the airwaves.

Bands sprouted like weeds in every neighborhood. Would-be rock stars let their hair grow, donned psychedelic "Nehru jackets," and attempted to emulate the musical heroes of the day. Mothers sewed costumes, and fathers hauled our equipment to gigs in the family stations wagons, never complaining.

Jack Jacobi Verde: Good Morning Sunshine

The 1960s were a time to play and listen to the hum of the world. I was born into circumstances that bent and twisted my soul with the magic of drugs. We were born from the experience of losing ourselves on the effects of a pill or a smoke. Free love was cool at that time with all the flowers and feathers in women's attire. Those were the moments of being high on some drug with friends who wanted me stoned and funny, as they said.

Yes, sex, drugs, religion, and the mystical sprung into our heads those merry days. Love and hate built a purple insanity of twilight encased by dreams that transformed our inner being into weird psychedelic forms. The bodies of hundreds moving to the sounds, and I was lost in the volume of crowds. I felt hidden within a singular form of one body of flesh held by the frame of bones as time passed like a river of foam high on LSD coming down. My soul looked at my throat filled with laughter, as the sound echoed across a quad of trees as the summer rain fell glistening like a billion stars.

I had the view of a child looking on towers of moving flesh in all directions with plans dancing in their heads, wanting to keep their children warm and fed. I was poor in the city, as any poor man in any city with roads and people wanting a change, to mold their lives into better fates. We are small things that dream of being kings, like those little birds flying amid the trees singing and holding on to their own private twigs.

Nancy Pruitt: Wild Thing

As the largest birth wave in U.S. history, the baby boomers, including hippies, were faced with a cacophony of societal ills, civil unrest, unexpected assassinations of our young leaders, an escalating war in Vietnam, and near nuclear devastation after the Bay of Pigs. Fueled by easy access to birth control, psychedelics, and marijuana, music and films encouraged our lifestyle.

As we tried to break free from parental yokes and outdated mores, feeling disillusioned with our government and teachers, encountering the "glass ceiling" for women, and enduring too much sexual harassment, we looked for nobler causes. Instead of finding truth and justice, we found a new mistrust in authority. Free expression in art, music, our bodies, and in our thoughts became the norm for finding true meaning in an ever-unsafe world. Spiritual goals became prominent, and gurus offered a "higher joy" than materialism and self-indulgence. Conflicted with how to behave like a "good girl" versus a "wild child," we found that real love could be evasive and unreturned. What was a teenager to do or feel?

Larry M: Be Here Now

The hippie movement was the offspring of the Beat culture of the '50s. It was a reaction to the virus infecting the body politics of the day. Initiated in the beginning for a simple request for free speech on the Berkeley campus, it quickly developed into movement to stop the Vietnam war that was driven by false claims of aggression, misguided policies of the containment of communism, developed in secrecy and presented with falsified facts. And this was advanced by a group of Kennedy's men who were supposed to be the best and brightest, followed by Johnson who had a pedal to the metal, no compromise policy.

This exploded into a complex assortment of protesters of various callings, environment/tree huggers, psychedelic adventurists, spiritualists exploring various Eastern religions, hipster/dandies eager to follow the latest trend, musicians on fire, blue jean intellectuals in the mode of Sartre's Paris-existential café, ready to discuss Ram Dass's "Be Here Now," teenage runaways looking for a new family, etc. The cement that held it together was the music and the drugs.

You either got it or you didn't. If you got it, it was a life changing experience, hard to explain to someone who was not involved. It was counterculture and underground and that was part of the appeal. The movement has been and will continue to be presented as a bunch of misfits that were concerned only with drugs, sex, and rock-n-roll. That leaves the question: Where would we be now if the country didn't have the hippies? In a worse position, I would claim. We added color and life into a system that was going in the wrong direction and set the model for push-back and common sense.

Jack Besser: Hair

To me, the concept of hippie represents the tribal values of a culture that had set itself apart by going natural. Growing your hair long, speaking the truth, being kind, showing compassion and understanding to all, sharing … they all mean integrity. This is and has been a challenge in a world where people put on a false impression of who they are and what is truth. In my early teens, I was a longhair, a freak. I had the longest hair in my school; and when I moved to The Farm, few guys had hair longer than mine.

My connection to The Farm started when I was 16 and Gaskin's caravan came through our town. I identified immediately. While my first son was born in Rhode Island, my second son, third son, and grandson were all born on The Farm. When I left that community after eight years, I greatly missed the camaraderie of an extended family that I had enjoyed.

I now live on the Hilo side of the big island of Hawaii, a place where hippie values of compassion and oneness are practiced. I regularly travel to Thailand where I find truth and guidance in the teachings of my Sak Yant, Buddhist teachers. To me, the dream lives on.

Acknowledging the past, being here and now, and looking towards the future and the unknown, I still refuse to sell out to a false identity. Being a hippie is a path to self-realization and unattachment, forever shedding your skin as your awareness grows, staying in right mind, taking the right action, growing stronger as we grow older.

Being a hippie is a spiritual path and, like a monk that shaves his head to show no vanity, so I still have long hair. It is an expression of that old non-conformist to a false identity. Let your freak flag fly and be true to the human being you are. Stand up for truth. We do not do it, because it is easy. We do it, because it is who we are.

I recently have created 501 c3 nonprofit in Hawaii called Antevasin, (Sanskrit word meaning: at the edge of the forest where the spiritual masters dwell). The organization serves as an awareness center of mind/meditation, body/health, and the exploration of the unknown coupled with sustainable building and lifestyle.

Perry Sobolik: Peace, Love & Tie-Dye

A blonde chick passing through the intersection in her VW convertible Bug flashed a peace sign as bright as her smile. "Good Day Sunshine" blared from her car radio as Danny smiled back. It *was* a good day. Sunshine.

"Hey, Zonker, you going to the rally tonight?" Danny asked his roommate approaching from around the corner. "Damn straight!" was the answer. "I wouldn't miss a Stop the War rally. How goes the petitioning?"

Danny had already spent two hours collecting signatures against the war on a mimeographed form he had typed the night before. Now he was thirsty and ready to go home.

"Ching-ching-ching" clamored the finger cymbals and tambourines heralding the gentle approach of Hare Krishna devotees in their Saffron robes extolling the virtues of Buddhism. Danny waved as the group nodded his way, not breaking their chant as they distributed leaflets announcing a local meeting and free dinner.

"Hi, my name's Ebony and I'd like to sign your petition," said the multi-hued dashiki-clad black woman with a resplendent afro hairstyle who had just walked up. "I like your poster," she said, gesturing toward the hand-lettered sign imploring "Make Love, Not War."

"Make the rally tonight," Danny encouraged. "We're planning a sit-in to block the freeway if the pigs don't jack us up too badly."

"How's it hangin', Danny?" hailed Kara, his old lady, who had just appeared with her friend Linda.

"Slow but steady," he answered as they shared a hug. "Did you score that lid of weed for tonight" he whispered. "Right on!" she replied. "Might as well go to jail stoned if it comes to that."

"We'll have some pot for that concert on Saturday, too," Kara suggested. "I can't wait to see The Doors live. 'Love me two times, babe,'" she added with a playful wink.

The phone and light poles along "The Ave" were plastered with fliers promoting concerts, gigs and gatherings from throughout the area. Adding a festive brightly-colored broadside to the street, the printed, garishly-displayed written word was the main conduit for communication. Tie-dye for telephone poles.

"So, what did your folks say about our plans to move in together?" Danny ventured, as Kara listened to the strains of a Jimi Hendrix tune as it floated out the door of the headshop next door like auditory incense. "Foxy Lady, yeah, yeah..."

"Daddy didn't think much about the idea, as you can imagine," she finally offered. "Mom was more receptive. But that's Mom. I still want to."

"Your old man is going to have a shit fit," added Linda. "Sorry I won't be here to save your ass. Can't stay. Harvest is coming up in a few weeks. I've got to get back to the farm. Plow. Plant. Pluck. That's my new mantra. If all goes right, we might exceed last year's canning record of 130 pints," she said crossing her fingers for good luck.

Linda's Medicine Wheel Farm required immense amounts of "sweat equity" to supply a family of four with over eighty percent of their sustenance. "I haven't had a vacation in four years," Linda said. "The goats need milking daily, and it's hard to find neighbors with time to help. Going back to the land turned out to be more work than I thought."

By now Danny had had enough petitioning for one day. "Kara, I've gotta split. Have band practice in half an hour. Wanna come?"

"No. I think I'll hang with Linda for a while. Will I see you tonight?" she asked.

"Right on," he answered, raising a peace sign over his head as he walked away mumbling "Peace, love, tie-dye, Hare Krishna, eat the Easter Bunny, fuck or fight, Rama, foo foo, snake bite, we don't wanna fight..."

Eric Proteau: When I'm 66

The young word peddler pedals his two-wheel bike fast
to the Summer of love sounds and Golden Gate Park's be-in.
Angels straight from hell hold peace securely.
Music rocks and wails off the banks of the meadow.
Hippies and groupies gather and gain momentum at the fevered pitch.
Viola Lee sings the blues.
The pig jumps out of his pen in a harmonic blues jag.
The Dead rock the sound of Jerry the guitar man.
He shapes us with his pure smolder.
Shiva dancers spin as flowing tie-dyes twirl.
Burning joints form clouds of smoke over the meadow.
Hippies sling stories and whisper wishes for a new way
where all of us choose what we want and with whom.
Love is in the air on this fine day in the Summer of sixty-six.
Now I'm sixty-six.
My visit to this same meadow in the Fall of my years
is quiet and peaceful
And I see half a dozen hippies passing a huge joint.
They see me and offer me a hit.
I partake and sit on the grass and listen to their tales and trials
just like we did.
It was nice to know there are still hippies swapping tales
and sharing their vibes.

All You Need Is Love

When I was 20, it was easy to believe in peace, love, and happily-ever-afters. I was in college (financed by dear ole Dad), living in a dorm, having fun, getting high, and doing as little school work as possible. With no responsibilities, I was free to chase idealism any time I wanted.

Looking back, I can imagine how "straight" adults, struggling every day to keep a roof over their heads and food in their children's mouths, must have felt about people like me. How naïve and selfish we must have seemed to believe that love was all the world needed.

When seen through the eyes on a soldier fighting for his life, a wife being beaten by her husband, a father unable to afford medicine for his child, a cancer patient riddled with pain, or other folks facing countless other terrifying real-world situations, the idea that "all you need is love" seems more than ridiculous. It's obscene; or at least, it sounds that way on the surface.

When I was 20, I wanted simple answers and immediate results. Today, I don't expect either.

Love isn't like pixie dust. It can't dissolve bullets in mid-air, turn monsters into pussycats, or cure incurable disease. Instead, love is like rain that nourishes the earth and encourages the seeds of happiness to grow. It can't stop a bullet; but practiced widely over time, love can dissuade shooters from picking up guns in the first place. Love can't magically stop all evil or end all wars. Instead, it can melt them over time.

In the end, love is more valuable than money, more important than fame, more powerful than authority, and more long-lasting than achievement. In the end, all we need is love.

I'm reminded of a day many years ago when my family and I were

23

visiting the Big Apple and decided to eat at McDonald's in Times Square. Before ordering cheeseburgers and fries all around, I asked the cashier how she was doing, no big deal, just my small way of recognizing her as a human being and not just another cog in the hamburger machine. She stopped, said nothing for a few long seconds, and then looked up with a combination of irritation and amazement. For the briefest moment, I saw something in her eyes that wasn't exhaustion or aggravation. I think it was the slightest hint of peace and comfort only possible when one heart connects to another.

Then, as quickly as it appeared, the flicker was gone. "Fine," she finally answered; and we both went back to being strangers again. I like to believe that my small act of kindness made a difference for her and, perhaps in the long run, that she would add a pinch of her own and pass it to the next person.

I've learned since my hippie days that only love can make this world a better place, simple acts of caring, delivered without fanfare or credit, shared in every day experiences by one person with another. I discovered that small drops of kindness can nourish the seeds of happiness even on the hard streets of New York City.

I've also learned that supporting the kind acts of others is as important as performing those acts yourself. Maybe this means adding your name to a petition or joining a group that others have organized. Personally, I try to encourage love in the world by praising others for the small things they do every day. I'm particularly fond of praising strangers who I see acting kindly in public places, people like the checkout woman who smiles sincerely at each customer or the guy who helps an old lady retrieve a grocery item from the top shelf. I make a point to stop and say "Thanks for being so nice!" or "That was a nice thing to do!"

I feel a powerful connection with these strangers that I don't feel at any other time. In some magical, invisible way, the best of me and the best of the other person are connected, filling us both with a moment of peace and reminding us that goodness is everywhere if we care to see it.

When I was 20, I was astonished at how smart I had become. I knew what was best for me and, therefore, knew what was best for everybody else. Given my obvious superiority, I tried to fix people who seemed to be broken. After all, I was just trying to help. The poor souls in front of me couldn't see what I could or thought I could. It wasn't their fault. They just needed me to tell them what to do.

This way of thinking can be particularly tempting when you encounter people who continually complain about their circumstances but never do anything to improve them. These folks are in a never-ending loop, crying over misfortune while refusing to change. Their wounds are usually self-inflicted as they repeat the same suicidal behaviors again and again. Over and over, you rack your brain for the perfect combination of words and actions that will convince these miserable people to get off the tracks before the inevitable train of disaster slices them in half. But they never change.

Eventually, when you're just too exhausted to go on, it occurs to you that maybe you don't know what's best for anyone else. Maybe you can't save people from themselves. Maybe they don't need saving or simply don't want to be saved. Maybe you're not all powerful. Maybe the only person you can save is yourself, if you're lucky.

I married a smart, talented, free-spirited hippie chick in 1975. I was sure that she was the perfect partner for the counterculture life I had imagined for myself. As with most people, the "I love you's" came easily in the beginning. I loved how she made me feel. I loved having someone to talk to, confide in, and laugh with. I loved the newness and the excitement. For some people, this kind of love grows and lasts until death do you part.

If you're unlucky, as in my case, you find yourself loving who this person was or who you want him/her to be instead of who the person really is. Sadly, when this happens, your romance becomes a home improvement project. The object of your affection becomes exactly that, an object to be shaped and molded instead of cherished and enjoyed. Instead of growing, learning, and laughing, you spend your time believing that the partner you want is trapped inside the partner you have. Again and again, you look for ways to release him/her from this psychic dungeon so that the two of you can live happily ever after. That's not love at all.

In the years since, I've found new love with someone I admire and like, not for who she could become but for who she is. Every day is a joy. I don't try to change her. If anything, she has changed me, in her subtle non-threatening way, to be less crazy and more loving, particularly to myself.

Abbie Hoffman was the master showman of the anti–Establishment/ anti–War movement in the '60's and early '70's. He orchestrated an incredible array of demonstrations, described as "guerrilla theater," illustrating materialistic absurdity and disrupting normal society. In 1966, Abbie and friends threw dollar bills onto the floor of the New York Stock Exchange to "see the capitalists scramble."

In 1968, his Yippie Party ran a pig named Pegasus for president. His ideas for paralyzing the 1968 Democratic Party Convention included putting LSD into the water supply and getting "hyper-potent" male Yippies to seduce the wives, daughters, and girlfriends of the delegates. In fact, he and *his band of players never executed these plans; nor did they need to. The threat was enough to drive the power brokers crazy.*

After the Vietnam War ended in 1975, Abbie championed environmental causes, but largely disappeared from the public eye. Today, he'd have his own show like Howard Stern. Instead, according to his autobiography, he felt lost and alone. After being charged with coke possession, he disappeared underground for several years, resurfaced, did a year in jail, and eventually hanged himself in 1989.

I feel sad when I think of his death. He was a valiant crusader and a source of inspiration. I wish he had saved himself while he was saving other people. I wish that he had realized that it's not enough to love others. You have to love yourself too.

Abbie didn't think he deserved to be in the boat, an emotion I understand all too well. For a long time, I imagined myself in the black icy waters of the North Atlantic as the Titanic disappeared before me. I saw myself clinging to the side of the last lifeboat where my family sat safely waiting for rescue, knowing that I would die so that they might live.

Looking back, I'm not sure why I felt the necessity to die for the cause. Maybe it was a hero complex, maybe a death wish, or maybe the realization that the desperate life I was living had to end sooner than later. Whatever it was, I got over it. Today, I know that being in the boat is a personal choice. There's always room for me. I just have to love myself enough to climb out of the water and take a seat. I deserve to live as much as the next person. Today, I know that the more I love myself, the more loving I am to other people.

On a hot spring day in 1971, actress and activist Jane Fonda delivered a speech against the Vietnam War at my university. I was there. She spoke in a small auditorium with four huge windows on both walls, pushed wide open in hopes that a breeze might rescue us from the oppressive heat. The room was packed, and we sat anywhere we could, in the seats, in the aisles, in the windowsills.

I was impressed with her presentation and her demeanor that day. She didn't seem to be better than us. In fact, I had the distinct impression that she felt as insecure as I did. I don't remember exactly what she said. But I liked it. And I liked her.

To this day, many folks can't forget—or forgive—Jane for photos taken of her in 1972 in which she is sitting on an anti-aircraft battery smiling and surrounded by North Vietnamese soldiers. When asked about the incident in a 2015 interview, she replied: "Whenever possible, I try to sit down with vets and talk with them; because I understand; and it makes me sad.

It hurts me, and it will to my grave that I made a huge, huge mistake that made a lot of people think I was against the soldiers."

I don't believe Jane meant any harm. She was doing the right thing, as she saw it, just like the rest of us. I hope she can forgive herself.

Recently, someone told me about the anger and pain that he felt about some things I did over 20 years ago. Everything he recalled was true, and his anguish was hard to hear. While I have apologized for my past on numerous occasions, that wasn't enough. For healing to begin, he needed to tell me how he felt, without reservation, and for me to listen without justification. It was quite a cathartic experience for both of us.

Helping an old lady across the street is easy. Admitting your mistakes is not. Failing to admit that you've hurt someone doubles the pain. Acknowledging the truth and taking responsibility for your actions allows you and the other person to heal.

We're all going to hurt somebody along the way, regardless of our intentions. The worse of us will inflict irreparable suffering; the best of us, hurt feelings. What we do or don't do will inevitably cause pain to an innocent person at some point; not because we're inherently bad, but because we're inescapably imperfect.

I know from personal experience that victims of abuse often blame themselves for the abuse they receive. When someone hurts you, you naturally wonder why. You think that, if you can just make sense of the whole thing, then it won't hurt so much. If you can just understand why it happened, then you won't feel so out of control and so afraid. Admitting mistakes and taking responsibility for them enables the people we hurt to regain a sense of self-control, something essential for healing.

We need healing too. Admitting our mistakes and forgiving ourselves is an essential part of our own healing process. In this way, we can see that doing something bad doesn't make us a bad person. We can see that we aren't doomed to make the same mistakes again and again. We can see that we are worthy of forgiveness and love. In the end, we can either punish ourselves and others for the guilt we feel or live humbly as kinder human beings.

Bad things happen to good people; and giving doesn't necessarily mean you'll get anything in return. Life isn't fair ... at least not in the most obvious, looking at the trees, perspective. But from the forest perspective, I believe that the kinder you are, the more kindness you'll receive and the happier you'll be.

In my experience, being kind has a positive effect on most people. Smiles create smiles. Openness, openness; connection, connection. I believe *that in our heart of hearts, everyone wants to be loved. Sadly, many of us wander this desert called life desperately seeking an oasis of love where we can drink our fill. Giving, even in a small way, is a cool drop on parched lips. In my experience, most weary travelers will return the drink with a nod, or a smile, or a thank you.*

With or without a kind response, the miracle of kindness is that the more loving you are, the more loving you feel about yourself. After all, we probably torture ourselves more than anyone else tortures us. Being kind to others quiets that self-critical voice inside, soothes the angry child, and heals the broken heart.

While I can't measure it, I believe that each act of kindness makes the world a little brighter and a little happier. Like sweet, cool drops of rain, our small, every day actions can create lush green gardens in the desert of hopelessness.—S.L.R.

Kahish: Love Is Sufficient unto Love

Caring about strangers without preconceived notions or expectations was the social norm in my circle in the 1960s. By the time I married, I had acquired many brothers and sisters.

My wedding ceremony was officiated by my mother, a self-proclaimed minister. For the honeymoon, we searched for a permanent home in a 40-foot school bus converted into a living space. Finally, we found 5 beautifully wooded acres in an old logging town in Oregon ripe with those yearning to get back to the land. I was part of this movement then and embrace it fully now.

As we face turbulence in our current time, love for one another seems to be a necessity more than just a polite cultural exchange. Each day, I have a choice to be nice, to be kind, and to show love over the current social norm. Being real and honest with people has had a transformative effect on my neighbors and on me.

Mari S: A Beautiful Morning

I believe that those of us who were young adults in the late sixties and early seventies really did think that the world was getting better and could get even better if we all chose to treat each other in a more loving manner. This included our families, our friends, and even strangers.

I still feel good when I stop to let someone pull out into traffic ahead of me, when I see someone behind me in the grocery line who has only a handful of items compared to my full basket and I offer to let him/her go in front of me, or when I go out of my way to drive around the block to stop at some children's street-side lemonade stand. Maybe those things don't count as "love" but they sure make the world a more pleasant place.

Rick Denney: Love Generation

When one thinks of the '60s, images of bell bottom jeans, hippie beads, and tie-dyed t-shirts come to mind. Growing up at that time, most of us were just along for the ride. Very few gave any serious thoughts to anything beyond getting "high," listening to music and finding the closest 7–11 to satisfy our munchies.

The term "Love Generation" became one of the popular phrases in the '60s. We became the generation that made love—not war. Violence of any kind was not cool. We were mellow. Love became a major part of who we were as a group. At the time it seemed so innocent; believing that, if we just operated with love as our guiding principle, we could change the world and that people would see the difference and be convinced to join us. At the time, most of us believed that, if given a choice, people would respond to love and reject hate and violence.

Over time, the purity of our message of peace and love became tainted, but my sense is that true love never dies.

Perry Sobolik: With a Little Help from My Friends

I wrote this the day Aretha Franklin died. Another icon gone. Sing on, sweet soul sister.

"Chain, chain, chain—chain of fools," Aretha sang. But we never thought of ourselves as fools.

It was a "back-rub chain" consisting of a half-dozen friends sitting in a line on the floor, each gently rubbing the backs, necks and shoulders of the grateful recipient in front of them. The "engine" would then eventually rotate to the back of the chain to become the "caboose" (to the benefit of the previously "un-rubbed"), and this could continue for an hour.

Even though we were hormone-engorged teenagers, there was noth-ing sexual about these events. We all viewed it as doing a "big something nice" for each other. We all felt better about ourselves and each other afterward. Brothers and Sisters.

These social gatherings and their resultant shared attitude were a significant emotional and fraternal "glue" that served as the mucilage of my youth. These relationships have endured for over 50 years.

Certainly, we are not the first folks to develop deep and lasting friendships in our youth. This point was graphically illustrated when I recently laid my 98-year-old aunt to her final rest.

Pre–World War II photos of her partying and cavorting with close friends were quite prominent among her effects. They apparently also drank a lot of beer. So did we. We smoked a lot of "weed."

There just seemed to be a particularly deep love and trust among our group of "Peace, Love and Tie-dye" friends that continues to this day. Even if we encounter one another after decades of separation, it takes only minutes before we become the same young adults of yore. It's almost like no time has passed at all (until we look in the mirror!).

We are bound by an ethos that is structured by music (Rock and Roll), dress (I still wear pony-tail length hair), slang ("Right on!" "groovy," "hippie," "pot," and countless others), and an open-minded awareness of environmental, social and cultural "liberation." We were at the forefront of social movements that spawned "Women's Lib" (remember "Ban the Bra"), "Stop the War!" (flag and draft card burning), "Greenpeace" (Save the Whales), "recycle," "free love" and "stoned again!"

Turbulent times fostered torrid relationships, because we felt we couldn't "trust anyone over thirty." That last one proved itself false; as we still trust old friends now in their sixties, seventies and beyond.

And to think that it all began with a simple, friendly back rub. "Come on people, now, smile on your brother, everybody get together, try to *rub* one another, right now." Maybe we should.

CeliaSue Hecht: You've Got a Friend

In 1975, I met Rannette Daniels (later Rannette Nicholas) who became my friend, mentor, coach, and teacher for 40 years. She passed unexpectedly in 2015. She was the most important person in my life who taught me a lot about life, spirituality and business, who always had my back, who supported me to go for my dreams, to write and finish college, and who challenged me to do things that I thought that I could not do. Her laugh was infectious and melodious, and she was the most kind, generous, patient and loving person I've ever known. She believed we live in a benevolent universe and helped me to heal my chronic pain (fibromyalgia) holistically. She had a sign on her desk that said "The difficult we do immediately, the impossible takes a little bit longer."

She also afforded me opportunities to travel around the world in the 1980's with an interfaith, international, interdenominational intercessory prayer ministry that she and her husband founded. I traveled to England, Germany, Greece, Holland, Israel, India, Singapore, and Thailand. I even visited Dachau in Germany. Earlier, a group of about 30 ministry members, including children, Jewish and German Catholic, visited and prayed for healing at all of the former ex–concentration camp sites in Austria, Germany and Poland. She encouraged us to do community service work, too. I volunteered at St. Vincent de Paul shelter for men in Las Vegas every month for two years and it was a blessing for the 150–300 men who attended the meetings as well as for me.

During Earthplay, a seminar company that Rannette created, she fostered an atmosphere where women encouraged and supported one another's growth and success. We also shared intimate personal details about being female and empowered one another. We were a spiritual family and community.

Rannette always encouraged us to get to know people we did not like and find what we had in common with one another. Mostly, we benefited from these interactions as we became more honest and got to know ourselves better. It was not always easy, even difficult, and sometimes a lot of fun. I enjoyed becoming friends with women from England, Germany, and other countries as we journeyed, worked and lived together.

My friendships with women (and men) have lasted a long time. Many are the kind of friendships where you may not speak for years; but when you do, it is as if you had just spoken to one another yesterday. My friends have come and gone. Some have died. Having been through so much together, I am very blessed to have known so many beautiful people in my life.

Ray York: Carry On

The best part of my hippie communal life was the music. We loved The Dead, and it was a revelation to listen to live music, so much more than what my cassette player offered. To have hippies with guitars sitting on the porch in the evening playing while we smoked pot and sang along was heaven. And the pot was free. Somebody always had some pot.

The volleyball was great, too. But as far as lasting values, I took away very little. I still have friends from the commune. They are good people. But the values of the group at the time were sex, drugs, and rock 'n' roll, with a garden.

The best thing I did on the commune was to build a house. I hung it out daringly over a rock outcropping: it extended horizontally well beyond its vertical support, and was an adventure to live in. At night, it swayed when the trees swayed; and we sometimes felt like we were aboard a ship.

It pains me to admit it, because I bought into it for years, but my hippie experience was a flop. When I faced real problems down the road, hippie slogans didn't help. "All you need is love" was just an empty phrase from a song.

When my time was up on the commune, I went down to the city, a burned-out hippie. I was angry about the wasted years I had used as an avoidance of the real world. I was unable to stand the pressures of the rat race I once again joined. My relationship blew up. I lost my children. I was doomed to start from scratch.

Unmoored, I smoked too much pot, worked as a cab driver and at construction, but couldn't hold a job, and had no money. Then word came down from the commune that a tree had fallen through my house, and it was ruined. It was as if the tree had fallen through my life. That event, that image, shocked me into a new realization. It galvanized me.

My hippie life was behind me. I stopped smoking pot and started to do right by who I really am: not a hippie, not a square, but a human being. I began to meditate. With meditation, there is no doctrine, no dogma. There are no ideals. There's just you and your mind. If you want to find your strength, you meditate. When you give yourself to it, it is pure and perfect healing energy.

Then came Parkinson's. And more limitations than I ever had to deal with. I've had three brain surgeries. I'm losing the ability to walk and to talk. I fear the isolation of being non-verbal. As my face becomes set in an open-mouth rictus, I'm losing the ability to smile. But I can still meditate, and I'm smiling on the inside. I can travel—I went to Baja last month— and I can write. I hate to look in the mirror, but you can't have everything.

Ray York: Happy Together

She was the Queen of the Rodeo and I was a cowpoke.
She said, "Howdy, cowboy."

I looked up and saw a vision of loveliness.

I built a house and she moved in. But I wasn't ready, and after a year, we split up. I went out in the world to get some seasoning.

And then one day, 25 years later, at a little Mexican restaurant, we met again. She was an airline pilot, a captain. I was a cowpoke.

"Hello, cowboy," she said.

"I'm ready," I said.

We've been married for 12 years.

Do Your Own Thing

Born butt-first in 1950, I've been a rule breaker ever since. The expression "Do your own thing" has always suited me perfectly. Yet, like most things, being "free" turned out to be considerably more complicated than I expected.

I think it's fair to say that most hippie-minded folks in the 1960s and early '70's were trying to be free of their parents, or at least, free of their suffocating rules and obvious hypocrisy. I was no exception. In 1970, I was sure that I wanted to get away from the cookie-cutter life my parents had designed for themselves and for me; although I was a little fuzzy about how to replace it. And so, like many others, I became an explorer of the new world, testing this and that to find the right fit, a process that continues today.

By my estimates, doing my own thing has cost me one marriage, 10 regular jobs, 15 businesses, 20 apartments, and all the money I've ever made. But who's counting? When I look back, the price of swimming upstream, day after day, past the carnage, oblivious to the pessimists, seems incredibly high.

But at the time, I didn't care. I wasn't going to let anybody else—particularly my parents and those like them—tell me what to do. Damn the torpedoes. Full steam ahead. "Leap before you look," was my motto. Sure, I hit the rocks a time or two—or 16. But hell, I was free!

In 1970, I couldn't imagine why anyone would choose to live a suffocating life of conformity. I was sure that the desire for freedom was innately programmed into every human being, until I read a book called Escape from Freedom *(1941) by Erich Fromm. Fromm's central message is that many people would rather escape from freedom than pay the heavy price of independent thought and action.*

"Modern man still is anxious and tempted to surrender his freedom to dictators of all kinds," he wrote, "or to lose it by transforming himself into

a small cog in the machine, well fed and well clothed, yet not a free man but an automation."

Fromm explains that, when we turn left while everyone else is turning right, we are alone and forced to struggle through life without the warm sense of belonging that we crave as social beings. In my case, that's true. I am a hermit of sorts, without friends, close only to my immediate family. Ironically, while editing this book, I've expanded my world somewhat through new connections with fellow hippies.

I was a practicing alcoholic and drug addict for 30 years. No one made me do it, and no one could make me stop. Poisoning myself was my decision. I was a free man, free to look for joy where I could, free to destroy myself if I wanted. I was tangled up in a net of my own choosing, without realizing I was just avoiding the fundamental changes that sobriety would surely bring.

I used to say that I would quit using as soon as the conditions in my life improved. When I had more money, my love-life improved, and I didn't feel so sad and desperate, I would give up the booze and the pipe forever. Of course, I was too deep in a hole to realize that my life would never improve until I quit getting high which, of course, would require making big changes, something I wasn't willing to do.

I know today, after decades of being clean and sober, that I can't be free unless I'm willing to change, willing to take a "leap of faith" out of the old into the new. I have to be willing to face the terrifying prospect of a life I can't imagine in order to escape the life I can no longer endure. I have to be willing to see things as they are, admit that I'm traveling in the wrong direction, and start again.

Today, I'm more careful about which rules I break and which battles I fight. I still don't let anybody tell me what to do, but I'm more willing to weigh the price before I jump. While my impetuous decisions over the years have certainly hurt others, they've hurt me the most. The terror of living on the edge for such a long time is simply not worth it anymore.

Today, I know that I don't have to prove anything to myself or to anyone else. I don't have to be rebellious just because I can. Today, I'm secure enough in myself to ignore the small stuff and focus on issues that really matter.—S.L.R.

Susan Hanauer: Free Bird

I've always done my own thing, much to the dismay and disapproval of my family. I grew up poor and exceedingly shy. I hated playing with girls, probably because I shadowed my two older brothers. I fed off their energy. Everything they did was exciting. My little sister always wanted me to play Barbies with her. Considering we didn't have much money, the two outfits for each doll were boring.

I got good grades in school, though I kept to myself. I didn't have any meanness in me; so, when the hippie movement got strong, I gravitated to it like a hungry child who discovered a buffet. I wanted peace for everyone and freedom and love in everyone's hearts. Maybe being the middle child and the peacemaker was the cause; but in the end, nobody was listening.

I grew up basically alone. By the time I turned 17, I looked around and discovered I didn't even have to run away. Everyone had left. My disabled mother was in a nursing home, while my father was busy with his mistress and their new baby. My brothers moved out to other states, and one invited my little sister to go with him.

I was in the upper 25 percent of my graduating class when I quit school. I was so bored. There were other dropouts to hang with plus drugs and booze and sex. Living in Montana put quite a damper on the whole hippie movement, but I still protested where I could against the Vietnam War and authority of every sort. I was doing this my way.

In the summer of 1972, I felt a strong need to get out of Dodge—or in this case, Great Falls. I wanted to go join other free birds, not in California, but in Arizona. So one day, I snatched up my six-week-old German shepherd Dica (acid spelled backwards) and my best friend Barb, who was only 15 at the time, and hitchhiked out of there. No one cared that I left. No one tried to stop me.

As we rode into Albuquerque from Santa Fe—my dog, my friend, and about six other souls stuffed into a car—I had this incredible sense of peace that floated over me. I was never at peace with my life. Now I felt I was given a new life.

In the next six weeks, I had an abortion, met David, hitchhiked back to Montana to tell my family we were getting married, hitchhiked back to Albuquerque where we got married, and then hitchhiked to David's Dad's house in Bethesda, Maryland. Since then, we've raised five home-schooled children and operated several of our own businesses. Yes, I do my own thing; because life is just too entertaining to go with the normal.

Susan Hawke: Be Sure to Wear a Ribbon in Your Hair

On Career Day at school, we had to write an essay about what we wanted to "be" when we grew up. I chose "Witch," because I was obsessed with them. Witches make potions and fly through the air on brooms! I dressed like the stereotypical witch every Halloween.

But my teacher made me change my topic. So, I replaced the title with "Mermaid." What little girl didn't want to be a mermaid? It'd be your job to swim with dolphins, string seashells, comb your hair in the sunshine, and sing with your pals! I remember my teacher picking up my paper then immediately flinging it back on my desk. "Write something real!" she demanded.

The usual jobs presented to girls—nurses, secretaries, waitresses, and yucky teachers—didn't appeal to me. I wrote "Flower Girl" in earnest as my teacher hovered. "Do you mean like a 'bride' in a wedding?" she'd asked.

To clarify, I wrote beside it, "Female hippie" along with a job description that went something like this:

> A Flower Girl is Mother Nature's daughter. She sings and dances for peace. She is kind and does not tell lies. She helps children and animals. She likes all of the colors in the world and rainbows. She is an artist. The Flower Girl is FREE!!!

Upon receiving my diploma, I thought I was free to "be" whatever I wanted. I bought a Camaro with the money I'd earned as a carhop (a waitress on roller skates). I worked as a secretary "downtown." On weekends, I dabbled in New Age religions and met actual witches. Then I attended a liberal arts college. I tried to please others and myself at the same time. Because I'd always been told I was "different" from my peers, social approval was important to me.

That changed when I became a journalist. I was part of the first wave of women in newsrooms. Not everyone welcomed us. Female reporters took a lot of crap back then. I appreciated those men who were supportive. I discovered "truth" can be perceived in many ways. Our world is both colorful and complicated.

I covered environmental issues in an attempt to be Earth's steward. Later, I worked with marine biologists in the Everglades. I got to swim with manatees in Florida's canals and dolphins off its coasts. According to history, sailors often mistook manatees for mermaids, which is hard to imagine. Yet I felt like a mermaid as I swam alongside them!

Later, I ironically became a teacher and learned new generations of girls do not appreciate the courage of their predecessors. Still I hope they will—someday.

I've performed multiple roles in my quest for truth. But have I ever truly been free to just "be?" So, when do I get to be the Flower Girl? Sometimes I wonder if she ever really existed—if only in the dreams of an evolving, female hippie.

J Laurence: It's Your Thing

If there was a single theme that permeated the hippie era, it was contradiction. I remember being told "smoking is bad" while watching my uncle light one unfiltered cigarettes after another and a family friend drinking whisky every day with a cigar between his teeth. I recall my parents pointing out the faults in others, while ignoring their own, and shopping carts filled with unnecessary items in the name of consumerism. The contradictions were everywhere. Hippies decided that enough was enough.

Our parents wore fashionable hairstyles and clothes. We let our hair and beards grow, wearing jeans, work shirts and boots instead. They listened to Sinatra, Garland, Bennett and big band. We chose folk, blues, and rock. They believed in patriotism and paying taxes. We were dead opposite. They demanded that we get a college education, a job and a family. We objected to it all. They believed in rules. We believed in questioning.

One of the things that irked me the most was how parents failed to observe. If they had paid attention and listened, they could have inspired and guided instead of cramming rules down their children's throats. Born into a family whose parents were creative, mine did everything to block my pursuit of a creative career. Once a candidate for a high school of the performing arts, I was forced to attend public school where art and music teachers were clueless.

Thanks to the hippies, everything that was written, sung about or done back in the day contradicted the status quo. Evolution, revolution, the times they are a-changin' ... we basked in contradiction of all sorts. Today when we observe the recent return to old world ideologies, complete with racism, consumerism and faltering democracy, hippie mentality is more important than ever.

As I think back, hippies launched the original grass roots movements. Observing today's youth wearing their hair long, seeing the contradiction in society and marching for what's right, I'm inspired knowing the hippies were the ones that broke through first. We saw the contradictions and moved in favor of change.

Rose V: Light My Fire

One day, I came home from school to find all the clothes I owned had disappeared. I looked out my bedroom window, and there was my Dad burning something in a huge metal trash can in the backyard. After opening the screened door on the back porch and cautiously walking up to the burning can. I saw part of my fringed jacket, a bellbottom pant leg, and a few tie-dye shirts melting in the flames. My dad didn't say a word as I stared at the fire and realized he was actually burning all my hippie clothes. Until that moment, I didn't realize how much he must have hated the direction his daughter's life was taking.

He handed me a credit card and told me to go buy some decent clothes that didn't look like a hippie. "All right old man, you asked for it," I was thinking, as I ran out to the fanciest department stores and bought an expensive fringe jacket, designer jeans with awesome embroidery all over them, and lots of other stuff that looked like a much pricier version of my old clothes. When I defiantly wore my new outfit the next day, Dad just shook his head. We never talked about it again.

Looking back, he must have thought that burning all my hippie symbols would make things normal again, that I would return to the sweet, conservative dutiful daughter I sort of used to be. He thought he could just burn away my new mantra of free love, free will, and free peace with a trash can. Sorry Dad.

Tea R. Peronto: Wouldn't It Be Nice

It was 1970, and the hippie movement was going strong. Joe and I had it all figured out, even though we were only eight years old at the time. We heard the stories about Vietnam, and the grown-ups did not seem to be doing much about it. We hated war and wanted to grow up to fill the world with peace and love.

During our school recesses, we would wander out to the field just beyond the sandlot and lay down in the tall grass. We were the rebels, down low where the playground attendants could not see us. There we would plot our grand plan for the future when we grew up. The sky was so blue as we talked and watched the clouds float overhead. I could hear flies and other bugs buzzing around us while we laid there munching on sour grass, free in our own little world.

We would collect money from returning recycled bottles and cans. We would get odd jobs and use that money to buy one of those cool VW vans. We would paint it in beautiful colors and camp in it while we traveled the country spreading our message of love and peace. We would be free to do our own thing and not live by anyone's rules.

A few years later, my plans changed. My parents found religion, and our life became full of expectations. They had rules about how we should act and dress, what to read, what music to listen to, and who to hang out with.

Then in high school, life got even more complicated. There were pressures to wear the cool clothes, have a car, and party like the other kids. I did my best to keep up and to follow all the rules, but I never was very good at fitting in. My anxiety went through the roof.

I ran into my old friend Joe in the halls of high school one day, and we had a good laugh. What happened to us? Did we even want to be cool and hate the people who were not? Instead, we decided to bring together the un-cool kids, show them some love, and invest in some good friends.

Today I am a grandma at the far edge of middle-aged. I still do not quite fit in. My blonde hair hangs almost to my waist, although I have been told that a lady of my advanced years should wear it much shorter. I wear a thumb ring and an ankle bracelet. I enjoy baseball, camping, and fishing. I do not care about fashion, makeup, cooking or shopping.

I am not really a hippie anymore since that is no longer "a thing," but I did carry something away from that part of my life. I still believe in loving those around you and in doing all you can to add to peace in the world. I still strive for freedom as well, the freedom to be unique.

Steve Trinward: People Got to Be Free

In the fall of 1967, I entered Tufts University. Almost immediately, I became involved in campus activism and protesting the war (even though I was at the time enrolled as a Navy ROTC Contract student). About the only thing about me that wasn't anti-establishment was my ROTC-mandated haircut.

Within a few months, I found myself engaged in defending the ROTC cause, opposing the attempts to "ban ROTC" from the campus. Even then, I knew enough about liberty to know that preventing someone from choosing to peacefully find a way to pay for an already pricey education by using a Navy scholarship was wrong.

As a freshman I joined Students for a Democratic Society (SDS) and went to lots of meetings and rallies. But from my Students for Tufts experiences, I began to see through the rhetoric. Seeing both the pro-peace and true "pro-choice" (on a wider scope than abortion rights) perspectives gave me a big step toward resisting the basically socialist message behind most of the "peace movement."

Like nearly all hippies, I also got involved in experimenting with psychedelics, beginning with cannabis, of course, then expanding my consciousness with mescaline, psilocybin, and LSD. I also went a few rounds with MDMA in its early forms, long before it became known as "ecstasy." In each case, the intention was more about looking for new perspectives than about "getting high"—well, most of the time at least.

Throughout college, I struggled between wanting to fit into the activist group and its mostly socialistic agenda, and my own basic common sense. I campaigned for Clean Gene McCarthy in '68 and continued to protest against Vietnamese and Cambodian incursions. I was also active right through Kent State, though Altamont dimmed the flame a bit.

A year after graduation, I was ready to stump for the next peace candidate, George McGovern, when I was invited to a gathering of a newly formed political group. I attended, and after about five minutes of conversation with the Libertarian Party's vice-presidential nominee, Tonie Nathan, there was no looking back. I knew I was, and had always been, a libertarian.

I've been with the Libertarian Party and the liberty movement ever since. The belief in a world based on choice, contracts, consensus and (voluntary) community is just so in line with what my "hippie" self was seeking. The Party's devotion to peace, civil liberties and economic sanity in a world where "everyone wins" is fully in line with my beliefs and desires.

Doors of Perception

After spending an afternoon tripping on mescaline in 1954, Aldous Huxley wrote a psychedelic classic called Doors of Perception. *In short, his drug experience changed his perception of the world. I can relate. The few but profound journeys I took with acid and mescaline jolted my senses into seeing reality in fundamentally different ways.*

Some will say that psychedelic visions were merely delusions, nothing more than a temporary rearrangement of electrons in a drugged brain. Whether what I saw and sensed was delusion, illusion, or confusion, I can't say for sure. But I am sure that the perception of a different reality was certainly true to me. Looking over the psychic fence and sensing something completely different was real to me and, more importantly, convinced me that "reality" could be seen in an infinite number of ways.

Unlike some folks in that day and time, I stopped taking psychedelics after a few trips. The journeys were mentally and physically exhausting, and I chose to climb out of the rabbit hole while I still could. Timothy Leary, psychologist and heralded proponent of LSD, leaked the truth when he wrote: "There are three side effects of acid: enhanced long-term memory, decreased short-term memory, and I forget the third."

Tripping was never the end game. It was only the beginning. Once you realize that a bigger, brighter, inconceivable world exists out there waiting to be discovered—and you realize that more and more psychedelics will eventually melt your brain instead of expanding it—you naturally begin looking for other ways to open the doors of perception. And there are so many.

I've learned that any time I experience a new person, a new place, a new idea, a new taste, a new smell, a new mood, I'm looking through the doors of perception into the infinite. When I open myself to others, I enter a world I've never seen before. When I let my imagination run free, I see new pictures and new ways of doing things. Every day is a new trip.

If one individual can see "reality" in different ways, then obviously two people can look at the same speck of reality and see different things.

Ken Kesey, author of One Flew Over the Cuckoo's Nest *and self-described hippie guru, lived communally with a group he referred to as the Merry Pranksters. In 1964, the group traveled across the United States in a psychedelic bus organizing LSD parties.*

One of Kesey's famous lines (per Tom Wolfe's The Electric Kool-Aid Acid Test*) was: "You're either on the bus or off the bus," ostensibly referring to Pranksters who wandered away when the bus stopped for gas, but probably directed toward those who failed to agree spiritually with the rest of the travelers.*

I interpret his statement to mean: "We're right, and you're wrong. You're either for us or against us. You either see what we see, or we don't want anything to do with you!" I hope I'm wrong about that. I hate to think that Ken could have been mouthing the same old delusional ideas that still lie at the heart of human misery.

Personally, I've come to realize that we're all on the same bus, looking out the same windows, but seeing different things.

In 1971, I took a philosophy course on "Existentialism," one of the few college courses I still remember today. In his first lecture, the frail-looking professor instructed us to count the holes in the acoustical ceiling tile just above our heads. After a few minutes, he asked a guy on the left side of the classroom. "How many holes did you count?" The student gave a number. Then, he asked a second question of the guy. "How many holes are in the ceiling tiles on the other side of the room." Sounding a bit aggravated with such a stupid question, the student answered, "The same number."

"Not necessarily," replied the old sage with a grin. "On your side of the room," he explained, "you define reality by the information emanating from your senses, in this case, your eyes. But you can't use that method to define reality on the other side of the room. The reality you see is determined. The reality outside your vision is determinable; i.e., able to be determined by your eyes if you moved your seat."

"Since no one can be in two places at one time, no one can know the reality experienced by other people in other places. Your reality is governed by your experience, not by a set of ultimate logical truths," he concluded.

It took me a while to understand what the prof was trying to say. But one day as I walked back to my dorm from class, Boom! I got it. We all see things in different ways, and our reality is governed by our experiences. The color blue I see when looking at the sky may not be the same color you see looking at the same sky. It's all about perception.

All of this sounds esoteric and frankly useless, until you apply the idea to relations between people. Those from one country, one culture, one religion, one gender, one age cannot know exactly what someone of a different country, etc., has experienced and believes to be true. Even those with similar backgrounds living in the same country can see the same thing and interpret it in different ways.

Several years ago, I came across a bumper sticker that read: "Militant agnostic: I don't know and you don't either." How true about everything!

As human beings, we're wired for certainty. From the moment of our birth, our busy little brains are trying to make sense of the world ... how things work, what they're called, which things brings pleasure, which ones bring pain. Without this kind of foundation, the world would be chaotic and unnavigable.

And yet, it is this insatiable lust for certainty that creates so many problems. Followers of one religion are so convinced that they are God's chosen ones that they want to destroy the non-believers. One gender, one race, one sexual orientation, one body type, one income group, one political party is so convinced of its superiority that it rejects all others.

In fact, nothing is certain; because we are limited by time, space, and the inadequacies of our brains. Imagine all the "facts" that human beings have accepted over the ages that later turned out to be ridiculous. The world is not flat. Bloodletting does not cure disease. Witches do not cause famine. The world did not end when the Mayan calendar predicted ... etc., etc.

Here we are in the 21st century, smarter than any generation before, but still ignorant enough to believe that we have all the answers. Perhaps, in our own way, we still think the sun revolves around the earth.

Over the years, I've found that the wider I open my mind to uncertainty, the calmer I feel and the more accepting of others I become. Unafraid of contradiction, I see new possibilities. Without preconceived notions of ultimate truth, I'm open to new ways of thinking. For me, true wisdom is knowing what I don't know.

These days, I have no interest in winning arguments or persuading other people to change their minds. I don't have to be right. They don't have to be wrong. I don't care what people believe so long as they don't hurt anyone else.

Because each person has his/her own unique perception of reality,

human beings will never agree on everything. Therefore, the road to peace
is not a one-world government or one-world religion, but a one-world will-
ingness to honor the perceptions of others.—S.L.R.

Ashley Kent Carrithers: Spinning Wheel

Today, a lovely lady asked me what I learned from my mind trip experiences. I told her that I had enjoyed a few encounters with psychedelic
drugs back in my younger days and was glad that I had, having gained
understandings which were, for me, evolutionary.

I explained that, wonderfully, in a corner of Creation, the keys to freedom and feeling good exist, delivered as magic mushrooms, certain cacti,
the root of some plant in the Amazon, and the ubiquitous weed, each
expanding consciousness delivered on the wings of love.

What did I learn? Let's start with the salubrious joy of laughter, where
one laughs and laughs at the silliest things, having glimpsed life's wondrous
absurdity and knowing that the miraculous mystery of love, so vast and
beyond belief, is best embraced with laughter.

Then, I said, as laughter runs its raucous and prayerful course, you
discover the Universe coursing through your body and creating a sense
of Oneness, not just with the beloved tripping fool sitting alongside, but
also with the birds, the plants, the rocks, the breezes, the trees, the waters,
and everything in creation. Awe ascends, and the mind opens to love and
life's raw majesty.

As I struggled to explain more, I found that words were inadequate
to describe the waves of love. I could remember the sensation, the slowing
of time, the waltz of gratitude and wonder, and the joy of being as celestial
songs cascaded, embraced, and transformed; but I could not describe it.
I could only recall how the world became a cathedral. God was everywhere,
but there was no "where" as Oneness had transcended awareness. Like a
sumptuous smile presented for my delectation, the portals of perception
had opened wide leaving me mute in its wake.

Beth Richards: Amazing Grace

We were wandering the halls of an old classroom building at The
College of William and Mary, admiring the walls. The dark wood was so
rich and deep with grains swirling about in their intricate patterns, snaking

dark lines in the rich mahogany color. It was the summer of 1968. My roommate Nina and I had agreed to accompany a friend to the college one Saturday and wait while he took a GRE test. We didn't tell him we intended to drop acid while we waited for him.

Nina and I had been living together for a year or so and got along with some difficulty. She had some hard edges and strong political and social beliefs. I was quiet and never very sure of anything, afraid to debate with her. There were often misunderstandings and uncomfortable moments, although we still had fun together playing pinball, slipping out for coffee at the White Castle in the middle of all-nighter, and trying to figure out how to come up with food and rent.

On this particular morning, I was uncomfortable tripping in public, paranoid that someone would catch on to some odd behavior. So, we decided to leave the building where our friend was taking his test and wander beside Matoaka Lake near the college. As our acid experience deepened, we found ourselves standing in front of an old gnarled tree stump halfway in the water at the edge of the lake. While we stared at the stump, I realized with a deep and complete awareness that we were looking at the center of the universe which resided in that stump and that Nina and I were of one mind, completely. It was as though we were one person in two bodies. I was overwhelmed with the profundity, with this newfound experience of knowing I am completely one with the universe. God was that stump and was everything else as well.

Gradually over the day, we drifted back to "normal"; and the cracks appeared in our euphoria until all was as it had been. But that glimpse into perception of our state of grace has never left me completely. I will always know that I am part of all that is. Although my life has moved onto many different places, and I've had my share of the woes of the world, I keep that seed of awareness, a gem of bliss at the center of this rough planet.

Ray York: Trippin'

I was raised in a strict Catholic family and went to Notre Dame. It was there, in that great bastion of faith, that I lost mine. I simply wasn't interested any more. And rather than feeling tortured, I felt free. So, I wrote a children's book and, with the royalties, quit my job and traveled around the country looking for someplace to call home. When I heard of an interesting community north of San Francisco, I went to visit.

By then, my hair was long. People looked on me as a hippie. I worked in the garden and hunted, with plenty of time to read books like *Be Here Now* and *Gravity's Rainbow* and authors like Carlos Castaneda. I ate mushrooms and had the most amazing experience of my life when I "saw God." I began to realize that the end of my faith was not the end of God in my life.

I took LSD, and the same wonderful thing happened, a peak experience, the pearl of great price! I intensified my reading: Teilhard de Chardin, St. Augustine, Gurdjieff, The Doors of Perception, St Therese of Lisieux, the excellent *Lazy Man's Guide to Enlightenment*, everything I could get my hands on along those lines. I found references to *The Cloud of Unknowing* and drove all the way to Berkeley to buy it.

Soon I realized that I was getting too dependent on acid and that I was going to have to find god without it. I was also out of money. So, I left my dear hippie friends, went down to the city, and cut my hair. I was back in the world, but no longer exactly of it. The world was the same as it always had been, bustling, neither friendly nor unfriendly. I ignored it as much as I could, read, and took acid once a month.

One night, my girlfriend took me to what she called a "satsang," a spiritual gathering of people into meditation with a guru. It sounded good to me. Meditation had to be the way, I thought, and signed on. It was what I was looking for: The kingdom of heaven is indeed within. My life smoothed out. I still did acid once in a while.

Today, hallucinogens have made a comeback as therapeutic drugs, used in hospices around the country and by the medical profession at such mainstream places as NYU and the Mayo Clinic. Hippie drugs have a new name: entheogens, i.e., a substance typically of plant origin that is ingested to produce non-ordinary states of consciousness for religious or spiritual purposes, including mushrooms and acid.

Having always felt alone in recognizing the value of these drugs as a gateway to the sacred and not just a form of recreation, I feel validated—tripping pointed the way.

Rick Denney: Long and Winding Road

Like many other students graduating from high school in 1967, I was filled with great anticipation. Finally, I was able to put high school behind me and focus on future endeavors. Plans were to take the summer off, regroup, and figure out what the next move might be.

I had my share of problems living at home. My parents seemed out of touch, driven by their excessive social drinking which turned out to be accepted alcoholism. I did experiment with drinking in high school but with little success. My parents had money, and I grew up in an influential neighborhood. My stepdad owned a construction company, and my mother never worked except for a part-time modeling job. She was your typical stay at home mom.

So, the journey began. I moved out, got a job, and rented a large house with four friends.

Grass became my drug of choice until peyote came along, followed by LSD, followed by cocaine. Wow, life was good! Our house had six bedrooms. On any given night, each one of them was the place to be, with all the drugs, rock and roll, and unfiltered sex one could handle. Looking back, it was a great time to be 18 years old.

Today, I know that, during those years, my core values were shaken, bent but not broken. Many of my friends became hooked on various drugs and experienced personality transformations that changed their lives forever. I never did any "hard drugs" like heroin and never injected a needle into my body. When I saw how that road affected my friends, I decided this was not for me.

Still, I felt something was missing, something spiritual; so, I began a search to find it. Drugs, especially LSD, gave me an inward perspective that fueled my search. But eventually, realizing that drugs were not the answer, I followed The Beatles into Eastern mysticism, an interesting path that seemed to work for many, but not for me. Not knowing why it didn't work only made me more intense in my search for "the answers."

After many different experiments stretching into the early '70s, I finally came to a place in the mid–80s where I realized that numerous forces both inside and continually around us gently guide us thru life's daily challenges. I have learned that, when I find a place where I can be still, meditate and listen, the answer comes most of the time. It may not be the answer I want, but it's always proven to be the answer I need.

The saying that "life is a journey not a destination" rings true for me. Yes, I grew up in the '60s and consider myself an old hippie who has evolved. I continue to evolve each and every day.

Wayne Lee: Good Vibrations

Recently, I watched a documentary called *The Sunshine Makers* about the two guys who made millions of hits of Orange Sunshine LSD in an altruistic effort to move America en masse away from violence and greed and toward peace and love. They were eventually imprisoned and their crusade ended, but to this day they still believe that theirs was a noble cause.

I never manufactured any psychedelics, although I took plenty of them. For me, as for most of my friends and fellow flower children, drugs were primarily a way of raising our consciousness, growing spiritually, finding God. We *knew* that by expanding our minds we were helping transform our country—and world—into a better, more peaceful, more enlightened place. We felt like spiritual pioneers, blazing new trails that would lead others toward God-centered lives devoted to creating harmony and connection among all sentient beings.

I no longer take chemicals, but I've never given up that desire to discover the path to transcendence and to share it with others. These days I use my meditation practice to find inner peace and connection, knowing that the vibrations I send out affect everything and everyone else in the universe, like ripples emanating from a pebble tossed in a pond. I practice Open Gate Meditation (opengatemeditation.com), a self-guided process of purification and renewal, much like opening the windows of a room to let a fresh breeze blow away the old, stale air from within. No matter what ordeals or challenges I'm facing on any given day; after I sit, I feel cleansed, rejuvenated and empowered to get up and go out there to continue the work of spreading peace and love throughout the cosmos.

I am that pebble, that agent for change. We all are. We all make a difference in the world, whether we believe it or not. Even if we don't call ourselves hippies anymore and we no longer seek to "drop out," we continue the work of tuning in and turning on, each in our own way. Yes, it's been a long, strange trip; and it isn't over. It will never be over.

CeliaSue Hecht: Human Potential Movement

The Human Potential Movement, so named by Aldous Huxley, began in the '60s and early '70s. Abraham Maslow taught self-actualization, the supreme expression of human life. The Esalen Institute in Big Sur offered diverse experiential interactive and transformational workshops. The purpose of these and similar teachings was to increase self-awareness and expand consciousness through the development of human potential. With such development, humans would experience an exceptional quality of life with peak experiences, leading to positive social change, also known as the New Age.

EST, one of these self-actualization approaches, was founded by Werner Erhard, aka Jack Rosenberg in 1971. His early influences included Zen, Alan Watts, Abraham Maslow, Carl Rogers, Napoleon Hill, Dale Carnegie and Scientology. The controversial EST training blended Eastern religions and Western thought. It was supposed to transform the way one sees and makes sense of life so that situations that one is trying to change can clear up in the process of living. It was a way to get in touch with the Real Self as opposed to the Mind-Ego. Statements by leaders of EST included: "What is is. What isn't isn't," and "It's a whole lot easier to ride the horse in the direction it is going." They taught that the spiritual path is a journey leading to enlightenment.

Stewart Emery, originally from Australia, was one of the first CEOs and trainers of EST. He co-founded Actualizations in 1975 in order to help people become more authentic through their actions in the world. "Don't resist your experience. Embrace it for what it is," he said.

I participated in Actualizations in San Francisco in 1977 where each person told the story of his/her life. The audience laughed and cried in response as they related to the person's story. The concept was: "The Truth may set you free, but it will piss you off first."

The Daniels Institute of Successful Living, a.k.a. Earthplay, was founded in 1975 in Beverly Hills by Rannette Daniels who had worked with her father Ranald Daniels from age nine. Ranald taught one of the most successful motivational training programs at that time and also hosted a radio show with Ernest Holmes, founder of Religious Science, a.k.a. Science of Mind, interviewing important thought leaders such as Dale Carnegie and Napoleon Hill.

Rannette created a weekend workshop called the Successful Living Seminar that expanded into a five-day seminar which became known as "the experience," designed to help people transform the way they experienced life. I was one of the Experience Leaders and led the seminar in Los Angeles and Munich, Germany. I also led other workshops including the Money Experience, the Family experience, Freedom Eating, Relationship Realities, and Assertiveness and Anger.

An organization called Concept Synergy began offering workshops in 1973 based on the teachings of Lazaris, a nonphysical entity channeled by an individual named Jach Pursel. Rannette introduced me to Lazaris in the 1980s. Over the years, Concept Synergy has conducted a wide array of workshops all over the world and offers tapes, books and videos. Lazaris says: "It was never meant to be this painful" and that "We are here to remind you that pain and fear are not the only methods to grow, but we can grow more elegantly through joy and love. You do create your own reality. And there is a God/Goddess/All That Is who knows your name and loves you. And you love good enough."

I did not consider myself a religious or spiritual person. At one time, I laughed at people who talked about past lives and other spiritual topics. Years ago, it would have been inconceivable to me to think I would become what I am today—a psychic medium, able to communicate with those who have passed, and to experience enlightenment, magic and miracles in my life.

Beth Richards: Piece of My Heart

A new song had been aired on the radio. It was different, very powerful; but the vocal seemed raw, harsh and piercing. I wasn't sure I liked it, but it definitely caught my attention. They said it was by a band called "Big Brother and the Holding Company" out of San Francisco, a city I revered for all the new ideas and styles it brought. The challenges to old ways of being coming from the west coast resonated with me. So, when my friend Linda asked if I would drive up to Alexandria, Virginia, to a concert by this group and its singer Janis Joplin, I eagerly agreed. She left me a message that we would meet a friend up there who would have some pot. I had not yet had a chance to try that and was eager to add it to my set of experiences.

We drove up to Alexandria on an October weekend, 1968, and stayed at my older sister's house. The concert was at a roller rink, no seating, and was held mid-afternoon. Jeff Beck's group was opening for Big Brother. At the time I was unaware of how amazing a guitarist I was going to see. But that's a side note. It was definitely weird walking into a roller rink and sitting on the floor in the afternoon light to watch such powerful music!

So, we smoked some weed on the way. It was my first time getting high, and I just remember walking through a lot of people with colorful clothes and wondering what all this was about. We went in where a makeshift stage had been set up at one end of the rink. I sat lotus-style right in front of the stage and waited. Shafts of afternoon sun beamed down on the old wooden floor around the crowd. When Janis came on stage and opened up her soul to us, it was like being flattened with the power coming out. I was instantly in love with her. Her long wild hair, exotic flowing poncho, and swigs on a bottle added mystery to the dynamic vocals. The music clearly came through her from some depth of feeling in the universe. It made me soar up to the rafters of the old rink and changed my life forever!

Since those heady days, music has had a powerful, visceral effect on me. It can take me to the depths of my inner spaces. Listening to powerful voices, deep drum rhythms, intricate string melodies or ringing keyboard notes can pull me into the Holy Spirit like nothing else. Janis Joplin played a major role in opening up my soul to the sense of wonder instilled in me by coming of age at this magical time in history. She definitely took a piece of my heart!

Barry Sommer: Yasgur's Farm

In 1969, at age 15, sick of school and urban life, I ran away from home in Los Angeles and made my way north to the land that gave birth to us hippies, San Francisco. The city by the bay was calling with a bullhorn. While I loved the new age life being created in Los Angeles, I felt the draw of the fog shrouded city and knew my life in LA was a precursor to a great adventure that awaited me. Filled with newfound wisdom, since all 15-year-olds are smarter than anyone over 30, and a burning desire to find love in all the right places, I stuck out my thumb somewhere along Highway 101 by Santa Monica and caught a ride all the way to San Francisco.

I remember getting into the VW van, brightly painted with the symbols and fetishes of my hippie brethren, and being offered my choice of mind-altering chemicals within 10 minutes. From that point on, my memory gets a bit fuzzy; but I do have small glimpses of the trip across the U.S. Of course, remembering exactly what was real and imagined after 50 years is a bit difficult.

Despite living in a slightly altered universe, the group in the van could be the poster children for the change we wanted to make in the world. Everything was shared, music dominated the air, and the problems of the day were discussed and solved. Corporate power structure, political graft, the war, jobs and the future were bantered about. We had solutions for everything. I was in heaven. I had found my new family and my place in the world.

Looking for food, rest, and more drugs, we went to Woodstock. As we made our way down the road to the farm of Max Yasgur, the first people we met offered snorts of mescaline from a small plastic baggie. Without hesitation, I answer "Yes," grateful for the generosity which was very different from the urban city where I grew up.

Love, respect, and dignity ... it was a beautiful thing that we all believed would last forever. I had to smile. The Age of Aquarius was upon us, and the world would be a better place for it. After three days of rain and mud, filled with memories of Hendrix, Joplin, Santana, Joe Cocker and Joan Baez, I made it home, still inspired by the spirit of love and cooperation I had experienced.

Fifty years later, my optimism has dimmed a bit and cynicism is creeping in. Faced with politics, social order, and cultural shifts, I am once again fleeing to a calmer place where people do care and love is part of daily life. I miss the old days but relish the new spirit that comes with new simpler ones.

Rick Denney: A Day in the Life

Growing up in Portland, Oregon, high school was a rebellious time for me. In 1966, I got suspended from school because my hair was touching my collar and I was wearing my new Beatle boots, both a "violation of the dress code." My friends and I were always pushing the boundaries and always in some sort of trouble over silly issues.

My mom was a part-time professional model and occasionally, she would travel outside of the Portland area to do a show. When she learned that she was going to Seattle in August for a few days to model a new line of clothes for a client, she asked me if I would like to go along. I agreed. It sounded like fun.

I discovered that The Beatles were doing a show in Seattle on August 25th, the same time we would be in there. Somehow, I got tickets for the evening show—two in fact. The plan was to find a girl in Seattle to take. But when that didn't happen, I went by myself. I wish I would have kept the extra ticket. It would probably be worth a tidy sum today.

I can't remember much about the actual show, because the noise and the girls screaming was so loud. When I got back to the hotel and my mom asked me about the concert, I remember thinking what a waste of $6 dollars, the price of the ticket.

At the time, I thought that seeing The Beatles was not such a big deal. Looking back, I now understand that it was a moment in time that started me on a road on which I am still traveling today. After the concert, I began listening to The Beatles and they became an important part of my life. Like many young people of my generation, I identified with the music and saw The Beatles as one of the first bands on the scene guiding us into an era that became known as the peace movement. I'm proud to say I was part of it then and remain so today.

Rose V: *The Ed Sullivan Show*

I was raised in a nice Southern house with a nice Southern yard and a nice Southern country club where I could hang out with my friends in the summertime. Our family was full up with nice cars, big house, impressive friends, and Bahamas vacations. I never thought life should be any different. Why should it be? My parents partied like rock stars on a continuous basis, leaving us kids to run wild all with minimum interference and shiny credit cards. Except for one event, I would have probably continued like that until I grew up and married the required doctor, lawyer, or business tycoon.

The defining factor of my path to hippiedom was seeing The Beatles on *The Ed Sullivan Show* for the first time. Sitting in our designer living room, glued to the black-and-white images on our Zenith TV, I was hooked. They were English, had long hair, and played music I could understand. I was instantly in love with all four of them. They didn't look or sound like anybody I knew. My only thought was that I needed to find myself more of those "beatniks," as my Daddy called them.

Many years later, I started my own landscaping business and hired every hippie and homeless guy I saw, thinking that maybe we could still make a life of free love and free will, but with a paycheck. Sadly, those people are not with me today. They got real jobs, drank themselves into oblivion, or moved back home to find an easier life. I've been looking for my hippie family ever since.

Flower Power

A familiar face on tee-shirts and posters in the '60s and '70s was that of Che Guevara, self-styled revolutionary with long black hair, a black beret, and black piercing eyes. In real life, Che fought with Castro during the Cuban revolution (1956–59) and was killed in 1967 while leading guerrilla wars against governments in Central and South America.

When I was 20, I wanted a revolution in America—not the violent kind, but the top-to-bottom reorganization of politics, schools, the economic system, and even families to solve the desperation and abuse I saw in the world. I didn't really know who Che was and didn't feel the need to wear his face on my chest. But I did like the symbolism that he represented.

Of course, I had no idea what Che's version of revolution really looked like. I didn't realize that upending a society overnight usually involved imprisoning or killing those who disagreed with the new direction. I didn't realize how often violent revolution simply replaces one dictator with another, one elite class with another. As The Who would say: "Meet the new boss. Same as the old boss."

As an impatient hippie, I wanted fundamental, long-term change, implemented immediately. Like many of my comrades, I was sorely disappointed that it didn't happen when I wanted and, in many respects, still hasn't happened today. But over the years, I've learned that "how" change is achieved is just as important as "what" is achieved.

Mahatma Gandhi and Dr. Martin Luther King understood that achieving peaceful ends requires peaceful means. They knew that, while short-term cosmetic changes can be achieved quickly by violently dismantling the status quo, long-term change can only happen when ordinary people change their hearts and minds, an impossible task when these people are consumed by fear and thoughts of revenge.

Poet Allen Ginsberg coined the term "Flower Power" to describe the strategy of combating hate with love. Grounded on the preposterous-sounding idea that non-violence could overcome violence, civil rights and anti-war protesters deployed wave after wave of "Flower Power" initiatives including mass demonstrations, rallies, sit-ins, boycotts, teach-ins, love-ins, guerrilla theater, draft card burning, self-help nonprofits, and even a psychic attempt to levitate the Pentagon. Between 1960 and 1975, these strategies contributed to ending the Vietnam War and legislating equal rights for minorities, women, the disabled, and the elderly. Never in American history had so many positive changes taken place in such a short period of time.

History tells us that Flower Power battles were often bloody confrontations in which police and angry citizens attacked unarmed protesters using clubs, bull whips, attack dogs, fire hoses, savage beatings, arson, bullets, and bombs.

One of the most dramatic of these battles happened on Sunday, March 7, 1965, when six-hundred civil rights demonstrators began a protest march from Selma, AL, to the state capital in Montgomery. In a spectacle of police brutality, later referred to as Bloody Sunday, state troopers attacked the marchers as television cameras conveyed the startling images into American homes. Consistent with Jesus's admonition to "turn the other cheek" and Dr. Martin Luther King's strategy of passive resistance, the protesters refused to fight back. What enormous courage and self-control it must have taken to stand there and be beaten without striking back!

I'd like to think that confronting violence with non-violence would have melted the hearts of the attackers that day, that the marauding police officers would have suddenly realized the error of their ways and traded fire hoses for hugs. That didn't happen.

What did happen is that previously silent citizens, after witnessing the sacrifices of the innocents, got involved in the struggle. Faced with gut-wrenching images of unarmed men and women being fire-hosed and bitten by attack dogs on national TV, kindhearted folks, who had previously been uninvolved, said a collective: "That's enough!" Laws were written. Justice was enforced.

Dr. King famously said: "We have to repent in this generation, not merely for the hateful words and actions of the bad people, but for the appalling silence of good people." As good people, do we really have to wait until we see the blood on TV before doing the right thing?

Most college students who marched on college campuses against the Vietnam War felt that we were safe from physical harm. We grieved for the civil rights protesters who were beaten, arrested, and sometimes killed; but we never thought it could happen to us. We were soon to learn the truth.

In 1970, Tricky Dick Nixon decided that the best way to end the war in Vietnam was to expand it into another country, Cambodia. That pissed off a lot of folks including college students across the country.

At the time of the Cambodian invasion, I was a sophomore at a small, liberal arts college. In the early morning hours, a day after The Prez had announced the escalation, a friend and I decided to display our opposition by erecting fifty small white crosses in rows outside our dormitory. We felt like real revolutionaries.

A much larger protest erupted at Kent State University in Ohio. On May 4, 1970, National Guardsmen killed four students and injured nine others during an anti-war demonstration on campus. The dead were standing 270–390 yards away from the Guardsmen. One was shot in the back. Of the injured, one was permanently paralyzed. Only one Guardsman was hurt, a minor injury occurring minutes before the shooting began.

In response to the massacre at Kent State, over 4 million high school and college students across the country went on strike, closing hundreds of public schools, colleges, and universities. Forty-eight years later, in March of 2018, a million students walked out of class to protest mass shootings and demand gun control. Once again, students led the way.

Elected president in 1960, John F. Kennedy was, for many, a symbol of the king we pretended not to want—handsome, strong, and decisive with a beautiful queen and adorable children. For many, he symbolized a new day for America. Many referred to his reign as "Camelot."

For reasons we don't understand, under circumstances still unclear, someone killed JFK in Dallas, Texas, on November 22, 1963. I will always remember hearing the news. I was 13 years old, sitting in my afternoon chorus class with about 50 other kids. Suddenly, the principal came on the loudspeaker. He said that he was sorry to have to tell us that someone had killed President Kennedy. He told us that school was adjourned and that we should go home immediately.

It was like an explosion in the room. No one spoke, but we were gasping for breath. My stomach hurt. Some girls cried. I didn't say it, but I was afraid. The Russians wanted to nuke us. Some maniac had killed the president. What was coming next?

An ex–Marine named Lee Harvey Oswald was quickly arrested for killing the president. Two days later, Oswald was assassinated by a mafia-connected bar owner in the basement of the Dallas Police Station. Go figure.

Five years later, in April of 1968, Dr. Martin Luther King, Jr., leader of the civil rights movement who had inspired and energized millions to confront violent segregationists with non-violent means, was killed by a second maniac. Two months after that, Bobby Kennedy, John's brother, was murdered by a third.

For many of us, losing these bigger-than-life heroes marked the end of our optimism about the future. Without their majesty and force for good, we felt lost and more afraid than ever. Perhaps we've been looking, unsuccessfully, for a new hero ever since.

I've come to believe that Flower Power works without great leaders. In the end, long-term change, the kind that determines our ability to live together happily and peacefully, evolves from how we treat each other every day. Laws can change actions, but they can't change hearts. Speeches can inspire, but individuals have to do the heavy lifting.

In the 1960s and early 1970s, Flower Power was employed most often as a group strategy. Personally, I'm more interested in applying Flower Power on a one-to-one level. Gandhi is quoted as saying: "Be the change you want to see in the world." I believe it.

A better me makes a better world. A more peaceful me soothes the rage of the fighters. A more accepting me enables the haters to be less afraid. A more hopeful me gives strength to the hopeless and power to the helpless.—S.L.R.

Risha Linda Mateos: Hippie State of Mind

I was very young when I chose the hippie lifestyle, because it offered more freedom of expression and appeared to be much more tolerant of race, class and cultural differences in a world in which I did not seem to fit.

I was raised in Miami, Florida, by a widowed, conservative, traditional Austrian mother. My questioning of authority seriously began in 1969 while attending a private Catholic school. My 8th grade class took a field trip to a headshop called the "Magic Mushroom" in nearby Ojus where the nuns planned to show us what dazed drug users looked like. When we walked in and I was greeted by my neighbor who worked there, the nuns immediately started second-guessing their choice of destination. I knew that my neighbor was a skilled craftsman who made lovely sandals for the shop and I was awakened to the fact that what the nuns had told us was wrong.

Soon, much to the consternation of my mother, I walked away from institutionalized religion and opted for public high school where the population was more diverse. At 17, I moved away from home permanently. After a rough start where I sometimes lived in abandoned structures or on people's porches, I embraced communal living with other teenagers who had also moved away from home for one reason or another.

I worked at several different jobs; but when I began working as a cook at "The Health Hut" and "Here Comes the Sun" health food restaurants, I fully realized the depth of my hippie soul. I became vegetarian and chose very unconventional clothing that spoke to my creative spirit.

After getting married in my 20s and having children, I began to look a bit more conventional; but my soul was still "hippie"; I began a spiritual quest that lasted through my adult years until I chose refuge in Buddhism 20 years ago at the age of 43.

In 1999, I met and worked with the Dalai Lama of Tibet at a twelve-day event called the Kalachakra for World Peace. For several years afterward, I hosted visiting Tibetan Monks who arrived in South Florida to teach about their threatened culture. I have also been an avid activist in environmental protection and politics since high school.

I lived in Queensland, Australia, from 1982 through 1984 and have traveled abroad extensively; but no location has taught me more about an authentic life than Mexico, a country rich in ancient history and indigenous culture. I am a photographer, herbalist and third-degree Reiki practitioner, grateful that I grew up in the "hippie age" and appreciative of life beyond the conventional.

Nancy Pruitt: Angela Davis

Her shrill voice soared into our heads, "Do you want to strike?" The sea of young students echoed her call: "Yes!" we shouted back, fists in the air. Angela Davis was ostensibly at UCLA in 1970 to teach existentialism, and I was sitting in her class when her question echoed the frustration we felt in our youthful exuberance. Our answer pleased her so much that she cancelled the class that day, blanketed us all with A grades, and encouraged us to join the campus tumult outside. The next morning, the Bruin student newspaper featured a picture of our teacher, beside a handcuffed SDS student, looking up to the heavens.

Growing up in Los Angeles, our young lives were branded by the assassinations of three key liberal leaders we revered; and our faith in government was dashed. Living through the Watts riots, we watched disadvantaged blacks fighting back, then oppressed even more by LBJ's underlying racism.

The Manson home invasion murders in 1969 attacked our sense of safety. That was so horrific and uncomfortably close, we were never the same after witnessing the depths of evil with his murder orgy.

It was a poignant time in our society, and we grieved losses of our idealism, trust in authority, safety anywhere, and calm debate over the pressing issues we all cared about. Sound familiar?

Our music was our safe harbor, a way to express our fears, our anger, and our hopes for humanity. Still, you have to wonder, then and now, is Peace-Love-Harmony even possible in a greed and hate-driven world? At 68, I still have faith.

Today, my advice is to use your mind. It's your strongest asset. Question everything. Think for yourself. Try to leave this magical spinning ball of rock called Earth a little better than you found it. Allow others to be who they are. Collaboration turns ideas into reality. Make a difference. Make art. Make music. Make love not war. Make your food whole. Live in the *now* and judge less. Help others. Push the boundaries from which we hold ourselves back. Remember history, respecting what all the armchair quarterbacks never saw or failed to learn. This too shall pass. Be kind. Act authentically with your core beliefs. Today, I remain a true flower child in spirit/heart.

"Cynthia," c/o Patricia Lapidus: excerpt from *The Farm That Tried to Feed the World*

I was always guided by a spirit to make a difference and a determination to make it happen. The Tennessee Farm and the New York Farm were vehicles to realize my dreams, and I continue to dream the dream. The dream was not the physical body of the farms but a spiritual bond we held in common and, for many of us, continue to hold in common. We made the decision to live on The Farm and try something new, something that would make the world a better place. I believe we did that and continue to do that. Yes, we made mistakes; but we were on a quest to change the world. We came to The Farm with all of our lives' baggage and had to sort it out the best way we could. I will always cherish my experiences on The Farm. I feel very fortunate to have had that opportunity.

CeliaSue Hecht: Be the Change

I once worked with a man named John who we called Gandhi. To this day, he has a very gentle spirit and is committed to various environmental causes and peace. He has a great sense of humor and utilizes it doing street theatre to raise awareness and educate people. I have found that numerous great leaders use humor to get their message across. We can often accept and laugh at ourselves when harsh truths are presented this way.

Most people abhor hypocrites, people who say one thing yet do another. My dad used to tell us, "Do as I say, not as I do." I loved my dad but hated when he would say that. "Walk your talk" is something to which I subscribe; although I also know that, as human beings, we do make mistakes. We are here on earth to learn, discover and journey to our Real Selves. No one is perfect. We never will be.

As a wonderful mentor, coach, teacher and friend for 40 years, Rannette Nicholas often talked about living our principles and striving to become our ideals. We will never attain the ideals, but we can become better human beings along our journey in life by going for what we want, our dreams. If you don't know where you are going, how do you know when you get there? She created a genius goal setting system called Directing your Intention that works every time. There are four possibilities: You get specifically what you think you want, or you realize you never really wanted it, or you obtain an aspect (perhaps a red car rather than a blue one) of what you want, or you discover what is between you and what you want.

Lazaris teaches us to Recognize (the problem/issue), Acknowledge (own it, how we are allowing or causing it), Forgive ourselves and others, and Change. We can work with these processes to heal ourselves and Become the Change we want to see in the world rather than just protesting, resisting or complaining about what is out there.

Surely, there are ways that we as individuals pollute our world. It's not just the toxic companies who dump poisons into our oceans, air and earth. Once, I challenged my aunt who was smoking in my face at the same time she was railing against polluters. She did not like being told that she was being part of the problem not the solution. But if/when we are part of the problem, we need to Change too. When we point our fingers and blame others, there are four other fingers pointing back to ourselves. Which makes me think of the Michael Jackson song, "The Man in the Mirror."

Author and social activist John Robbins, once heir to the Baskins-Robbins ice cream fortune, had a dream years ago about a cow. From there, he visited factory farms with an open heart, not to blame but to consciously see what was going on. He saw how horrifically the animals were being treated. He did not hate the workers nor did he blame anyone. Instead, he created a nonprofit organization called EarthSave to educate people about their diets and how to eat healthy (without meat). His book *Diet for a New America* tells this inspiring story. Ironically, when his father had a heart condition, his father's doctor recommended John's book without realizing that John had written it.

Our actions do speak louder than our words. If we really do want to change the world, it begins within our own selves. After the student murders at Kent State, the Vietnam War and Watergate, many of us hippies realized that we had to change ourselves to best effect social change. We realized that we cannot bring about peace or justice with hate in our own hearts and war raging internally. As we become more peaceful individuals, there is more Peace in the world.

Ron R: Transcendental Meditation

I graduated from high school in Deadwood/Lead South Dakota Class of '69 and became a hippie in August of that year, when my friend David and I managed to drive my Dodge Dart all the way to the Atlanta Pop Festival. That historic event was a month before Woodstock and included all of the Woodstock stars except for Jimi Hendrix. Music became my inspiration and guide into the free-thinking, free-loving, boundary-breaking sixties world. Led Zeppelin played at 11 p.m. one night, and a girl dressed in colored ribbons shared a joint with me.

The next day, in the midday heat, people I didn't know shared watermelon, water and even food with everybody around them. This detail, in 1969, was a revolution to me: "Wow, I don't even know that guy, and he passed me a watermelon!" The simple act of sharing was a rebellious act in the materialistic '60s. It was the Counterrevolution, and I lived it; I became, at that moment, a hippie.

A year later, I got kicked out of South Dakota State for anti-war activities on campus and finished my education at University of South Dakota in Vermillion. My "peace & love" self-developed even more. Tired of the stoner lifestyle at college and very aware of the contents of the Herman Hesse book *Siddhartha, The Master Game*, and Carlos Castaneda, I was looking for more; something deep.

In my senior year at USD, I came across a poster that was kind of glowing that said "Peace Love Happiness—Transcendental Meditation—Maharishi Mahesh Yogi." I got right into it; and after another two years, I was a teacher of TM. A friend at Maharishi University in Fairfield Iowa told me, "Ron, you speak some Spanish. You should go to Colombia and teach TM. They need a teacher." So, in 1974, with all the hippie idealism that only a 23-year-old could have, I went to Colombia to save the world by spreading the inner experience of unboundedness. I was a hippie with a haircut.

In Colombia, my reception was embellished by the truism, "Nobody is a prophet in his own land." I was immediately busy teaching TM in Manizales and Medellín. Maharishi was a figure of the '60s hippies, and I was his ambassador to Colombia. My hippie ideals were channeled seamlessly into my time in South America. The Beatles, Donovan and Mike Love of the Beach Boys were meditating at that time, and I was motivated despite the hardships of living on rice and beans in a foreign country.

I rolled with the TM crusade, teaching meditation in El Salvador, Guatemala and Mexico until three years later when I realized that those countries had their own teachers. So, I back went to California where, as it turned out, they didn't need any more TM teachers either. So, I found a job at the Gemological Institute of America (G.I.A.) in Santa Monica where diamond grading and colored stone identification are taught to the gem and jewelry industry. It was just a warehouse job, but I learned from their books that the best emeralds in the world come from Colombia. I slapped my forehead; and within two years, I had quit and returned to Colombia with plans to become a gem dealer.

This time, my hippie ideals were compromised and replaced by raw survival. Surrounded by liars, smugglers, killers, and the Medellin cartel, l occasionally heard car bombs from the TM Center and found that most of my friends are "too busy" to meditate.

I don't evangelize TM anymore; but I still hold values of the heart in the highest esteem; and music still moves me like always. Now at 67, I proudly witness my hippie ideals flourishing. My 3-year-old nonprofit, "Clayhands," is giving back to Colombia by providing employment and sustainability by teaching and promoting alternative construction with adobe, pressed earth and bamboo. I still meditate every day and still feel idealistic about the U.S. and the world.

J Laurence: Summer of Love

As I looked back to the couch surfing days of the '70s, I realized I had overlooked the importance of gratitude and giving. A dinner chat changed that forever.

Weeks later, I became involved in the formation of a nonprofit dedicated to sending disabled and poverty-stricken children to summer camp, a cause that opened my heart. I utilized my God-given creativity helping to produce events that raised thousands for the organization. Witnessing the ear-to-ear smiles of over 100 children during the first summer camp was an experience of pure joy. In the years that followed, the number of children eclipsed 500, while the summer camp term was extended to 3 weeks. Needless to say, there wasn't a dry eye in the house.

As time played out, I took on every single opportunity I could find to volunteer, even when time was precious or nonexistent. Events such as "Open Heart Open Home," a tour of artist Eichler's home in the county where I live, raised thousands. Soon after, I helped with the area's first "Concours d'Elegance," a classic car competition and show that raised nearly a quarter million dollars to benefit Hospice.

Regardless of the nature or size, I find great joy in contributing to others, even if my gifts are only information or insight. I've discovered that the most important treasure we can receive is that of giving, something that is truly part of Who I Am.

Mari S: Doctor My Eyes

It was 1967. I was 19, sitting in the living room of my small house with a sleeping husband in the bedroom. Where I wanted to be was in San Francisco with all the flower children and crazed hippies that I was being shown night after night on the news. That freedom and creativity and adventure was what I craved. It took me another two years and a baby before I realized that I had no business getting married at 18.

I had a lovely daughter and a good husband. We lived in a small town in Washington State, so it took a while to meet "exotic" New York hippies who had moved with their traveling light show to find a communal space in the Columbia Gorge where they could create the "off the grid" lives they wanted. It was also in about 1969 that my first friends started coming back from Vietnam with their awful stories and their trunks full of weed and hash and their enthusiasm for psychedelics.

I couldn't wait to try them, although it turned out I was not as turned on by the drugs as by the free-wheeling lifestyle. I did have a few lovely evenings on mescaline or mushrooms, however.

I ended up leaving my marriage, but stayed in the area to be close to my daughter. I was extremely anti-war and participated in the first large peace march in Portland, Oregon. In the years following, I continued to be active in political movements but became very disappointed when the Reagan era rolled around. Most of my generation had moved on to pretty middle-class lives in order to support themselves and their families. What had seemed like a movement before that would make the world a better and kinder place just seemed to fall apart.

I rarely used the word hippie to describe myself, but others certainly did. I didn't put myself in that category, because I always worked and maintained a stable home. I still believe that activism (including voting) is the only way change will happen. My friends and I feel the United States' political system is in a dark place right now, so we are becoming more active in contacting our political representatives. We are also realizing that we need to enjoy every moment, because who knows what is to come.

Now at 70, I am proud that I have a liberal daughter and two liberal grandchildren who I hope will continue to fight for what is right and kind and just ... with the help of us old hippies of course.

Ashley Kent Carrithers: World Peace

I have developed an entire new, revolutionary and visionary, global governance model which I am trying to effectuate as it guarantees world peace, de-militarization, species preservation, climate stabilization etc. Durn it! I am still trying after all these years.

Beth Richards: Revolution

It was a dark night in May 1970. I was on a low hill just outside the building that housed the ROTC office on the campus of the University of Virginia, nervously watching a rowdy horde attack the building. There was fire, police in riot gear, and people screaming—NO MORE WAR!! GET OUT OF VIETNAM!!! The scuttlebutt running through the crowd was that protesters had gotten inside and were occupying the building already.

It was the most chaotic scene I had ever witnessed, and I was feeling extremely uneasy, wavering between feeling I should participate, stand my ground, make a statement and not be a wimp versus torching or taking over a university building. The latter seemed counterintuitive, sending the wrong statement and making us all look stupid.

The massacre of four college students at Kent State in Ohio by the National Guard had electrified the whole country just four days prior to this talk, so everyone was extremely fired up. Tension over the invasion of Cambodia was filling the news propelling the anti-war movement to an historical peak. I wanted to be part of the action.

We had gone to Charlottesville from Old Dominion University to hear a talk by Jerry Rubin and William Kunstler, colleagues of Abbie Hoffman. Rubin, a highly visible activist and icon of the anti-war movement, was an inspiring speaker and roused the crowd to a fever pitch. He had testified before the U.S. House Committee on Un-American Activities wearing the garb of a Revolutionary War soldier, passing out copies of the Declaration of Independence. He and Abbie Hoffman had brought the NYSE to a halt by flinging dollar bills down onto the stock exchange floor to make a statement about the role of money in social injustice. Rubin had founded the Yippie Party with Hoffman in 1967. It is no surprise that he was able to inflame many of us in the crowd, a group already attuned to insisting on social justice and peace.

As the years have passed, I can see that speaking out so strongly was important in making changes to the direction of this country. If we had quietly and peacefully written articles, waited politely for change, and shared our opinions amongst our like-minded selves, the war would have gone on much longer and civil rights would have been granted at a snail's pace if at all. Intensity, passion, and outrage are often necessary to spark change, to drive people to push their cultural values in the direction of a safer and more just society. This is still true today. I find myself outraged by some of the injustices that are taking place in my country, but still struggle with the tendency to stand back and quietly complain from a distance to keep from looking stupid, when expressions of outrage are more likely to bring about change.

Gordon Muir: Get Up. Stand Up.

There have been periods of time when men having long hair was fashionable and acceptable, but the 1950s and '60s were not one of those times. Coming straight out of the war years, the usual look was either a brush cut for the mainstream, or an Elvis duck tail for the rebels without a cause. Long hair was for girls.

When hippies started to grow their hair, I well remember the violence directed their way. Forgotten in the fog of time is the fact that, to be a real hippie, you had to have the backbone to stand up for your beliefs in the face of hatred, catcalling, and more often than you would think, violence.

"I can't tell if it's a girl or a guy." "Get a job, asshole." "Get a haircut, ya freak!" For a while, punching a hippie was a thing, made easier by the fact that hippies believed in non-violence. "Long haired freaky people" were not wanted and their views on life were too threatening to be tolerated. So, violence, the non-thinker's answer to everything, became one answer.

When I was five, my family separated; and I was sent to live with relatives I didn't really know in a mining town way up in the cold North. One of the life-changing events that occurred there was my being beaten up by a boy just a little older than me. I don't remember how it started, but I do remember being face down in the dirt road with him on top of me. I wasn't angry with him. It was more about shock, miscomprehension and wonder. I wondered how one human being could do this to another.

Today, I somewhat understand the urge to violence. I have spent the majority of my life as a hippie warrior, a martial artist in the true sense of the word, not a thug, not a fighter, but a warrior able to protect myself and my loved ones. Fighters live to fight. Warriors avoid fights when they can but are prepared to fight if necessary.

My personal belief is that humans are, at their core, good. But in many cases our early training may lead us to undervalue or even hate particular groups. Whether this is race, status, gender, or education-based, it still leads us to look down on others. The spiritual masters have explored the training required to build and maintain communities and tribes that may be the answer to world-wide anxiety, fear and greed.

The real answer is Spiritual awakening; and this, like being a hippie, is only for the brave and committed. Let's fix that and build on mistakes of the past to set a course to The Dawning of the Age of Aquarius.

Beth Richards: For What It's Worth

Here I am, a 16-year-old wannabe hippie chick in a red plaid schoolgirl skirt, lingering in wonder on the wide granite steps in front of the Pentagon on a bright October day in 1967. Down the steps in front of me writhes a rabble of brave war protesters waving signs—"Get Out of Vietnam NOW!!" "Give Peace a Chance!!" "No More War!!"—and shoving back at the phalanx of uniformed soldiers in full gear, bayonets pointed toward them. U.S. Marshals with padded chest protectors are stationed among the soldiers, standing on a low wall, their billy clubs swinging through the air and landing on the shoulders and heads of the protesters. Screams of pain and spatters of blood fly around the scene. It seems unbelievable to me that this is happening in my country.

Suddenly, an order is shouted out and a small contingent of soldiers separates and steps ahead. There are just enough of them to form a barrier from wall-to-wall across the stairs where I am standing. Their bayonets are pointed directly at me, and they are advancing slowly with steely eyes staring straight ahead. Survival instincts kick in, and I realize that I had better do something quickly. I flatten myself against the side wall and hold my breath as the whole line seems to completely ignore my presence. The soldiers brush right past me and proceed up the steps. This is the point at which I bolt down and run back into the larger crowd, numbering over 100,000, gathered in an approved area.

In 1967, the Vietnam War was nearing its height; and the protests against the war were growing as well. One of the biggest antiwar mobilizations was the March on the Pentagon. Since The Beatles appeared in the U.S. in 1964, we young folks had become increasingly aware that things were changing around us—something was happening here. I had some solidly rebellious tendencies, and the culture was giving me a lot of fodder to indulge them. From listening to Bob Dylan's unmelodic but cryptic voice to sporting navy surplus bell-bottoms to plunking Woody Guthrie protest songs on my guitar, I was ready to change the world. Sneaking up to Washington, D.C., with my sister to attend this protest was definitely on the agenda!

The trajectory of my life from a 1960s adolescence to my current old age was started in this era, and I never looked back. I have spent my entire adult life living on a cultural edge, dressing, eating, traveling, birthing and raising children in a manner that challenged the idea of normal that was so set in prior generations. Here I am still, fighting against control by those who would choose power over my life for their own personal gain. I remain committed to living outside "the system" that tries to keep our creativity and our oneness suppressed, to keep us locked in a consumerist, warmongering society.

Free Love

You've got to hand it to the 1950s. They sure knew how to regulate sex. At the dawn of 1960, consenting adults couldn't legally engage in same-sex sex, sex with someone of a different race, anal sex, or oral sex. Married women couldn't buy birth control or obtain a medically sanctioned abortion. Though not outlawed, sex before marriage, sex for pleasure, non-missionary sex, masturbation, and multiple sex partners were widely considered immoral. Guilt and ignorance about sex were the standards of the day.

By 1970, I heard about something called "free love." The idea was simple: Consenting adults could make love in any way they wanted with anyone they chose, free of fear. Cool!

While some considered "free love" as an invitation to 24/7 orgies, most of us simply wanted parents, preachers, and politicians out of our beds. While some free lovers indulged in multiple partners and hedonist escapades, I missed that part of the revolution. I just wanted to take the fear out of the whole thing.

For some men, free love simply reinforced what they already wanted to do. But for women, previously locked away as baby machines and male property, the concept of free love was a radical idea. For the first time, women were encouraged to enjoy their sexuality, to have sex before marriage if they wanted, sex with a stranger, sex on top, sex with other women, and sex with themselves. Free love meant that women could openly enjoy sex for the first time and unashamedly seek satisfaction.

Instead of supporting the idea that women could enjoy sex without fear, some guys used the idea of free love to make sex even more fearful. They figured that, if a "liberated" woman was free to have sex with anyone at any time, she wanted to have sex with everyone all the time, just like they did. She might say "No," but she really meant "Yes." Obviously, she wanted it. Why else would she be wearing a halter top and hip hugging jeans?

Today's "Me Too" movement highlights what millions of less famous women have known for eons. Some men will harass, assault, and rape women if they can, not just the dark alley types, but all kinds of "respectable" predators, church going, wealth dealing, important men who seem incapable of hurting anybody. If Dr. Huxtable can do what he did to 60 unsuspected women over decades, anything is possible. If any date can turn into a nightmare, if any sign of interest can be construed as permission, if "No" has no meaning, then the whole idea of "free love" for women is a sick joke.

Ironically, as women became more assertive about their desires and more determined to remove fear from the sexual equation, some men went in the opposite direction, becoming more fearful and less sure of their ability to please these "liberated" females. Suddenly, he had to worry about her orgasm without really understanding how her body worked. Concepts like "foreplay" and "g-spots" entered the unspoken conversation beneath the covers, while he desperately struggled to keep an erection. Instead of making sex less fearful, free love for some men amplified their already simmering terror of being an object of ridicule in her eyes and, somehow, unmanly in the eyes of the world.

First published in 1972, The Joy of Sex *was an illustrated sex manual by British author Alex Comfort. This graphic, self-help guide for open-minded adults not only celebrated intimacy but also educated its readers about the "ins and outs" of "doing it," a radical departure from the under-the-covers, in-the-dark version of sex on which most of us were raised. Its purpose, I think, was to help ordinary people experience less fear and more joy by bringing the whole topic into the open.*

In fact, openness and playful curiosity about one's body was, for many, a fundamental tenet of the hippie perspective. As one contributor says elsewhere in this book: "We wanted a culture which acknowledged the human body, not just for sex, but to hug each other, to be naked without shame, to revere the body with natural foods, beneficial exercise, herbs, baths, massage, deep understanding."

Sex without fear, I've learned, is not sex without consequences. I'm not talking about pregnancy and disease, although these issues will always be important when people hook up. Instead, I'm talking about the idea that sex can ever be completely casual, that people can connect their bodies in the most intimate ways and not be emotionally affected.

Casual sex sounds good on paper and when drunken lips meet in the heat of passion. But it seems to me that the only people who can be com-

pletely unaffected by a sexual encounter are psychopaths, incapable of empathy or self-awareness. Thankfully, few of us fit in that category.

Whether we realize it or not, lovers feel something when they connect, a primal, unconscious, often unexplainable reaction that can't be duplicated in any other way.

Many years ago, I thought an "open" relationship might work. It didn't. In fact, the little bit that we tried poisoned everything from then on. In a perfect "free love" world, couples would be free of jealousy. One "open minded" partner wouldn't care what his/her mate does sexually with another person. That's a fantasy. Having been on both sides of the cheating game, I can tell you that nothing hurts more than imaging your significant other making it with somebody else. It's a picture you can't un-see, a wound that never heals.

I grew up believing that you should only have sex with someone you love. I still believe that, not because I should; but because the safest place for my emotions in that intimate moment is with someone I trust and, in a real sense, love.

Call me old school, but I've found that being physically intimate with someone you love in a monogamous relationship is definitely the way to go. In that kind of environment, sex is free of fear, free of guilt, and free of convention. Couples are free to communicate about their sexual desires and preferences, free to explore each other's bodies, and free to experience pleasure in ways that no other type of encounter can match.

In loving relationships, sex is about connection, not performance; safety, not fear. The goal of free love is not simply to make it with anyone we want whenever we want, but to love whoever we want and express that love freely in a sexual way without fear.—S.L.R.

J Laurence: Art of Loving

Eric Fromm's book, *The Art of Loving*, was published in the late '50s and grew very popular during the hippie years due to the "make love not war" ideology. A favorite book quote, "Love is the only sane and satisfactory answer to the problem of human existence" is a perfect example.

The rise of both spiritual and "personal growth" dynamics during the hippie years radically changed the way that many of us saw relationships with a "significant other." We realized that trust, shared interests, compatible values, and friendship were more important in gaining and maintaining a loving relationship than physical appeal. As a devotee of Eastern thought and student of the human condition, I also knew that non-violent communication is the best possible strategy for resolving conflicts. Remembering that my parents never debated their differences, and therefore never resolved them, was a red flag I failed to see. Without a willingness to understand another, love can't survive.

For many, this new awareness led to the rejection of marriage's legal ties and the adoption of cohabitation. Despite being blasphemous to the hard-core religious, unwed child rearing also grew rapidly. Having lived with a loving woman for over 10 years, I was grateful there were no legal ties.

Relationships are ultimately a mirror, allowing the opportunity to grow, develop listening skills, and love without condition.

While a "soul mate" is ideal, true friendship is more important, resulting in a connection that grows, endures and brings mutual joy. For those who are "complete" within themselves and not looking for someone to complete them, love becomes available and flourishes.

Eleanor Roosevelt said it best: "Many people will walk in and out of your life, but only true friends leave footprints in your heart."

Mari S: Anticipation

As a child in the 1950s and early '60s, sex and reproduction weren't discussed in my home. I used to read medical books trying to gather the facts. When I was 16 and began babysitting on a regular basis for a young couple with three children, I discovered *Playboy* magazines stacked in their bedroom nightstand, I thought I had died and gone to heaven. While there is now much debate about Hugh Hefner's actions, misogyny and attitudes about women, his magazine seemed to be coming from a very liberal place at the time. I found it appealing.

Craving the sexual freedom exposed by the "Summer of Love" and the happenings at the Esalen Institute in Big Sur, I was married and divorced by 1970. Soon, I was living with a charismatic man who seemed to feel the same way I did about sex. I thought that I could maintain a primary relationship with this person, who I loved, and still have sex with other men on occasion. This arrangement might have worked, but it turned out that my partner was the weak link.

Our first foray into "free love" was giving him permission to sleep with another woman who was visiting. Later, she told me that he had performance problems due to nerves. In our second sexual experiment, the two of us attempted a foursome with another couple who were casually dating. After a short time with the four of us in bed, my partner stormed out of the house and ruined the evening. I was never sure if his problem was jealousy or performance anxiety.

Third time's a charm, right? We decided to share ourselves with the couple who were our best friends. This time we went to a hotel together and divided into our separate rooms. Once again, the experience was ruined when my partner came back to my room and made a huge commotion; although I'm still not sure why.

Well, that should have been the end of that. And it was, as far as open sharing was concerned; but I began a tryst with the man who was part of our failed four-in-a-bed experiment that has lasted since 1972. Finding that we were—and still are—very attracted sexually to each other, our relationship has consisted of occasional sex, sometimes with years in between, lots of laughter, and comfort during hard times.

He eventually moved several hours away, and sometimes many years would pass before we would see each other again. But with the advent of the cell phone, we have been able to stay in touch and tease each other. Today, at the age of 70, I'll be meeting him in a couple of weeks at a beach hotel. The thought of it still gives me shivers of anticipation.

Steve Dickson: Like a Rolling Stone

After I got out of the Army in '74, rambling was on my mind. I'd previously spent time with some free spirits in California and thought about them after being discharged. I spent a year learning how to cook in an Italian restaurant and hauled hay and worked with livestock on a big ranch near Dallas.

In May of '75, while I was hitching from Florida back to Texas, an old blue-painted school bus pulled over and offered me a ride just as it was starting to rain. The two guys inside were on their way to Austin to pick up another fellow then going on the Rolling Stones Tour of the Americas selling bootleg T-shirts and posters at the concerts. They were looking for help, so I jumped onboard.

As we headed to Austin, we stopped in the middle of a back road surrounded by cow pastures and gathered a whole bunch of magic mushrooms. After we picked up John, the guy that organized the whole gig in Austin, and waited for him to finalize details for the tour, we drank mushroom tea and partied with his friends. The tea was amazing and really opened us up to each other.

High as kites, my new compadre, Woody, and I sat outside with a girl who was a student at the University of Texas and her two girlfriends. After a while, they decided to have an orgy. Woody and I had never been involved in an orgy; so, we agreed after making a deal between us not to orgy each other. It worked out pretty well, and the mushrooms enhanced the experience greatly.

The Stones tour started in Baton Rouge, and we followed it around all summer, selling t-shirts for three bucks along the way. We lived in the bus and stayed in hotels every few days to get cleaned up. At the big stadium venues, we traded shirts for tickets; so, I saw the concerts about eight times. The cash was good, and we spent it on hotels and drinks and pretty much wasted the rest.

There were many groupies who traveled from miles around hoping to party with the band; but of course, most hopes were dashed. So, some settled for us. Being in the days before AIDS, sex was easy and free. However, after the violent incident at the Stones concert at Altamont in 1969, the mood and the perception of the Rolling Stones changed. That summer, we had experienced the lightness of the hippie lifestyle and the darkness that was changing it as well.

The Stones have endured and so have we; although in my opinion, today's music can't hold a candle to that good ol' rock and roll; and Keith Richards will probably outlive us all.

I never did really settle down in one place. I've been married three times and, for the last 28 years, I've worked as a U.S. merchant mariner wandering the world delivering cargo. I've learned that there is much more that we humans have in common than that which separates and divides us.

Beth Richards: Living in Sin

In the 1950s and '60s, it was expected that people would marry in their late teens or twenties and likely have a family. Those occasional women who did not marry, a.k.a., the "old maids," were schoolteachers or WACs and were generally looked on with pity. And even a small whiff of unchaperoned time between genders was regarded with suspicion.

The sudden explosion of change that came about during the 1960s opened everything for discussion. All of the social rules that we had grown up learning were to be questioned, tested, experimented with, and just maybe thrown out entirely. It all seemed so uncertain yet so thrilling to be involved in changing the world.

Our parents and their parents were the problem. They had lived by certain rules and mores and taught them to us. And here we were, throwing them out the window with no regard for the consequences. How dare we!

At the age of 20, I found myself writing a letter to tell my parents that I was *living in sin*. I had rented an apartment with my boyfriend Ernie in Massachusetts after riding my bicycle up from Virginia and meeting him while rock climbing. I felt entirely justified in my choice.

I waited a week and phoned them. We chatted about mundane things like the weather and how the dog was faring. Then, with both of them on the line, my Dad asked me about what I was doing. During my explanation of cohabitation as being the right thing to do, they both hung up at the same time. My first thought was that this was the first time I'd seen them do anything in unison. At least I'd brought them together.

I had no word from them for several months. I did keep writing letters to advocate for my situation. I was deadly serious about the moral rightness of my stance. My blindness to the dramatic upheaval in social mores that was happening at this time period startles me now. I knew things were changing, and it seemed so right to question everything.

But I did reconnect with my folks in the end. I wrote to tell them that we were spending 2 weeks climbing in the Teton Mountains that summer of 1972. On our return to our Massachusetts apartment, I found a letter from my mother. She had enclosed a few pages torn from the *Reader's Digest* with a story about a young couple who became stranded and almost died while climbing the Grand Teton. She knew it could have been about me. Apparently, she had decided it was time to accept what she couldn't change.

So after that, we talked on the phone and wrote letters. When we went to visit them later, they wouldn't let us sleep in the same room together; so, we slept on the beach with the sand crabs.

Oh, and we did finally get married. But that's another story.

Rick Denney: The More Things Change

We had been taught that marriage was a sacred institution, a lifetime commitment with one person; but in reality, we saw this wasn't true with our parents. Many of us grew up in homes where their parents preached messages they did not follow themselves. It seemed hypocritical. Many homes became fractured, sometimes with parents divorcing and moving on with a new lifetime partner. If marriage was a lifetime commitment, it didn't make sense that our parents could push the reset button and have a do-over. In the '60s, we could see how phony that was.

If our parents could switch partners, then why should we be any different? Why should we get married then end up in divorce? So, we decided to be different. Welcome to the sexual revolution. Having multiple sex partners became the thing to do, especially after getting high and listening to our favorite music. Free love was available to us all, guys and gals, with no guilt or strings attached. At the time, we were living care-free. Life was great.

Then we got older. Some of us actually found lifetime partners, and attitudes began to shift. The thought of having multiple sex partners faded in favor of relationships based on criteria other than sex. The '60s were great, but time marches on. Now, many of us now have settled into our lives, reverting back to living much the same way our parents did. Funny how that works.

Nancy Pruitt: I Can Bring Home the Bacon

It began as a bustling evening at a popular Italian restaurant in Del Mar, California. I had been part of the original crew, working dinner shifts; so that I could attend college classes at San Diego State University (SDSU). On this particular Friday evening, I checked my next week's schedule and noticed that the manager had changed all my shifts to days when he knew I was in school.

As I was picking up two lasagna dinners from the kitchen, I asked him why he had changed my hours. He laughed and blurted out, "You didn't give me a blow job," loud enough for everyone to hear. He was trying to be funny, I suppose; but it wasn't.

In fact, we had no personal "relationship" and he had never pressed me for one in the first place. As my humiliation level climbed, it was all I could do not to dump those very hot plates on him. Instead, I quietly delivered the food that my customers awaited, fighting my instincts to fight back.

A few days later, I went to the Labor Board to file a written complaint about the manager's behavior, explaining that he had given me hours he knew I could not keep because I had not "serviced" him. The clerk slid the form back to me under the glass partition and said, "If you file this, you will never get another job here in San Diego." Her words pierced my ears.

Not working to support myself in college was hardly an option. Seething with anger, I pushed the form back to her and walked out bewildered.

Was it her concern for me or something more sinister?

This wasn't my first experience with men feeling they could satisfy their sexual appetites unimpeded. In 1971, a previous boss had aggressively pushed me into a broom closet feeling my breasts as I fought my way out. An English professor at UCLA had done the same in 1969. In another instance, I was chased around a houseboat in Sausalito by a famous author of children's books.

Somehow, I couldn't help thinking that powerful men were using women's liberation as an excuse for sexual abuse. After all, in their minds, women "wanted it" according to the new morality of the late 1960s fueled by easy birth control. "Sex, Drugs and Rock and Roll" was the loud shout of our generation. We balked established norms and rocked the sexual status quo. Now women were free to act on their urges too.

Ironically in my case, women's lib was unrealistic. I began working in male dominated job situations at 16 and never stopped until I was 66. I couldn't go bra-less in my jobs as an office worker, nutrition speaker, and restaurant chef manager or afford to quit after being harassed.

My little experience with "free love" was always painful knowing it never brought real love. If I did experiment, I did so with the desire to be loved by one individual. Expressing my sexuality with anyone who came along just wasn't me. Each experience closed me off more. It seemed that men gave love to have sex, and women gave sex to get love. What is liberating about that?

Yet for many working women, being attractive seemed necessary in order to succeed in the male dominated workplace. Dressing for success meant being desired for our femininity, and submitting to unwanted advances was the only route to favor and promotion. Advertisers told us that we could have it all if we were just sexy enough. Enjoli perfume, for example, assured us that the new women of the '70s could "Bring home the bacon, fry it up in a pan, and never let him forget he's a man."

Historically women fought hard in this country for all of our rights; but under the surface, sexual harassment was the secret story. Largely unknown in the mainstream media, the Clarence Thomas/Anita Hill hearings put the issue front and center into our living rooms in 1991. I remember watching the hearing and thinking, "Maybe now this won't happen so much." I was wrong.

In today's milieu of flying allegations of sexual abuse and harassment, it is still often a case of "she said, he said." But the true victims of unwanted sexual attention need to be heard. The unspoken legacy of women battered by unwanted sexual advances in the workplace is billowing out of the Pandora's box opened by the Me Too movement. Personally, I feel that my justice finally came in the explosive cases of others. My shame is now shared which I find liberating.

In the last 25 years of my career, I worked as a saleswoman where I could pick my customers and shed those who showed me unwanted attention. I dressed as least provocatively as I could and developed my job knowledge to dazzle my customers with brilliance rather than breasts and short skirts. In all my jobs, I only wanted a fair chance to show my skills and earn a secure income, not be the butt of jokes and sleazy come-ons. My hope for my children's children is that the ideals of truth and human dignity, echoed in the '60s, will finally apply to everyone, women and men alike.

Wanda H: Love the One You're With

As a 17-year-old white girl from a small Catholic town, I started college in 1964 with only the most rudimentary knowledge of "sex." Most of my dorm mates were more sophisticated than I. By the end of freshman year, I was 18 and had decided to get with the program. For my first experience, I chose a young man who I knew to be greatly enamored of me, one I knew would be loving and sweet, and, above all, would take care of me in the event of any unforeseen results. I had no interest in marriage, but I felt safe with him and just wanted to get this milestone over with. It worked out fine for those times.

Over the next few years, I thought of myself as an intellectual progressive and a true hippie. I marched in sympathy with Selma. I attended the Newport Folk Festival. I made efforts to befriend Black people. I (sort of) learned to play folk guitar, bought all the albums and learned all the words. I grew my hair very long. I dressed in blue jeans and peasant blouses. I dated only boys from our subculture. During this idealistic time, I had one or two sexual encounters, but only with partners I really liked, as I was focused on making a statement and living in accordance with my ideals. To me, "Make Love, Not War" meant simply "Love other humans, don't fight with them." Naive?

Eventually, I left school to marry my favorite hippie. With friends, we traveled in a van to protest the Vietnam War in Washington where I marched up Pennsylvania Avenue carrying a sign that read "END THE

DRAFT." We counseled other kids on becoming Conscientious Objectors. When our son was an infant, I took him around the neighborhood in his stroller to collect signatures protesting the War and Kent State. When Crosby Stills Nash & Young recorded "Love the One You're With" after Woodstock, I took the lyrics to mean, "Enjoy the moment with others, because life is short." Silly me. It was the dawn of the '70s, and things were about to change big-time.

Busy with a toddler and my return to school for my degree, I hardly noticed that "The Establishment" was co-opting hippiedom. The Vietnam War was losing favor with the Silent Majority. Male newscasters were beginning to sport long hair and bright colors. Tie-dye design shirts started to appear in discount stores. *Everyone* wore jeans and boots. Popular music morphed from "Love the One You're With" to "Me and Mrs. Jones," "Stand by Your Man," "Lyin' Eyes," and "Lucille." Infidelity had become the new normal, because that's where our society chose to take the "Make Love, Not War" concept. Only the onset of AIDS in the '80s got folks back into their own beds. I shudder to think of all the unwanted pregnancies/babies/abortions, STDs, and divorces that resulted from that misguided time.

I've never equated love and sex, so I've never understood the evolution of "Love the One You're With" into "the sexual revolution." My own hippie days did not include "free love," just music, marches, hair, jeans, and driving my parents crazy. My take today is a bit cynical: Somehow, human endeavors always seem to devolve to the lowest common denominator. Sad.

Give Peace a Chance

Early in the 1960s, Americans finally realized that the world could easily destroy itself with nuclear weapons. Practice air raid sirens on Saturdays and duck-and-cover drills in classrooms became common place, capped off by the Cuban Missile Crisis of 1962 that led us to the edge of extinction. At the same time, a storm built on paranoia began brewing in a far-off country called Vietnam which, in time, would kill millions and leave America doubting its leaders and its moral authority.

Efforts to end the Vietnam War united those of us who considered ourselves hippies at that time. We had common goals and common enemies like Johnson who sacrificed his good intentions to avoid embarrassment and a guy named Nixon who would do and say anything to stay in power.

Over time, we realized that peace between countries starts with peace between individuals and that love for others is only possible when you love yourself. And so, we began the long journey of introspection, forgiveness, and personal transformation which continues today.

As a child, one of our favorite games was playing "army," in which one team searched for the other in the thick overgrowth behind our houses. One group would start at my end of the block, while the other approached from the other end, silently creeping toward each other until one of us was confronted by an enemy combatant's loud impersonation of machine gun fire.

"Ek-ek-ek-ek," the shooter would say in a stuttering voice from behind a bush. "You're dead." And we were, sort of, falling down with a long fake cry. That's all I knew of war. As far as I could see, the whole thing was bloodless, painless, and lots of fun.

It seems to me that most Americans are ignorant of the realities of war. Unless we know someone who's served, we pretend to understand what's happening thousands of miles away; but we really don't. We see news footage, read reports from imbedded reporters, and perhaps salute the flag at ball games. But very few of us see the blood or the missing limbs or the shattered brains of real soldiers returning home.

As much as it pains me to say it, perhaps we like it that way. This whole war thing is just too stressful. We have jobs to do, families to raise, bills to pay. We don't have the emotional bandwidth or the courage, on the whole, to dig in deep. We can ignore America's wars. After all, the fighting isn't happening on our streets. Our houses aren't being bombed or gassed. Lots of us are just playing army, letting bright-eyed patriotic kids do the killing and dying somewhere out of sight.

By 1960, the USSR (aka Russia) and the U.S. were busy having a pissing contest with the fate of the world in the balance. At noon on Saturdays, an air raid siren would blast through town to test our civil defensiveness. Everyone was told that, "Had this been an actual alert," we should "take shelter"; because nuke-loaded ICBM's were heading our way. Exactly where to hide, we weren't sure.

At school, we were instructed to duck under our desks and cover our heads with our arms in case of nuclear attack. Some families built fall-out shelters in their backyards and filled them with canned goods. In fact, my parents bought a house with a partially built shelter that the previous owner had frantically started but never finished. Deciding that it wouldn't save us anyway, my Dad filled in the hole.

The whole nuclear scare came to a head in October of 1962 when the U.S. learned the Soviet Union was building missile and bomber bases in Cuba. After demanding their withdrawal, President Kennedy ordered a naval blockade of Cuba. For 13 days, officials and the American public feared that the two Super-Powers would start a nuclear war as a result of the conflict. On November 10, the Russians began withdrawing their men and equipment from the island, defusing the confrontation.

I was 12 at the time and remember those scary days, talking in small groups before school, wondering whether the earth would be destroyed, knowing that we couldn't do anything about it. As I remember, the adults were afraid too. They didn't do much to reassure us. Finally, one day, the principal came on the school intercom and told us that the crisis had passed. Without discussion, we went back to being sixth graders.

Today, nine countries have a total of 14,000 nuclear weapons, each more powerful than those used by the U.S. to destroy two Japanese cities at the close of World War II. The United States possesses about 6,500 of these with the capability to target any location on earth within minutes.

As the Cuban Missile fiasco illustrated, bravado and miscalculation by big kids can destroy the rest of us. Today, we have an irrational bully in the White House promising to annihilate a sadistic North Korean demi-god if he doesn't give up his nuclear toys. It's just a new pissing contest, more dangerous than ever.

Do we really need over 6,000 ways to kill every man, woman, and child on the planet? Do we really think that we can keep this many rattle-snakes in the house without at least one of them biting us?

More war in Vietnam demanded more soldiers. On December 1, 1969, the first military draft since the Korean War was televised throughout the country.

Previously, the U.S. Selective Service had been issuing cards to draft-eligible young men. Burning these draft cards soon became an important statement against the Vietnam War. Congress outlawed the practice, and activists like Dr. Benjamin Spock and the Berrigan Brothers were arrested for doing it anyway. I was too afraid to burn mine.

The draft system worked like this: 365 ping-pong balls, each with a distinct date, were placed in a cylinder. In a televised broadcast, the National Selective Service director pulled out one ball at a time. The first ball pulled was labeled Number 1, meaning that everyone with that birth date would be called into service first. The process continued until every birth date was assigned a number. As I recall, my birthday was matched to number 278 on the big board; my college roommate, 13.

In theory, my roommate was much more likely to be drafted than I. But in reality, neither of us was called; because the law exempted college students. That was good for us, but decidedly unfair to the guys who couldn't afford higher education.

Would I have enlisted had I been drafted? No. Or at least I don't think so. Most likely, I would have taken a vacation of some duration to Canada with most of the other "draft dodgers" at the time. Or maybe, like the Rasta converts I met in Jamaica, I would have gone South for a permanent relocation.

Today, the draft is gone; and the Vietnam War was "lost" decades ago. Still, we as Americans are faced with the same moral dilemma: What wars should we be fighting? For what cause am I, as an individual, willing to risk my life? For what cause am I willing for other people to risk their lives?

I supported my Father's military service in World War II. We were attacked at Pearl Harbor, and the Nazis represented an existential threat to America and the world. I would have certainly fought in that war had I been able.

When I was 20 or so, I couldn't imagine intentionally hurting, much less killing, anyone. I believed that enough love would convert an evil doer into a kind person and that wars could be banished forever. Sadly, my views have changed over the years. Today, I believe there might be times when I could kill another human being to save myself or someone else from imminent harm. But like the happy little boy playing army, I still have no real-world idea of when that would be necessary or how I would feel about it.

In the case of Vietnam, we were told that the Communists had made an unprovoked attack on an American warship. This wasn't true. We were told that all of Southeast Asia would fall "like dominoes" to the Commies unless we stopped them in Vietnam. Today, Vietnam still has a Communist-type government; and the United States is one of its major trading partners.

I wasn't willing to die in Vietnam to right a wrong that never happened or prevent an outcome that wasn't any of my business. I opposed the Iraq War for the same reasons. We weren't attacked, and we have no business telling the Iraqi people how to live. In Afghanistan, we achieved our initial objective to punish those behind the 9-11 attacks. I supported that. But continuing to sacrifice American soldiers to transform a country that doesn't want to be transformed is stupid and immoral.

The bottom line is this: If I am morally unwilling to fight a given enemy, how can I support sending someone else to do it? If those who authorize wars are unwilling to fight themselves, why should anyone fight?

On March 16, 1968, Charlie Company, under the command of Lt. William Calley, massacred 300 unarmed civilians in the village of My Lai, Vietnam. Charged with murder in 1969, Calley testified that he was ordered to kill everyone in the village by his Captain. He was convicted of murder and sentenced to life in prison but was released five years later. None of Calley's superiors were ever charged.

Was this soldier inherently evil or a product of war in which we ask ordinary people to kill for us in the most terrifying of circumstances? Personally, I don't believe that Calley is even vaguely typical of the good men and women in our armed forces.

But if we look deeper at the epidemic of PTSD cases arising from our worldwide war games, we can see that we are turning good people into tortured souls, some of whom will kill themselves; a few of whom will spew their uncontrollable rage onto others.

At its core, military strategy is simple: Kill the enemy. If a few other folks get obliterated along the way (referred to as collateral damage), well, that's just the way it is. War is hell.

After a U.S. bombing campaign in 1968 that killed hundreds of civilians in a small Vietnamese village, an American officer reportedly explained: "It became necessary to destroy the village to save it." This kind of twisted logic seems to underpin the reality of war, then and now.

While we're driving out "insurgents" embedded in small villages throughout Iraq, Afghanistan, Yemen, and other war zones, we're killing thousands of other folks, innocent, uninvolved, everyday folks who just want to raise their families in peace.

When the fighting finally ends in these places, do we think that the innocents who live through our assaults and their children are going to thank us? Are we that stupid?

On May 8, 1970, a large group of construction workers attacked antiwar protesters in New York City. Encouraged by President Nixon, they beat the protesters with their own signs while City police watched.

A favorite shout from these "hard hats," as they were called, was: "Love it or leave it." Recently, I've been hearing the same thing again when The Donald proclaimed "maybe you shouldn't be in this country if you don't stand for the National Anthem."

At the 1968 Summer Olympic Games, two American athletes (Tommy Smith and John Carlos) each raised a black gloved fist in a "Black Power" salute while receiving their Olympic metals. After an initial silence, the crowd began booing and screaming the Star-Spangled Banner as the American flag was raised on the podium. For this simple, peaceful, political statement, both athletes were banned from the Games.

You would think that screaming "patriots" might have learned something since then, but no. They're at it again, booing black NFL players who choose to "take a knee" rather than stand during the National Anthem. Who made these folks the Loyalty Police? And if they don't believe in the right of all Americans to peacefully express their opinions, even unpopular ones, then I question whether they really believe in America at all.

What does it really mean to "love" your country? I love my family, but I don't agree with every one of them all the time. I'll do what it takes to protect them, but I won't help them abuse other people. If that's what patriotism is, I'm good with that.

But if loving America means I have to salute the flag, ignore the injustices of its past, overlook the problems of its present, and blindly support every ill-conceived impulse our leaders might have, I'll pass. Guess what? I don't have to love it, and I don't have to leave it.

Walter Cronkite was the anchorman of CBS Evening News from 1962 to 1981. Based on opinion surveys at the time, he was considered "the most trusted man in America." Every night, he reported the "facts" at home and abroad including the bloody hidden reality of the Vietnam War and the mind-numbing tragedy of President Kennedy's assassination. No one disputed the accuracy of his reporting or called it "fake news." He famously closed each newscast by saying: "And that's the way it is." If Walter said it, we believed it.

By 1968, the United States had over 500,000 combat troops in Vietnam. While President Johnson and his generals bragged about their victories, Walter visited the country in early February of that year to see for himself. After speaking with commanders in the field, Walter learned that America was not winning the war and likely never would. In an on-air editorial on February 27, Walter gave the facts to the American public, a development that significantly shifted public opinion against the war and played a major role in Johnson's decision not to run for another term.

In 1971, the U.S. Defense Department finished a top-secret report, later named the Pentagon Papers, *that analyzed the Vietnam War since its inception. Dr. Daniel Ellsberg, one of the civilians involved in the project, gave a copy of the report to the* New York Times *and the* Washington Post, *who began publishing it on June 13, 1971. Consequently, the public learned that the President and his people had consistently lied about the causes and conduct of the war. Of particular shame was the official conclusion that the United States continued the war primarily to avoid the embarrassment of losing. On August 30, 1975, the last Americans withdrew from the country followed rapidly by North Vietnam's final victory.*

If the American public had known the truth earlier than 1968, would the war have ended sooner? I like to think so. If we had known that Iraq had no "weapons of mass destruction" decades later, would we have invaded? I hope not.

Regardless, it's clear that truth has always been a powerful non-violent tool in the struggle for a more peaceful world and that some leaders will say anything to get what they want. It's also clear that, if we want a kinder more peaceful world, we are obligated to separate facts from propaganda.

Originated by our national leaders at the time of the Vietnam War, "peace with honor" was a flowery slogan designed to hide the ugliness and stupidity of the War from the American people. In reality, there is no honor in killing people who are not threatening you. In fact, I don't see the honor in killing other people for any reason.

Not having been a soldier myself, I don't pretend to understand the experiences of returning soldiers or the feelings they carry with them. If I had to guess, I would think that many of them feel guilty, no matter how justified their battlefield actions may have seemed at the time.

Soldiers know that, in order to save their own lives and those of their colleagues, they must do what they would never do at any other time. They know that killing a stranger is always personal, whether executed face-to-face or at a distance. They know that all soldiers are basically the same, regular folks trying to survive in hell until they can return to their loved ones. Our "enemies" are also our neighbors. We must find ways to settle our disputes honorably; i.e., without violence.

One of my favorite tunes from the early '70s was "Peace Train" by Stephen Demetre Georgiou, better known as Cat Stevens. After years of hard partying, the songwriter converted to Islam in 1977, changed his name to Yusuf Islam, and stopped recording non-religious music until 2004. Although he condemned the 2001 attacks, he was placed on the "no fly" list and refused entry into the United States from September 2004 until December 2006. He still performs today.

Yusuf's story reminds me that, if we can't tell our friends from our enemies, we'll always be at war. Yes, I understand that some people hate this country and won't hesitate to kill as many Americans as they can. But who are they really? Surely our enemies don't include every Muslim in the world or every person who looks and sounds differently than we do. If we look at the world without fear, we'll see they're a lot more of us who want to be on the Peace Train than want to derail it.

In 1961, President Kennedy created the Peace Corps, one of the few government programs from that era still doing good work around the world. The concept is simple: Americans with skills and compassion volunteer to help local leaders in struggling communities to solve challenges like disease, unsafe drinking water, food shortages, and limited economic opportunities. While that's taking place, regular folks in other countries see Americans for who they are, compassionate sharing individuals, not bomb-dropping, heartless colonialists.

The Peace Corps illustrates a practical expression of the classic slogan: "Make love not war." While some folks may think of this catchy phrase as an invitation for sex, I think of it as a prescription for peace.

Here's an idea: What if we spent as much money helping desperate people as we do on ways to kill them? True, getting this help to the people who need it will always be tricky. Corruption, logistics, language differences, and cultural misunderstandings will make the mission difficult. But aren't we a country of problem-solvers? Do we really want to kill people, because we can't figure out how to help them? If we devote our resources and national will, isn't it possible that we'd make less war and more love?

So, what's the alternative? Do we really think that we can kill all our enemies? *I learned recently that the military strategy in Vietnam was to "break the back" of the enemies by killing 10 of theirs for every one of ours. What happened? We killed millions of Vietnamese, lost 54,000 of our own, and they still "won" the war.*

Why? In the case of Vietnam, farmers, who had initially stood on the sidelines, became soldiers after American napalm burned their villages. As their men died, women and children joined the fight, driving trucks, delivering food, and doing whatever they could to defeat us. In the end, America's "kill ratio" strategy succeeded only in uniting the country against us.

Today, the same strategy is yielding the same results in Afghanistan, Iraq, Yemen, Syria, and every other place where we try to bring peace with violence. Once again, trying to kill all our enemies isn't making us safer. It's just making more enemies.

As Dr. King once said: "Darkness cannot drive out darkness. Only light can do that. Hate cannot drive out hate. Only love can do that."—S.L.R.

Raina Greenwood: Better Dead Than Red

I grew up in the moral universe of Irish Catholicism and its political corollary anti-communism. Although my father was a less-doctrinaire Midwestern Baptist who had converted to marry my mother, both parents shared this Catholic world view when it came to politics. They were both intelligent and capable, but given to alcohol-fueled rages and physical abuse of their children.

My feelings for them were anxious and uncertain; but their status as moral arbiters and authority figures was intact, enhanced if anything, by the abuse. Their sole experience of travel had been a cruise to Hawaii, an experience they both cherished and tried to re-enact with regular partying with their cruise mates. None of their fond recollections of Hawaii ever touched on its racial mixing, except for a few anecdotes about the cute little Japanese girl who could belt out a song just like Ella Fitzgerald.

Catholicism and Americanism converged around the central tenet of anti–Communism. Communism was Satan's invention and its opponents the righteous. Dr. Tom Dooley was a Catholic icon and Cold War poster boy whose books and speaking tours detailed communist atrocities in Vietnam, Cambodia and Laos as justification for a decade of American "advisors" in the region. Dooley's focus on international politics also drew attention away from his own complicated and compromised life as a CIA operative and suspected pedophile. In that moral universe, the United

States *had* to be in Vietnam, *had* to oppose North Vietnam and reunification, *had* to drop napalm upon the Vietnamese, *had to* invade, kill, massacre its people, offering up America's sons to this endeavor. War protesters were American traitors and godless hippie punks, long-haired, unshaven and oversexed. Intervention and invasion of Vietnam was a religious and political obligation.

But for many in my generation, there was a disconnect. There was no political or ethical universe that could ever justify what photos showed of Vietnamese victims of American intervention. Life, Look and Time magazines published photo essays depicting a visceral reality of children with melted flesh from America's biochemical weapons. Pictures of Buddhist monks setting themselves alight on Saigon streets to protest Diem, documented actions truly incomprehensible to most Americans. It seemed implausible that an industrialized and rich nation like the U.S. could be threatened by a small agrarian country so far away. Moreover, America's combatants, some of them deserters, were returning with thousand-yard stares and atrocity stories that belied the official version. Networks of American teenagers and college students were spiriting them away and actively opposing the draft.

At my house, Vietnam was good for a full-blown argument on a weekly basis. I took it as my own moral obligation to raise these discussions with my parents. My two teenage sisters had "secret" boyfriends, one of them a Mexican-American actually facing the draft. They didn't want my parents finding out what they were doing after Catholic high school, so they flew under the radar on this issue at home. My oldest sister would step up to the plate with civil rights issues, the Negro and white civil rights marches, the black voter registration drives, the Birmingham bombings and the three slain civil rights workers. But Vietnam was mostly "my" contribution to political arguments.

Things came to a head one evening in my fifteenth year, shortly after I had read the new issue of Ramparts, a "left-wing" Catholic magazine which offered hard-to-find articles and liberal commentary on Vietnam. In fact, the magazine had been formed to reflect and promote a more liberal Catholic viewpoint. It was totally against America's involvement with the then–Catholic Ngo Dinh Diem's dictatorial regime, soon overthrown, which led to the expansion of America's covert actions in South Vietnam. Copies of Ramparts were passed around Whittier High School, where I transferred after my mother was informed by the principal of St. Paul's that my essay on the sacrament of the Eucharist indicated I would be a better fit for public high school.

Ramparts was a seminal force in opposing American foreign policy in Asia and Central/South America during the '60s and '70s. The publication detailed the political efforts of the Catholic church to derail all population control research, culminating in the mid-sixties when oral contraceptives came on to the market. Reading Ramparts was a revelation to me. For a long time, my parents tolerated my having it, mostly because I could tell them with conviction that it was a "Catholic" magazine. They never bothered to wade through its erudite analyses.

That evening, however, my parents called me after dinner into the living room, always a bad sign. While the downstairs den was child-friendly, the living room functioned as a formal entertaining space and informal interrogation chamber, essentially, my parents' domain. Evidently, Mom and Dad had connected the dots between student protests on TV, anecdotes shared among their bridge-playing friends, and the intrusion of Vietnam into the everyday conversations of everyday families throughout America.

"But what makes you think you know anything?" sneered my mother that fateful evening. She had a way of pursing her lips and injecting the venom of contempt into her speaking voice, enhanced as ever by the highballs consumed before, during and after dinner. I showed her the pictures of burned and maimed Vietnamese from *Ramparts* magazine and *Life*. I fully expected her to share my horror and disbelief, feeling that they would affect her as much as they had me. She flipped through them. "Yes, I've seen them."

My father attempted to "reason" with me. "What do you think will happen if Vietnam turns communist? All the other countries will go Communist, then what?" I showed him the pictures. "Well do you really think you know more than our leaders about this?"

I tried again. "But what about the people we're hurting? America's not supposed to do that. We should be helping them, not sending bombs!" My two cousins were shortly to enlist in the Army; and they, in fact, became some of the people the U.S. was hurting. One of them went through three wives, took himself to the Idaho woods, and appropriated his siblings' inheritances, but that would happen later.

My parents, normally at odds with each other, offered a united front, each with the same curled lip in the face of this Vietnamese suffering and my "naivete." I can't remember their exact words; but clearly, they weren't feeling the pain I felt.

I was dumfounded. I couldn't understand the deafening lack of regard for the horrible suffering we were inflicting on the Vietnamese. My parents had always presented themselves as deeply Catholic, righteous people, despite the continual fights heard all over the neighborhood, the nightly drinking, and the bruises and cuts they inflicted on their children. The disconnect between what I thought America symbolized and what my country was actually doing was so extreme. My parents, who may have been as confused as I was about Vietnam, both affected the facial expressions of spectators at a gladiatorial combat, sneering before the thumbs up or thumbs down.

Part of me wanted to sob and rage. A year earlier, I would have dissolved in tears and run to my room for a luxurious cry. I didn't do that this time. I just sat, looked at them, and really saw them for who they were: limited people with a low ethical IQ despite all their churchgoing. I realized they were no longer the moral arbiters of my life, but people who were deeply flawed and clueless, people who didn't care to know anything disturbing or anything requiring empathy for people they would never meet. They were moral idiots.

The last pieces of regard I had for them fell away. I felt very stupid to have been so afraid of them, so cowed throughout the alcoholic rages, their scorn, even the physical abuse. I regarded them with more adult eyes and understood I had nothing more to learn from them. Although the political skirmishes continued until I left for college, I never again felt that a dialogue was possible or that they would become what I considered "good people" to be.

It wasn't until later that I considered their seeming unconcern might have been a form of panic, a reaction to facing the profound changes in values that occurred in the sixties and seventies. Not only were their children rejecting their values, but there was a real iconoclasm going on. Like strangers in a strange land, their goals, dreams, ambitions and reference points were being deconstructed on all fronts. No wonder they started drinking at 5:00 o'clock weeknights, earlier on weekends. They had landed, not in middle-class America, but on an ice flow melting beneath their feet.

Vietnam was *the* watershed event of the Sixties even more than the Civil Rights movement which was, after all, an American movement claiming equal rights for all. Vietnam was the first real faux conflict initiated for ultimately capitalist reasons, the first time America became the "bad guy," no longer the hero of World War II and the Marshall Plan, but the Darth Vader of capitalism.

That watershed evening with my parents also recalibrated my internal settings from the moral trivia of my Catholic upbringing and its ineffectual pieties. It expanded my spiritual universe and deepened it. I converted to

Buddhism a few years later and found a more complete and accurate view of life, a view in which clarity and wisdom were actively sought and in which an active practice of compassion was the antidote to the moral autism of American politics during and since the Vietnam Era.

Susan Hawke: Our House

I was a 1960s child greatly influenced by my hippie grandmother. She'd chucked her brassiere, wore love beads, bought books on African art, and sang along with Joan Baez's songs on the radio.

Grandma taught me to ride the bus downtown to attend city council meetings and scold the Mayor. Grandma pressured my grandfather to vote Democrat, lest the sanitation trucks or snowplows skip their house. In Chicago, politics rule.

My grandmother picked fights with my politically conservative grandfather about the Civil Rights Movement. Things got intense in 1966, when Dr. Martin Luther King, Jr., marched in Marquette Park, just blocks from their bungalow. King and his supporters were pummeled with bricks and bottles. I don't remember whether Grandma went, but I *do* remember Grandpa insisting it was too dangerous for *me*.

My grandparents' divided home exemplified how conflicts that seemed far away exploded in America's living rooms! I tried to understand, but found only confusion instead. According to Grandma, hippies were righteous, which seemed obvious when they were giving riot police flowers. But hippies also burned the American flag, which brought my World War II veteran grandfather to tears.

I loved them both and wondered why they couldn't simply "Give Peace A Chance" like John Lennon and Yoko Ono declared from their bed! Decades later, I contributed to Ono's efforts to memorialize the movement at "The Peace Museum." Yet today, I remain confused and impatient for the peace we sang about. I shall not burn our flag! But I may pick flowers.

Steve Dickson: Fortunate Son

I joined the Army in 1971 at the age of 17 in the state of Georgia after living there for four years. We'd previously lived in Washington state and Montana. When my father who sold heavy equipment was transferred to Georgia, the racial tensions and the intolerance of those times in the deep

South was a shock to my system. Segregation was still in full effect, and I just didn't understand it or want to be a part of that mindset. The military was my ticket out.

I was sent to basic and advanced infantry training at Ft. Ord, California. During my first weekend off, I hitchhiked into Monterey, a great way to travel back then. A couple of girls in the plaza near Fisherman's Wharf asked me if I had a smoke, so I passed them my cigarettes. One of them took me by the hand, and we walked up the hill into a grove of trees and met up with some other people living in a camp.

They rolled a joint and passed it around along with a bottle of Boone's Farm wine. For the first time, I was smoking pot and being around such free-spirited people. The six girls and four guys who lived there spent their days panhandling from tourists at the wharf. In the evenings, they got stoned, drank, sang and danced around the fire.

During the week, I spent my days training to be a soldier under strict regimentation, with the expectation of going to Vietnam. During the weekends, I hung out with my new friends and listened to their stories, learned why they lived rough, and pondered their way of life, uninhibited and living for the moment. Most had left home due to bad experiences and wanted to be free. It was ironic that they spent their nights camping in peace and joy, while I was in the field preparing for war

After a few months, I had orders to go to Vietnam. My friends asked me if I wanted to join them on the road and head down to Big Sur. I considered it but didn't want to become a deserter and end up in jail. Soon thereafter, Richard "Tricky Dick" Nixon de-escalated the war; my orders changed; and I was to be sent to Panama. My Monterey friends were cool with the new orders and wanted me to send them some pot from down there. I never did.

Nancy Pruitt: Agent Orange

It all seemed impossible to believe in 1972. Veterans of Vietnam who wanted desperately to forget the horrors they survived never expected to bring the war home to their families, but too many did. Told by their superiors it was harmless, the use of Agent Orange in Southeast Asia left millions of deforested acres and horrible side effects to this day ranging from birth defects, mental health issues, cancers, and diabetes for the people of Vietnam, the U.S. and Australia.

During the heaviest use of Agent Orange from 1968–71 in "Operation

Ranch Hand," my husband Steve traversed through countless areas which were sprayed as he "walked point" for the USMC as a dog handler. He became one of the "Walking Dead," meaning his life was marked for killing by the enemy. He survived three tours, returning with multiple health problems that surfaced much later. We married in 1972 and were never to have children due to our fear of multiple birth defects warranted by his exposure. It took over two decades for the Veterans Administration to finally acknowledge the effects of dioxin on our troops. Unacceptable.

My political views were permanently altered by my husband's experience and countless stories of survival in hostile conditions. I had been a vocal anti-war demonstrator years before I met him, but soon realized that it did not reflect my new life with a veteran. I had a lack of understanding what the war was like for soldiers like Steve. Joining into the group-think of anti-war sentiment in 1968–70, many beliefs I held true became hollow. I soon edged away from the disrespect and contempt I held for the war. But the trust in our government was dashed as their denial rained large, blanketing the truth particularly about Agent Orange.

Today the deliberate denial by our government reaches into the food industry, Big Pharma and Healthcare. Insidious and cowardly, the leaders we look to for protection prefer to keep us in the dark and medicated so we don't care, a slippery slope indeed when our great country is controlled by lobbyists dictating to the politicians we elect to represent us, unthinkable yet our reality.

When I would explain "I didn't think that this would happen when I did XYZ," Steve would pause me and say, "Stop with, I didn't *think*." Profound and biting as it felt, I have to say I am grateful for the many gifts he gave me, including his loyalty even after our divorce in 1980 until his untimely death in 2008 from Agent Orange.

Tara B: Peace Sign

My path to becoming a hippie began in April 1958, the first time I saw the peace sign. I watched a report on the TV evening news that showed a huge rally in London where hundreds of people were walking along a highway carrying banners and signs with words like "No Nuclear Testing" and "Action for Life." They held aloft hundreds of large round placards that displayed an unforgettable image.

These citizens represented the Campaign for Nuclear Disarmament who were walking 52 miles from London to the Atomic Weapons Research

Establishment in Aldermaston, Berkshire, UK. The symbol on the round signs eventually became known as the peace sign, but its introduction to the world began that Easter Sunday in 1958.

I was mesmerized by what I was seeing. I had never seen or heard of anything like this before. These marchers were articulating something I could not yet voice. They were united in a peaceful campaign to bring awareness and change to the world, demonstrating their conviction that humanity needed to create a new way of being on Earth if we were to survive.

They not only spoke out against war. They spoke *for* peace. I was touched to the core and deeply impressed by the courage, intelligence, and intentions of these folks and their signs. I felt something I had never felt before: connectedness and a vision of a bigger picture. Even as a young teen, I knew I was part of this and always would be. It wasn't a matter of joining anything. I was already a part of it. It was who I was and still am.

We were the first kids born under the shadow of the A-Bomb, the first to bear the burden of knowing we could destroy all life on Earth. The image of that mushroom cloud was burned into our brains. Unlike today, the dangers of nuclear war were presented front and center in our politics and in our education. These images made a deep impression on us as children.

I'm convinced that this perspective contributed greatly to the rise of the hippie counterculture. It made us receptive to a new way of thinking. In a few short years, the graphic design presented that day became the iconic emblem of peace around the world. For me, a seed was planted that year which has borne such fruit. I have learned so much on this journey, most importantly, that peace begins with me.

After 60 years, the Campaign for Nuclear Disarmament is still active today and their walk from London to Aldermaston is held every year.

The peace sign is kind of like the hippies. We're still here, and we still mean the same thing, maybe now more than ever.

Carol Seaton: Military Industrial Complex

In ancient Rome, being a Christian meant taking a stand against the spreading, immoral Roman Empire. Now, Christians believe our engagement in wars is the will of God and that our wealth, dependent on a strong military, is a blessing from God. So where do we turn except to the hippie movement?

I remember my mother and stepfather discussing whether we should enter the Vietnam War. In my home, the answer was: No. Down the street lived a nice young man who was determined to become a police officer in order to avoid the draft. I had a strong feeling that this was a corporate war taking the young men from my school against their wills.

One of the worst days of my life was the day that the television broadcast live from the battlefield in Vietnam. I watched a mother run from her burning village with her baby in her arms. The cameraman zoomed in on the baby's limp hand. To this day, I cannot remember that scene without being consumed by the emotional horror and compassion for all mothers struggling to keep their children alive. At that moment, a feeling of dread spread through my body; and I thought that this intense cold might spread to my heart and I would die.

Today, it is horrifying to have a president who demands that other nations spend more to prepare for war. Surely, the U.S. needs immediate psychoanalysis. When the military strength of nations was measured before World War II, the U.S. was a low 17. Small countries had greater military strength, and the U.S. was known for its anti-war posture. For a nation that began by throwing the tea into the sea to protest being taxed to support England's military might, how did we get to escalating war around the world with our industrial deals (oil) and supply of weapons?

Eisenhower ended his presidency by warning us about the Military Industrial Complex. Today, we are the world's largest supplier of arms. The Military Industrial Complex is Eisenhower's term for what Hitler and George Bush called the New World Order. We adopted Germany's models for bureaucracy and education, and we are now what we defended our democracy against. We could throw every weapon into the sea; and we would still be organized by military order, not the family order that once organized our nation.

As my generation dies, so will the memory of the democracy we once had. Hippies were against the Vietnam War and still oppose war today. How can wanting peace be un–American? Today, I am really angry with my hippie friends who shrink from sharing their hippie values with those around them. In their old age, they have become cowards, passively allowing the evil we stood against to sweep over us.

Susan Hawke: Man on the Moon

A half-century ago, a half-billion awestruck people clung to their televisions as astronaut Neil Armstrong took humankind's first-ever step on the moon.

"Look at the astronaut—he's on the moon!" I remember my mom excitedly calling me. To make sure I didn't miss the moment, she'd tapped the black-and-white T.V. screen with her finger.

"On the moon, Mamma? Is there *really* a man on the moon?" I can hear the echo of my own child-voice asking. I remember running to a window to see the waxing, white moon in the Midwest sky. I'd alternately looked from the orb to the flickering screen as an astronaut climbed down a ladder then thumped his pillow-foot onto "moon dirt." I was astounded that the glowing mass in the sky and the landscape on T.V. were *both* real! From the window, I'd strained to see the American flag the astronauts hoisted, or even their rocket ship. But I couldn't. President Nixon called to congratulate the crew—live! Then a teary-eyed newsman came back on. Finally, my mom turned the T.V. off, because it was time for bed.

"Will they ever go back, Mamma?" I remember asking. "We'll have to see," was all she'd said.

In my room, I'd listened to The Fifth Dimension's "Age of Aquarius" song on my transistor radio: "When the *moon* is in the Seventh House ... then peace will guide the planet and love will steer the stars. This is the dawning of the Age of Aquarius!" I'd thought about the moonwalk I'd just watched and compared it with the usual news: bloodied soldiers hauling stretchers in Vietnam, angry protestors being whacked by masked police with batons, and colorful hippies with flowers singing about peace for the cameras.

I'd listened thoughtfully to that song on that night and consciously realized that I, too, wanted "harmony and understanding, sympathy and trust abounding" and "the mind's true liberation" like the lyrics said. In my innocence, I'd wondered: If people could ever live on the moon, would they bring *war or peace* with them?

Going Up the Country

Thousands of hippies took Timothy Leary's advice and "dropped out," trading lives driven by money and conformity for new, simpler ones in rural settings. Their critics labeled this strategy as self-indulgence, "running away" from the world's problems instead of fighting the good fight on the streets of Babylon. What these naysayers failed to see is that, in order to radically change the world, you need pioneers to invent new ways of living and loving for the rest of us to emulate. By adopting simpler lives off the grid and redefining what it means to be family, these drop-outers showed us that life can be more joyful than we thought possible.

Along the way, these pioneers became increasingly aware that what some call "progress" was, in fact, destroying the water, the air, and the soil. And so, they took personal and collective action to protect and conserve our increasingly fragile planet.

When I was 20, I didn't care where our food came from or where our trash went to. Except for Smokey Bear, I never thought about protecting the forests or keeping the air clean. They were boring subjects, as far as I was concerned. Besides, looking honestly at my personal habits and how they affected the greater good would have required me to change how I wanted to live. I wasn't willing to do that.

Today, my older son and his wife are leaders in the campaign for energy efficiency in both homes and commercial buildings. Their personal habits match their professional responsibilities. They recycle everything they can, reduce their water consumption, and eat locally-grown organic food. In many ways, they are the next generation of hippies, still dedicated to love and peace, but doing what I did not, protecting Mother Nature.
—S.L.R.

Barry Sommer: Incense and Peppermints

Hitting age 64 means I can now look back on chapters of my life and wonder: What the hell was I thinking? That I survived to be able to look back is a testament to the hardiness of the human mind and body and the stupidity that tests those physical (and mental) limits.

It is said that, if one claims to remember the '60s and '70s, they couldn't possibly have been there. I remember, because I lived right in the middle of it all. My family had a retail store in Hollywood selling beauty and barber supplies. Helping people look good kept the family busy, while my task was to explore and embrace all that the new hippie movement held. In the end, I ate, slept and danced to the beat of my hippie brothers and sisters, enjoying all the "happenings" and protesting the Vietnam War at the Federal Building on Wilshire Boulevard in Los Angeles.

Surrounding my youth were crash pads, head shops, love-ins, free drugs and all the free music one could ingest. The Sunset Strip was the place to be seen and make a scene, only eclipsed by Haight Ashbury in San Francisco which turned out to be the jumping off place for my sojourn to Woodstock. I'm pretty sure I was the only one at Woodstock who didn't get laid, and I have but fleeting memories of Hendrix, Joplin, Santana and the rest.

In the intervening decades, societies have changed and so have we hippies, sometimes good, sometimes not so good. But the foundational beliefs that were new then—peace, love and brotherhood—are still part of me despite the world around me.

Making sense of the absurdity in the 21st century is a tough road to master. So much so that, in order to survive, I had to leave the big city and find quieter pastures. I found them in Oregon in a little town of less than 400 people on the central coast. My bliss has increased, and communing with people who appreciate the slower lifestyle appeals to me greatly. I try to stay away from politics and concentrate on the beauty and grandeur of nature, letting it wash over me, bringing me contentment and happiness.

I've managed to keep the eternal optimism and belief in the goodness of humans I learned in my youth and have been able to maintain equilibrium of sorts. Now retired, I spend my time in volunteer work and the quiet pursuit of life that comes with time well spent.

Ray York: Take Me Home, Country Roads

I was a hippie, and I wasn't. That was for others to say. I dropped out, left my family and career behind and rode a motorcycle to California. The only thing I brought was my hatred for Nixon and the War. I wore my hair long and ended up on a ranch that was a commune; but it wasn't, with people who were hippies; but they weren't. It was a second childhood and a learning experience. I learned to ride horses, care for them, and even shoe them. I smoked dope and did LSD with my new friends, worked very hard and tried to Be Here Now.

I was dazed by the ranch, dazed and dazzled. I came planning to stay for a weekend and ended up doing three to five. I loved every minute of my time there. When we made a pyramid of men and lifted the ridgepole onto our new barn, I was proud as Iwo Jima.

I grew up in a men-don't-cry culture, but I learned to cry at the ranch. I found it helpful, even essential, to be able to cry when doing frequent hallucinogens. Besides, the ranch was a pressure cooker. The release was essential. Emotions built up that I couldn't easily disperse.

I remember sitting at the Big House kitchen table one morning after an all-night trip, with my head on the table, crying quietly; when Twink came through the kitchen reminding me gently of the onionskins of existence; and Russell came over to say he loved me before he made coffee. It was okay to cry. This was a good crew to trip with.

A few years after the ranch, a less idyllic reality began to envelop me. I went down to the city where all the things I had mocked and used the ranch to avoid were waiting for me, snapping back into place with a vengeance after our funny little commotion. For a while, I felt a slight hatred of everything.

We were like a hippie think tank. There was an air of openness, a feeling of adventure. Anything could happen, and it often did. There was magic in the air. The rhetoric of the times was in the air too; but in spite of its gentle anarchy and hippie drag, the strange fact is that the ranch, built on private money, was really a Republican enterprise that operated by trickle-down and pre-figured the days of Reagan, Bush, and Bush. The key difference is simply that ranch trickle-down, unlike the bogus Reagan trickle-down, was real. People were generous. I was a beneficiary of that largesse for many years.

Today, I'm a reporter in a small town where nothing much ever happens, good work for a fiction writer. I'm raising a fourteen-year-old boy, a scholarship student who plays bass and has already been arrested. He's teaching me about what he calls "real anarchy." I'm struggling to learn.

Douglas Stevenson: Joy to the World

For over 45 years, I have been engaged in one of the boldest social experiments to blossom from the idealism of the 1960s: The Farm Community in Summertown, Tennessee. Our 200 residents collectively share this modern Ecovillage comprised of over 1700 acres protected through a Trust. For the first 12 years after its founding in 1971, everyone who joined The Farm signed a vow of service to humanity. We created our first nonprofit, Plenty, believing there is enough of everything if we all share.

Living on The Farm has allowed me to be a part of something greater than myself and given me the chance to put my energy toward positive change in the world. In 1978, I spent six weeks driving an ambulance in support of 4000 Native Americans marching on Washington. It was my first exposure to the mindset of Indigenous Peoples, and the experience had a deep effect on me, furthering my promise to dedicate my life to making a difference.

My wife, Deborah Flowers, and I also spent two years as volunteers for Plenty after a devastating earthquake in Guatemala. She was our team's lab technician, helping the group stay well so that we could help. I provided radio communications and did the electrical installation for a soy foods production facility we built, a cottage industry for the Village of San Bartolo, now in operation for over 35 years.

When we got back to the U.S., I started a company producing educational videos; and Deborah became a Certified Professional Midwife, serving mothers and babies who come from all over the world to experience a spiritual birth.

Many years later, Deborah and I were again volunteers for Plenty International, spending seven months in Belize. Deborah taught childbirth education to Mayan women from a dozen remote villages, a project supported by UNICEF. I assisted a Mayan Ecotourism organization attract visitors through online marketing, bringing tourist dollars directly to the villages.

From 2004 to 2016, I served on the board of the Swan Conservation Trust helping to establish the 1400 acre preserve that now surrounds our community. Our seven board members raised over $1.5 million to buy the land, teaching me, once again, the power of working together.

I was also a founding member of PeaceRoots Alliance, established after 9/11 to counter the shift toward war. Part of my responsibilities involved posting of over 200 billboards around the county as a way to reclaim the flag in the name of peace. I also worked with PeaceRoots to establish the

Farmer Veteran Coalition, designed to help veterans heal from PTSD by putting them in touch with the earth. Today, FVC is a separate non-profit, managed and staffed by veterans, with chapters all around the country providing funding to veterans for educational and establishing small farms.

This is all to say that surrounding yourself with like-minded people enables you to stay true to your hopes and dreams, whether that means finding work more in tune with your beliefs or dedicating your time and energy in service of the greater good, the path that I believe leads to true fulfillment.

Change begins with you. When you find peace within, it will radiate peace to those around you; and this is how we can bring peace to the world. Take it from an ol' hippie.

Richard Schoebrun: Living the Dream

I was a Weekend Warrior, a grocery clerk in the San Fernando Valley. The Watts Riots on TV were only 30 miles away. On a Friday morning, we got the call that we were activated. I joined the Army Reserves right out of high school, trained in heavy equipment in Missouri, and later transferred into the National Guard. In my last year of active service, I was suddenly part of a deployment of 4000 Guardsman, marching into the streets of Watts, shoulder to shoulder with fixed bayonets. I was 21.

The next 5 days changed my life forever. I became a combat veteran on American soil. There were dead bodies on the streets, burning buildings, empty shells of burnt buildings, and even more significantly, I saw for the first time that people lived in Third World conditions in my own city.

Seeking change, I tried marijuana and laughed so much it became my choice over alcohol. In 1967, I participated in the Great Peace March against the Vietnam War from downtown San Francisco into Haight-Ashbury and eventually decided to move into the district. Someone suggested checking out this teacher at San Francisco State. Stephen Gaskin, a Korean War vet and Creative Writing instructor was holding meetings in a student lounge, tying people's psychedelic experiences to the ancient teachings of the world's religions.

My most profound spiritual experience on LSD was on Mount Tamalpais communing with a cow, which left me a lifelong vegan. Stephen's following grew, and he went on a national book tour with a large Caravan of rolling homes. When he decided to find land in Tennessee, our bus, with two couples and a small baby each inside, joined in.

In 12 years, The Farm was the largest spiritual community in the U.S. with over 1500 people. I was the first Store Manager, drove heavy equipment, and learned how to be a house mover, transporting the Gate House/Welcome Center onto The Farm from the town of Columbia, about 40 miles away.

We had medical staff, but no dentist; so I got a BS degree at the University of Tennessee and went to dental school. I couldn't finish but joined the hygienists in the dental clinic, learning extractions from a Farm doctor and figuring out root canals and fillings on my own.

In 1983, The Farm had to restructure from a Collective to a Co-op. I had five years of experience in dentistry but could no longer practice for free and wasn't licensed to charge for my services. I worked my way through nursing school by painting and construction work, then practiced at a nearby hospital.

After 23 years on The Farm, my family relocated to California where I discovered Sufi Dances of Universal Peace, now my spiritual practice. I continued nursing, eventually doing Hospice Care and Geriatric Case Management. This enabled me to retire comfortably enough to travel and volunteer at free medical and dental events, the joy of my life in my mid-seventies. I am living my hippie dream of service.

Judah Freed: Mother Nature's Son

As one who came of age in the Sixties, I loved nature long before I ever turned on, tuned in, and stepped up into mature global thinking.

I'm a midcentury Colorado kid, raised in Denver, University Hills, if that means anything to you. My father shared his love of the land. He taught me fieldcraft on family and scout camping trips in the Rockies. I earned merit badges for outdoor skills and knowledge, but there was no merit badge offered for common global sense.

Growing up in the Fifties and Sixties, I trusted all the anti-littering campaigns on radio and television as well as in newspapers and magazines. Whenever the family went on road trips, I always made sure the family car had a clean litter bag hanging from the window crank. I felt it was my patriotic duty to my country and the countryside.

Until adulthood, I didn't learn that the "Keep America Beautiful" campaign was really was an industry initiative to forestall laws proposed to regulate waste. Polluters hid the profit motive behind the campaign, making the promotion about as genuine as the Italian actor hired to portray a "crying Indian" in the TV commercials.

Similarly, I did not learn until much later that the "Green Revolution," touted in the 1960s for feeding the starving millions around the world, actually was a plan by the agrochemical industry to replace traditional earth-friendly farming methods with overreliance on expensive and toxic fertilizers, pesticides and herbicides. The green being pursued was money.

The first Earth Day in 1970 changed how I made sense of threats to Mother Nature. I was a freshman at Adams State College in Colorado's San Luis Valley. Outside the student union, a series of tables alerted me to national organizations unknown to me before. I recall talking with student members of Sierra Club, the Wilderness Society, Audubon Society, Greenpeace, Friends of the Earth and other groups.

Also that day, I was introduced to the thinking of Senator Gaylord Nelson. His work in Congress would lead to creation of the Environmental Protection Agency (EPA) along with passage of the Clean Air Act, Water Quality Improvement Act, Endangered Species Act, and other environmental legislation.

The first Earth Day was the first time I heard the name of organizer Denis Hayes. Today, he leads the worldwide Earth Day, attracting a billion people globally every year.

Earth Day also kindled my interest in such books as *Silent Spring* by Rachel Carson, *The Population Bomb* by Paul R. Ehrlich, and especially *Walden* by Henry David Thoreau. The notion of living deliberately at Walden Pond, or anywhere, sunk deeply into me. I next read Thoreau's *Civil Disobedience*, that led me to Emerson and the Transcendentalists, which eventually would lead me to the spiritual path called "New Thought."

In the following decades, my intermittent activism focused mostly on issues of war and peace. I marched against the war in Vietnam and in Southeast Asia. Later, I worked in the Nuclear Freeze movement, supported Jimmy Carter's tour of Denver's solar-powered restaurant, and managed an environmentalist's grassroots campaign for the Colorado state legislature.

My focus on ecology kicked into high gear from the late 1980s into the 1990s, when I became involved in the Windstar Foundation, the Aspen-based environmental education organization co-founded by Aikido master, Thomas Crum, and singer-songwriter, John Denver.

Every summer, I attended the "Choices for the Future" symposium in Aspen. As the event's pressroom aide, I coordinated media interviews for such thought leaders as David Brower, Ben Cohen, Matthew Fox, Jay Hair, Jean Houston, Barbara Marx Hubbard, Wangari Maathi, Jeremy Rifkin, Stephen Schneider, David Suzuki, Dennis Weaver, and others. Each speaker inspired me.

The heart and spirit of John Denver and the Windstar community penetrated into me and remains at the root of my evolving consciousness today. These influences and more today combine in my writings under the catchphrase of "global sense"—a sensibility that says we're all interconnected on earth, that what anyone does impacts life for everyone, and that we need to live responsibly free.

The social and ecological ideals I adopted in the "hippie" era still guide my life and work. I may be only one more voice in the wilderness; but as we face the growing havoc of global climate change, I cannot stay silent and still be true to my soul. Can you?

Carol Seaton: A Hard Day's Night

My relationship with Mother Nature began when I was too young to have words for memories. I would not have remembered this story if my father had not told me of recovering from the psychological trauma of war by putting me on his shoulders and walking through the woods with me. At age 4, my parents divorced; and my mother moved my sister and me to Hollywood, California. I was not to know my father again until I was 18. At even though I have no memory of my father walking with me in the woods, trees trigger within me a feeling of being deeply loved. There has to be some kind of psychological word for this transposing of a lost father's love into nature, and being a hippie is very much about nature and love.

The transposition of my father's love into trees was a life saver for me. My husband moved our family from Oregon into a summer cabin between San Francisco and Reno, Nevada. When it snowed, he had to drive a tow truck; so he slept at Nyack. For days, I was alone with the children; and I quickly learned Mother Nature doesn't care if you live or die. She gives us liberty. It's up to us to know what to do with it.

The cabin was heated by gas; but when a big snow hit, the gas company could not deliver, and we had to rely on a Franklin Stove. Ripping wet wood out of the forest with my bare hands, I would dry it on top of the stove so it would burn. Sometimes the cabin filled with smoke, so I taught my children to crawl out the door when there was smoke. Do you understand the power of this survival experience? Mother Nature was teaching me to be strong and how to survive with two little children.

In a few years, we returned to Oregon; and Mother Nature taught me another lesson. We lived in a mobile home that sat where a farmhouse had stood. My husband turned over the soil for a garden and then left me the care for the garden. I had had some experience growing vegetables, but nothing this big. The aged chicken poop in the old chicken coop was a great fertilizer, and Mother Nature blessed us with a bountiful crop. But when it was time to harvest, I wasn't ready to do it.

By the time I decided to stop being a spoiled brat and refusing to do things Mother Nature's way, it was too late. The harvest was lost, and I had learned another hard lesson. Now I have to chuckle, because I know many fellow hippies also learned from Mother the hard way. Mother Nature teaches us to grow up. We cannot manipulate her like we can humans. She does not accept excuses. You do things her way or suffer the consequences. It is all clean and honest. She gave me a bountiful garden and the wood in the forest to keep my children alive, but it was up to me to take the right actions at the right time. Our liberty depends on knowing that. I think those who find fault with hippies just don't understand what a good teacher Mother Nature is. Going from the city to rural areas, we had a lot to learn.

Ashley Kent Carrithers: Life Is for Learning

I went from a little red brick schoolhouse on a hill in our little village to a fancy, well reputed, "prep" school where I put on a jacket, learned how to tie my tie, and entered sixth grade. There were sixty guys in my class, and I was supposed to beat my classmates, academically, physically, and socially, whenever and wherever possible. The school placed a premium on erudite knowledge and learned talk, an anchor that lasted until my hippie days when I was finally able to transcend that academic nonsense and begin to forget what I had so studiously learned years ago.

True, I may be guilty of an increasing inability to discern the undiscernible; but it seems to me that what some people call wisdom sounds like the gibberish of like-witted dudes competing in a semi-puerile, tongue-measuring, circle jerk, endeavoring to out-jabber their colleagues and win. Win. Win.

As I wander through the dense forests of their machine-gunned words spewed casually from higher grounds, I shake my head and wonder: Is this really wisdom?

I graduated in psychology from Duke University, a renowned institution where a degree should mean something. It turns out that what I learned in those ivy halls provided basically nothing of value when compared to the classrooms I encountered in deep Nature's wilderness with senses wide open or in a lover's eyes where secrets unasked are shared without wily words.

Tom S: Somebody to Love

When I decided to move on from psychedelics, I wanted to get high on the natural world and become a sorcerer, someone who dwells on the margins, an intermediary between two realms, a person who could describe how nature makes itself evident and meaningful to our senses.

One day hiking, I came upon a trail I'd never seen before. It led away from the railroad tracks up on to a rocky overlook where I found a comfortable boulder where I could sit and look out across the breadth of the shadowed plateau and surrounding hills. In the morning sun, seeing the bright green treetops and the mist rising off the river; I could sense the intensity of it all, powerful and constant. Far enough off the road where no one would see me, it was a perfect meditative spot.

Not long after settling down, I heard a huffing sound. The noise turned out to be a logging truck coming down off the mountain behind me, brutally interrupting my solitude as it roared past. Then I heard rocks scattering and saw a deer rushing up the hill beside me, followed by another deer and its fawn.

As a hawk soared above us all, the mother and fawn suddenly split apart, the fawn going up over the ridge and down the cut between our neighboring ridges. I wondered. Why had the pair split apart? Then I hear the mother on a small ridge about fifteen feet away, sniffing at me. We looked at each other, eye to eye. Then I blew a horse-breath, and she was gone.

Twenty-five years later, all I could see around me is the desolation of the natural world and too many people I knew. "Bent out of shape by society's pliers," as Dylan sang. There was too much alienation, mixed with alcohol, infused with fear and paranoia.

I think back on the time when I was close enough to feel a part of the natural world, if only for a few seconds before returning to my man-observer frame of reference. Today, I wonder: Why can't we communicate with the wild instead of exploiting or killing it? What could we learn? Maybe we'd see how to survive peacefully on our own planet.

Damaged as it is, I do love the land here. I've learned from reading Meeker's *Comedy of Survival* that I have to accept nature "as is," even if she's scarred by logging and too much asphalt. It's like loving your mate. If he or she were to suffer a horribly disfiguring accident, you would still love that person.

You would still see the beauty within. After all, nature doesn't exist to please me. It's eternal; but I am mortal, only here a speck of time. It's up to me to make my time meaningful.

"Mark," c/o Patricia Lapidus: excerpt from *The Farm That Tried to Feed the World*

One winter, we single guys decide to live in a teepee. I figured if the Plains Indians could do it in winter, so could we. The teepee was maybe fourteen feet across, and we may have had some sleeping platforms. I don't remember. We had sleeping bags and blankets. Sometimes visitors would want to sleep in the teepee with us to get the experience.

One day, I was up at the top of our land; and I met one of our neighbors. I told him we were sleeping in a teepee in winter. He said, "What are you guys gluttons for punishment?" But that was the winter when everybody got the flu, except for the guys in the teepee. That taught me something about health and hardship.

Tom S: Dazed and Confused

My hippie adventure began in January of 1970, when I left the tradition-bound conformity of the suburban Midwest for the road westward to California, having no preconceived expectations, open to whatever came my way.

I'd read about hippies living off the grid in Taos; so when I got to New Mexico, I detoured up there to see the scene for myself. It was all I had imagined it would be. Then leaving town, I picked up two hitchhikers, Paul and Star. Star wore moccasins, an Indian poncho and feathers in her hair. They both had that psychedelic wisdom in their eyes. We drove through the night swapping stories of what we were going to bring to our fellow "freaks."

I spent a year and a half in California. I met a lot of loving, kind and gentle free spirits, imbibing and inhaling every chance I got. The first time I dropped mescaline, I was at the San Diego Zoo; and I told my friends, "Being this high must be illegal." I wasn't talking about legality though. I meant that feeling this joyful and uninhibited could never have happened to me living back in the burbs.

New Year's Eve, I was cleaning some peyote buttons with a friend before heading over to Winterland for a Dead concert. She asked me how many more times was I going to do psychedelics. She said she'd gone as far as she needed, and I agreed. We were both searchers, enjoyed the trips, but looking for more than just that.

I'd missed the Haight-Ashbury Summer of Love, but felt I'd caught up with it when I moved up to an old logging town at the end of the road in the Cascade foothills. Most nights, we sat around the wood stove in someone's kitchen, drinking herbal tea, passing a joint around, and enjoying the "communal vibes." Not long after that, I was living in a cabin near Mt. Rainier. My neighbor John, an old Scotsman, liked to play his bagpipes while meandering around the woods late at night. By the end of my winter up there, I'd learned what Kerouac meant when he wrote: "The wilderness is a void we put our own stamp on."

Time moved on. I cut my hair, each year smoking a little less pot. One day, I saw some poor lost soul wandering dazed and confused, hair matted, shoes flapping with each stumbling step. I realized I couldn't drift forever. I'd have to make my way in this increasingly mean-spirited world. I went to college and wound up teaching writing skills to suburban teenagers, encouraging them to think for themselves.

Eventually I found a place far enough off the grid to feel some sense of place. It took me awhile to get used to my neighbors' conservatism. In fact, they were a lot like the blue-collar people I'd wanted to escape from when I first moved west.

Then one day, I was asked to be a pall bearer for a fellow fraternal member. He'd lived in the same house for all of his 77 years. As we rode out to the cemetery, I noticed the snow-glazed mountains to the East and the peaceful morning sky revealing nature's sublime cycle of life unfolding before your eyes. I realized that my odyssey had led me to one of those moments of bliss and rapture that define our life. I was wiser in ways I never really imagined I'd be.

Beth Richards: California Dreamin'

I was terrified. We were driving along in our International Scout, a toddler and infant sequestered in the back seat and all our earthly possessions piled in the rear. Ernest was at the wheel, and I was anxiously peering down into the chasm of Butte Creek Canyon, sometimes called "the Little Grand Canyon." The road beside me dropped steeply, straight down to the almost-dry creek bed. The rock walls were beautiful, but all I could picture was our car hurtling down over the cliff.

The fact that Ernest had shut off the car ignition, rendering power steering and power to the brakes useless, added to my anxiety. But he masterfully negotiated the twists and turns of the winding road from the small village of Paradise into metropolitan Chico trying to preserve the little gas we had left, knowing we had little money to buy more.

Weeks before, we had set out for California from my parent's house in Virginia to see friends who had been urging us to join them in the land we thought might be paradise. After a long journey, first camping in corn fields and then sleeping on the cold sandy desert in New Mexico, we finally found ourselves in a worn-out tipi during a California drought. Scant rain was the only source of water and our dwindling funds meant eating soybeans and vegetables scavenged from grocery store dumpsters.

After a week, we discovered the depressing truth about California being a promised land. So, we took that crazy drive into Chico to sell the two things of value that we still owned, a Pentax camera purchased during our working days and a couple pairs of brand-new down mittens given to us as a gift (and not needed under the present circumstances, to say the least!). We drifted into the first gas station near Chico, pumped the rest of our money into the tank, drove to a local pawn shop where we sold our meager goods, and caught the highway south to Arizona where we knew of a commune that might take us in.

When I was growing up, California seemed like the Promised Land. Having spent a couple of years near San Francisco, I always dreamed of going back. When the Summer of Love splashed across the news, it was a clarion call for me to join this wonderful movement towards peace and freedom. I was then on the East Coast and desperately wanted to be part of the scene out west, wearing granny dresses and beads and dropping acid with Janis. So, when Ernest and I finally had the chance to go west many years later, it seemed like a good idea.

I still love California but have few illusions about it anymore. I find that I love many places, but my illusions of any of them being paradise are long gone! Each place I've lived possesses its own beauty and its own difficulties.

I Have a Dream

On August 28, 1963, a quarter million Americans joined a civil rights march in Washington, D.C., highlighted by Dr. King's famous "I have a dream" speech. The march was opposed by President Kennedy who feared that it might cause race riots in the streets. Much to his surprise and that of ordinary white Americans, there was no violence, only the thundering call for equality and economic opportunity.

To me, King's dream is the American Dream. The promise of equal opportunity for all makes this a great country, not its wealth or military might. We're not special because somebody's God has blessed us, but because there's room for everybody's God. We're not successful because we locked the outsiders out, but because we let the outsiders in. We're not patriotic because we salute the flag, but because we're free to celebrate or criticize the nation in any peaceful way we choose. We're not united because we speak with the same voice, but because all voices are allowed to speak.

Much criticism has been directed toward the hippie movement for being "anti–American." In fact, we were—and remain—passionate believers in the principles of equal treatment upon which this country was founded. As defenders of fairness and kindness, hippies have always supported the Civil Rights movement, women's liberation, gay rights, and any other effort that compels America to honor its commitment to equal opportunity for all.

Some of us were more visibly active than others in these struggles, attending demonstrations, joining voting rights campaigns, going door-to-door gathering petition signatures, and trying to elect sympathetic political leaders. Others did what we could on a day to day basis, illustrating our solidarity through our words and deeds.

Warren Buffet, one of the richest men in the world, was recently asked by a reporter to name the most important factor contributing to his success. Listening to the interview on TV, I expected him to say his parents, education, hard work, or maybe even the capitalistic system. Instead he answered with one word: "Luck."

"You see," he continued. "I was born a white male in the United States of America and that gave me an advantage over most of the world's population."

While I appreciate Warren's recognition that he began life with special privileges he did not earn; what he attributes to "luck" is, in fact, unequal opportunity and hateful treatment of those not so "lucky." Warren reminds us that women, people of color, non–Christians, the disabled, LGBTQ folks, ethnic minorities, Native Americans, old people, the "unattractive," and poor people must endure life at a profound disadvantage. Lacking economic and political power, often socially feared and vilified, they have to run faster and longer to "make it" in America, if they can make it at all.

I grew up in a white world. My parents were white. My relatives were white. Every student in my school was white. Every teacher, every neighbor, every storekeeper, every politician was white. Every policeman was white. The only black people that I saw were emptying trashcans at the curb, mopping the floors at my school, changing tires for my Father's business, or working as maids in our house.

As a kid, I loved going to the Carolina Movie Theater on Saturdays to watch the all-day cartoon shows. The theater was downtown in the most spectacular building I had ever seen. Gold columns stretched up two stories, red carpet was everywhere, and a huge crystal chandelier hung from the ceiling, I was in awe of the place. My parents happily gave me $5 and transportation to be safely gone all day.

By nine o'clock on Saturday mornings, the line of children wanting all-day cartoon passes would stretch around the block, rain or shine. After waiting for what seemed forever, we bought our tickets in front of the theater, opened the tall glass doors, and entered the red and gold majesty of the movie palace, not leaving until late afternoon.

One Saturday, I noticed that the black children didn't walk through the front doors like we did. Instead, they seemed to enter the theater through a partially hidden door on the side of the building marked "Colored" I didn't know what that word meant or why they didn't come in the front door like we did. I didn't ask. I didn't care.

One day, after a particularly good episode of "Rocket Man," the theater lights came up for a brief intermission. I glanced up at the balcony and saw a group of black children sitting on the top rows, laughing and eating popcorn.

"How come they get to sit up there?" I asked my friends. No one answered. Finally, as the lights dimmed and Bugs Bunny returned to the screen, I took one last look at the forbidden balcony and shook my head in disbelief. "It's just not fair," I grumbled. "How come they get the best seats?"

A few years later, in 1960, a group of black students from a local university sat at a segregated Woolworth's lunch counter in my hometown and refused to move. Soon the protest spread to other Woolworth locations, including one that I frequented every day after school.

On this particular day, I was sitting at the counter, intensely reading a Superman comic and sipping on a cherry coke with crushed ice, when I looked up and noticed that everyone had disappeared, including the two old ladies that always worked behind the counter.

I remember sitting on the stool and noticing how quiet the store had become. "They must have forgotten about me," I thought, as I slowly walked toward the front of the store. When I reached the swinging glass door to the outside, I saw a large group of black people walking around with signs. The white folks seemed to be watching.

Without thinking, I slipped through the unlocked door, weaved through the crowd, and headed home as usual. It was just another day for a happy white boy who could sit anywhere he wanted.

In the years that followed, I became increasingly aware of the segregation around me. As a self-proclaimed hippie in the early '70s, I considered the struggle of black folks for fair and equal treatment to be an essential part of making the world a better place. Because the injustice was so clear and the perpetuators so visible, it was easy for many of us with lighter complexions to feel passionate about the struggle, even if we never marched with Dr. King.

I have since realized that, no matter how strongly I feel about another person's pain, I cannot fully understand it unless I have endured it. As a straight, white male, raised by two loving parents in a middle-class life, I simply cannot comprehend what it means to be a person of color in America, or a child abandoned by his parents, or a parent struggling to feed his family on a minimum wage job, or a gay boy hiding in the closet, or an obese girl shamed on the Internet, or a working woman groped by her boss.

I was born and raised in North Carolina, one of those delusional racist places that joined the Confederacy in the "War Between the States," as some folks like to call it. While my Mother thought Gone with the Wind *was the best movie ever made and that Sherman was the devil himself for "raping* the South," I wasn't raised with any hatred for "Yankees" or any pride in being a Southerner. The subject was simply never discussed. I never learned any details about the Civil War, slavery, or Jim Crow laws in school. Unknown to me, my elementary school was named after a seriously racist governor. Since no children of color ever attended my school or lived in my neighborhood, the whole subject of "Southern-ness" never came to my attention.

When I got older and learned the hidden history of the "Old North State," I took assurance in the belief that none of my ancestors owned slaves. They were too poor, I thought. Only recently did I discover that both my great grandfather and his father were slave owners. So much for that delusion. I feel like many Germans must feel today who discovered Nazis in their family trees.

While I don't feel collective guilt about the evil deeds of my ancestors, I do feel compelled to do something about its effects in the here and now. That includes being honest with myself about racist messages imbedded in my brain from my Southern upbringing, recognizing the harm that past racism still inflicts today, and doing what I can to show kindness and respect to everybody.

From what I can tell, women have been mistreated since the dawn of time. The 1960s was no exception. In those years, employers were allowed to discriminate against women in hiring, wages, and promotion. Women had no legal rights to communal property. Courts could exclude women from juries. Married women were not allowed to use contraception. Employers could refuse to hire women with pre-school children or allow a woman to work in her last 3 months of pregnancy. Medical schools and law schools legally excluded women from attendance. Abortion was illegal.

In 1962, Betty Friedman wrote the book Feminine Mystique, exposing both the legal and cultural abuse of women in American society. In the years that followed, Federal legislation and court rulings, including the Equal Pay Act of 1963 and the Roe vs. Wade abortion decision of 1973, removed many of the legal obstacles women had faced earlier.

And yet, today, almost two decades into the 21st century, women are still the most abused group on the planet. They still have to fight for equal pay, unlimited career choices, and full respect as human beings. They're still being harassed, abused, raped, and murdered. I heard former President Jimmy Carter say in a speech recently that millions of girls worldwide are being aborted in the womb or strangled by their doctors for no other reason than being female.

So, who are these oppressors? Do they live in a certain country or belong to a certain religion? Are they black or white? Rich or poor?

Surprise! Surprise! The culprits are men, all kinds of men. Obviously, not every male person is an abuser; but too many are, in big ways and small. When I think of all the cruelty and pain that men have inflicted on this earth with their wars and their relentless abuse of women, I'm ashamed of my gender. I call myself a feminist, not because I'm female or because I think that women deserve better treatment than men. I'm a feminist, because I support everyone's right to kindness and fairness.

Even though lots of us wore bell-bottom jeans and tie-dye shirts, there was no hippie dress code back in the day. In fact, we were pretty much against anybody telling us what to do, what to say, and what to wear.

Meanwhile in London, the 1960s fashion world anointed its own definition of hip in the person of Lesley Hornby, better known as "Twiggy" for her ultra-thin body. Weighing 112 pounds in a 5'6" frame, she was thought to have the ideal body shape to which young women should aspire. Seriously?

Traditionally, power defines beauty. Movie studios, television networks, magazine publishers, and cosmetics companies have historically defined "beautiful people" as having white skin and straight hair. In the '60s, women of color shouted "Black is Beautiful" and adopted ancestral hairstyles and clothing to create their own definition.

I have no problem with how anybody wants to look. What saddens and angers me is the idea that women have to look a certain way in order to be attractive and that so many women who don't look like emaciated models feel bad about themselves. It seems so self-abusive and unnecessary.

It's not my job to tell women how they ought to look or how they ought to feel about how they look. I can only share my reaction to watching women struggle with the shape and "attractiveness" of their bodies. When I see women frantically adjusting their hair and make-up, I have to ask: Why are they working so hard? Do their jobs depend upon it? Their relationships? Their happiness?

Today, some adolescent girls are hounded so terribly online by anonymous trolls that they would rather die than face another day of "ugliness." Anorexic women starve themselves into thinner and, supposedly, more beautiful bodies. Older women contort their faces with Botox into sad versions of themselves to avoid the ravages of time. For what reason? Is this obsession social or biological? Is it forced on women or self-inflicted? I don't know.

As an outside observer, I can only say: If women are torturing themselves to please men, we're not worth it. You don't see us torturing ourselves to be beautiful.

This whole idea that women should be like Barbies on a shelf waiting to be picked by a man should be left to the past where it belongs. Yes, some men are only attracted to "living dolls." But in my experience, these are exactly the kind of men that most women don't want—the shallow, selfish, here-today-gone-tomorrow kind who are more interested in conquests than relationships.

Sure, we all want to look good. With unlimited funds, I'd probably buy new clothes for every day of the year. I'm 100 pecent supportive of women who dress up and wear make-up for their own enjoyment. Feeling beautiful is a great way to be kind to yourself. Worrying whether other people think you're beautiful is not. Complimenting the looks of others is kind. Degrading them for how they look is evil.

When I was in school, the worst thing you could say about a guy was that he was a "queer." When one guy said that about another, a fight inevitably broke out with an intensity not witnessed for other insults.

The truth is that I never really knew what a "queer" was for a long time. I just knew it was bad. None of my friends were homosexual (to my knowledge). My parents never mentioned the topic. When I was 17, I finally learned what the word "homosexual" meant thanks to a crude sex ed presentation by our Phys Ed teacher.

I had a friend in high school who was overweight, unathletic, and inclined toward "girly" things like art and clothes. He was never able to fit in with the other guys. His father was a retired, military-macho type who was painfully disappointed in his oldest son. After graduating in 1968, my friend moved to Boston.

The next year, after suffering unrelenting harassment, beatings, and arrests by homophobic cops, gays and lesbians fought back at a club called the Stonewall Inn in New York City. The "riot" that followed is considered the beginning of the gay liberation movement in America.

That same year, Billy Jean King, winner of 30 Grand Slam tennis championships and ranked for many years as the #1 women's tennis player in the world, was challenged to a "Battle of the Sexes" by Bobby Riggs, former pro tennis player and professed "chauvinist pig." Billy Jean won. Eight years later, she was "outed" as a lesbian by a former lover in a patrimony lawsuit. After losing tennis sponsorships and exhausting her tournament winning for legal fees, she became, and remains, an outspoken advocate of LGBTQ rights.

In 1973, my friend returned to town and sought me out. "I'm gay," he said. "And I'm much happier," he added with an easy smile, the kind of smile I had never seen on his face before. I congratulated him, and we soon went our separate ways again. A few years later, I heard he had died of some mysterious disease, AIDS, I think.

In some ways, America has come a long way since then. LGBTQ folks have certainly gained more legal rights and social acceptance over the last 60 years, but lots of straight people still seem infuriated by what "they" may be doing in bed. Why?

Perhaps the real problem isn't gay vs. straight sex, but sex in general. Let's face it. Sex can be scary and confusing. We're driven by forces we don't understand to please ourselves and our partners in unknown ways while balancing guilt with desire. We want to be wanted, but not too much. We want what we want but don't know how to get it. We confuse lust with love, permission with submission, and positions with feelings. We have no one to teach us and no way to escape our instincts. Perhaps straight folks need to solve their own sex problems before they tell everybody else what to do between the sheets.

Now free to marry, gay and lesbian couples illustrate that love in a committed relationship is more important than sex, no matter how you express it.

Growing up, I never saw disabled people. Maybe they were absent in my world, or maybe I just didn't see what I saw. When I finally did encounter folks without arms or legs, people with scarred faces, or kids in wheelchairs, I was shocked but only temporarily. I quickly looked the other way.

That all changed when I met my wife, a beautiful bird with broken wings, tormented by crippling arthritis for the last 40 years. Her fingers have deformed into claws, and her spine is reinforced with titanium. Like Keystone cops, her white blood cells are manic and confused, attacking healthy joints and bones until the connections are eventually severed, an agonizing and slow process, always painful, always unpredictable. This disease, like so many of us, is constantly creating the very problems it's trying to solve.

If anyone has the right to curse heaven and earth, it is my beautiful angel. And yet, she is the sweetest, kindest person I have ever met. Through her, I've learned acceptance, humility, patience and courage. Through her, I've come to realize that we all have disabilities. Some are physical; some, mental. We all have limitations. We're all "handi-capable," as my wife likes to say.

Frankly, it was easy to accept disability when it wasn't happening to me. After all, I didn't have any physical limitations for the vast majority of my life. But then, almost imperceptibly, my body stopped cooperating. Welcome to old age. Today, arthritis controls my joints. I can't hear without my hearing aids or see without my glasses. Even my teeth are plastic slip-ins. I have half the energy I used to have, and the whole thing pisses me off.

Of course, my bod still works better than my wife's; and I feel silly complaining about my minor ailments compared to hers. Still, this is my first go with disability. I liked hearing about it better than experiencing it.

Now more than ever, I believe that securing the rights of the "handicapable" is the next civil rights mountain we must climb. We've made important progress in guaranteeing the rights of racial minorities and persons with different sexual orientations and gender identities. While work in these areas must continue, I think it's time to focus attention on those whose bodies and minds no longer function as they would like. After all, that includes us too.

When George McGovern was nominated as the Democratic presidential candidate in 1972, he selected Senator Thomas Eagleton as his vice-presidential running mate. A few days later, he changed his mind after learning that Tom had received treatment for mental illness many years earlier.

About 20 years later, I accidentally met George on a street corner in Washington. We spoke briefly until the light changed. I was too awe struck to ask him anything profound. He seemed like a nice person, a humble person, a fair person, just as he did on TV back in 1972. I voted for him then. He was the "Peace candidate."

I wonder how he missed the point. As history has shown, you can't have peace without justice. And there's no justice when disabled folks, like Tom, are unwelcome.

In 1964, Jack Weinberg, a student activist and civil rights organizer, was being interviewed by a newspaper reporter. After hearing questions insinuating that the hippie movement was orchestrated behind the scenes by Communists, Weinberg recalled his reaction this way:

"I told him we had a saying in the movement that we don't trust anybody over 30. It was a way of telling the guy to back off, that nobody was pulling our strings."

After the interview was printed, Weinberg was irritated that his quote had received so much notoriety. "I've done some things in my life I think are very important, and my one sentence in history turns out to be something I said off the top of my head which became completely distorted and misunderstood. But I've become more accepting of fate as I get older."

I admit it. When I was 20, I thought that younger folks were inherently smarter, kinder, and more truthful than older folks. To paraphrase Mark Twain, it's amazing how much wiser I've gotten since then.

Getting old? I never thought it would happen to me. I certainly never planned it. It just jumped on me somehow when I wasn't paying attention.

When I was 20, I didn't have any interest in old people except for my Grandmother who made bacon sandwiches for me when I visited her. I had nothing in common with the rest of the gray-haired codgers in the world; and because my parents died in their fifties, I never saw old age up close.

Of course, my definition of "old" has evolved considerably over the years, usually from one decade to the next. Still, almost 70 years young, I don't feel old. I'm still the same person I was at 20 and still believe in the same things, more or less.

But I think I'm smarter than I've ever been, not in a way that means anything in the marketplace or enables me to answer all the Jeopardy questions, but in a way that keeps me out of trouble and allows me to enjoy the beautiful life I'm so lucky to have today.

When I was 20 or so, I ignored old people whenever possible. Today, I'm one of them. Old and gray myself, I've come to appreciate how many glorious minds and hearts are locked in worn-out bodies, alone and forgotten, waiting for the end.

Recently, I was plant shopping with my wife when I came across a wrinkled survivor sitting on a bench looking at the ground. For fun, I stopped and said: "Good morning. How are you?" to which the aging dude looked up, smiled, and began to talk about his day, his wife, and his bad knee. After a few minutes, each of us, richer in spirit than we had been, said good-bye. Walking away, I was so glad I stopped to say "Hello" and hoped that, when I become withered and white-haired sitting alone on a bench, someone will say hello to me.

Born to Mexican-American migrant workers, Cesar Chavez dropped out of school in the 7th grade to work in the fields. In 1962, he and Delores Huerto, an organizer of agricultural workers in California, founded the National Farm Workers Association that led a non-violent struggle for higher wages, better living conditions, and more respect for those picking the country's fruits and vegetables. The group later became part of the United Farm Workers (UFW).

Not much has changed over the years. A bunch of white folks, screaming "America first," want to build a giant wall to keep the "foreigners" out which is a bit ironic considering that every one of us was a foreigner at one time, except of course, the "Native Americans" who lived here for centuries and, tragically, were naïve enough to think that white folks would share.

Some say today's Hispanic immigrants are taking American jobs. That's the same reception that Poles, Italians, Germans, Irish, and every other immigrant group received when they first got here. The fact is that no one wants the back-breaking jobs that newcomers perform for the rest of us. Legal or illegal, immigrants have always been willing to do the hardest work for the least pay so that their families can have a better life.

America is a nation of immigrants, a kind and generous nation with a unique ability to assimilate diverse groups of people into a "melting pot." It is this amazing ability that makes us strong and prosperous, not the size of our military or the "purity" of our populous.

When I was younger, I didn't pay much attention to the "invisible" people who built and maintained the life to which I was accustomed. I didn't think about the hardworking, low paid labors who pick our vegetables, slaughter our meat, sew our clothes, collect our garbage, or sweep our streets. It was easy to see the mundane work being done without seeing the people who do it. For me today, making this world a better place means recognizing the humanity and dignity of everyone, especially those who carry the heavy loads for the rest of us.

The people who lived here first, the "Native Americans," didn't pretend to "own" the land. Time after time, parcel after parcel, they agreed to share it with white settlers who, as it turned out, had no intention of sharing and instead used white solders to eliminate their hosts.

Imagine a beautiful house overlooking a fertile majestic vista. The inhabitants are kind and generous who live a quiet life of self-subsistence. One day "outlaws" discover their hide-away and murder every man, woman, and child. They destroy all reminders of the people who built the house and declare themselves to be the legitimate owners.

As the descendants of these "outlaws," do we have a moral claim to the land that we stole? Of course not. That being the case, the least we can do is to ask the original "owners" for forgiveness and compensate them fairly while opening our arms to other immigrants who come looking for a new home.—S.L.R.

Wayne Lee: Color Blindness

It was October 1968, the start of my sophomore year at my hometown college. My best friend and I had just moved in to a four-bedroom rental house off-campus (for $120 a month!) and we were waiting to see who else would be moving in. Three mornings later, the downstairs bedroom door opened and out stepped a 6'6" black man who had moved in during the night. We were surprised, but not shocked. After all, we had learned during our freshman year that the world was considerably more diverse than we had experienced in our lily-white public schools; and we welcomed the multiculturalism.

A month later, I had a live-in Hispanic girlfriend; and throughout the remainder of my college years, I developed friendships and occasional romances with minority students. It just didn't seem like a big deal. I mean, interracial love was *groovy*, man. This was the heyday of the Black Power, Indian rights, women's lib and free-love movements. All of us counter-culturists were united against a common enemy: The Establishment. Whatever the color of our skin, we fought side-by-side as brothers and sisters in the Revolution to end not only the war in Vietnam, but also racism, sexism, the military-industrial complex and a mainstream culture we judged to be plastic, uptight and sold-out to wealth, power and "the American way."

My non-white friends were no doubt the victims of racism, but I was so caught up in the altruism of universal brotherhood and sisterhood that I didn't notice most of it. As a long-haired peacenik, I believed that we flower children were equally discriminated against; and maybe we were. After all, Democratic Senator Robert Byrd of West Virginia had twice referred to us as "white ni***rs."

It wasn't long, of course, before all that peace-and-love idealism gave way to the harsh realities of a racially and ethnically conflicted country. I missed, and still miss, the unified struggle, the us-against-them camaraderie, the colorblindness. We revolutionaries may have looked differently on the outside, but in our hearts, most of us shared the same power-to-the-people values of fraternity and equality.

I don't look like a hippie anymore. Most of us don't. But when I look around at today's liberals, progressives, environmentalists, feminists and others who are still working to make this a better, hipper, more diverse republic, I know that many of them once wore flowers in their hair. Our rainbow coalition fought the good fight together. They will always be my brothers and sisters.

Wanda H: We Shall Overcome

I became a hippie during high school in the '60s. I had a passion for folk music and protest songs. My favorite voices were those of Bob Dylan, Joan Baez, Judy Collins, Pete Seeger, and others in their genre. I especially embraced the concepts of "equality," "fairness," and the American ideal of "all men are created equal" (we weren't yet too worried about women). "We Shall Overcome" became one of my cohort's anthems. It wasn't until much later that I questioned "Who are 'WE?'" and "What does it mean to 'OVER-COME'?"

We had only two black families in my hometown. They identified themselves as Blackfoot Indian and blended in everywhere. But I knew from folk music that black people were downtrodden and needed to be acknowledged as equals by white people. The summer between high school and college, I waitressed with a young black woman at a diner in the nearby city. One day after our shift, I offered her a ride home. She demurred, but I pushed and drove her into her all-black neighborhood. On my way out alone, I noticed faces watching me with what seemed to be resentment; and I felt a deep sense of menace. It occurred to me that maybe this "love your neighbor" thing was not so cut-and-dried after all and should be handled with care.

In college, I joined Freedom Marches and loudly espoused integration of schools, housing, and workplaces. Once in the work force, I agreed with our government that sex and race-based Affirmative Action in education and hiring was essential to achieving "equality." I blithely ignored the possibility that less qualified individuals might be chosen over more deserving candidates for jobs and college placements just to meet quantitative goals. After all, men are created equal and, given an equal opportunity, will perform with equal skill and dedication.

Only later, as a manager in a large corporation, did I experience the folly of such programs. Women were hired because of a litigated consent decree. Some succeeded, some failed. Blacks were hired because of affirmative action. Some succeeded, some failed. In one instance, a black man with a Harvard MBA had to be let go. He could barely fill out his Day-Timer. Another time, a highly educated white woman was released after her probationary period. She picked fights with co-workers and supervisors, exhibiting zero social skills or common sense.

I now understand that being "created equal" means deserving equal treatment under the law and equal opportunities to excel in life. It does *not* mean that everyone *is* equal in all matters, will succeed in all endeavors, or must be given equal goodies by society. I'm skillful in some areas, but an absolute klutz in others. The same applies to everyone else, regardless of race or gender.

I now believe that "We Shall Overcome" should be understood to mean "We all deserve the opportunity to overcome our own limitations and disadvantages, to become our best selves, and to receive equitable recognition and compensation for our contributions to society." White supremacy and Black Lives Matter are counterproductive. Instead we need institutionalized opportunities for individuals to succeed in their own ways. I'm still "hippie" enough to hope we as a people get there soon.

Carrie B: Get Together

In 1963, I started college in the Midwest and felt the shock of John F. Kennedy's death that November. It seemed that you couldn't trust the world to continue moving forward. I wrote poetry, played guitar, and sang. The love of my life dumped me in 1965, an ego shattering from which I never recovered. I smoked a lot of cigarettes, gulped speed for exams, and almost got thrown out of my sorority for smoking weed. I loved The Beatles, Donovan, and reckless living. For Spring Break, I hitchhiked to Ft. Lauderdale, then flew to Nassau where I hung out on the beach, slept on floors, hooked up with whoever, and rode motor scooters around the island.

By my Junior year, the hippie movement had spread nationwide; and I was fully immersed in California dreaming. In 1966–67, we smoked dope, took acid and lost ourselves totally. I bartended at the local bar & grill where I studied and wrote poetry. With hair down to my waist, wearing long paisley skirts, I hooked up with any handsome dude I wanted. We didn't have AIDS then and knew little about STDs. It was just about havin' fun and rebelling from societal norms.

In October of 1968, my friends and I marched against the Vietnam war in Washington, watching police beat some people on the edges of the crowd and listening to Joan Baez sing. It was time to set a new world order, to crash the suburbia vision of how adulthood would be. Everyone caught the fever.

By the end of 1968, I couldn't stand being freezing cold or my boyfriend; so, I dropped out of the graduate program, loaded up my car and drove to California. I picked up several hitchhikers along the way, including a priest who left me with his Bible. I stopped in towns along Route 66 and I-8 and hung out overnight with whoever. In LA, I stayed with friends for a week; but I couldn't stand that city. So...

I drove to San Francisco with under $100 in my pocket, stayed with strangers for a week, got a job, and moved into a studio apartment for $90 a month in the first months of 1969. By this time, the Haight-Ashbury "love" scene had been replaced by hard druggies and filth. As someone who loved being around persons of color, I adopted an abused mixed-race child and lived with men of color until the early 80s.

Fast forward: I have become more a libertarian, believing that people should be able to live their lives without societal constraints as long as they obeyed the golden rule and did no harm. Now in my 70s, I'm still working, healthy, and enjoy rather unusual hobbies. I've become more conservative in the past 5 years, mostly because my Democratic party now extols socialism and has Marxist-like views on the capitalist economic system. I'm not willing to throw out the entire system because Trump is a blathering idiot.

Today free speech seems in jeopardy, with more emphasis on race, culture and identity politics. Productivity and meritocracy are being thrown out as "whiteness." Yet, those very qualities are the key to bringing all people of color into the American economy. What I inherited from the 1960s and still carry today is a willingness to fight against bigotry and intolerance of all stripes. I see today in California an incredible bigotry of the extreme left, vastly different than our free-wheeling culture of the sixties that simply set off in new directions without demonizing everyone who wasn't a hippie.

I want both Bernie Sanders and Ann Coulter to feel "safe" presenting their respective points of view on college campuses or elsewhere, without having paid agitators disrupting what they have to say. I hope for a world where transient political positions do not destroy lifelong friendships or family bonds. I wish that more of us can be like Ruth Bader Ginsberg and Antonin Scalia, polar opposites in opinions and politics, but nevertheless remaining enduring friends as long as Scalia lived.

Linda R: Up Against the Wall

One day while walking home from school on Main St in our tight knit community, my friend/neighbor saw a black family get out of their car and walk into the only restaurant in town. "Quick" she said, "I need to write down their license plate and tell the police." We were 10 years old! This was the mental attitude of the average citizen in our small town, 50 miles west of Detroit.

Years later when I entered high school, I began to question why my parents and town's elders raised us to fear black people. After all, we all bleed the same color. And so, from then on, I became the school rebel, constantly asking "Why?" I stood up to anyone in defense of black people, although I didn't actually know one personally. "Those people" lived far away in Detroit; and even after the Detroit riots of 1968, I continued to tell everyone: "If you oppress people long enough, they will revolt."

Over the next few years, a series of events changed my perspective.

When I was 18, traveling with a friend in his Chevy Van from Michigan to Arizona, he picked up a black couple on the freeway while I was sleeping in the back. After a while, we stopped at a restaurant to rest where my friend bought the couple something to eat. As we continued our trip, the black man told my friend to "pull-over" and walk down the road away from the Van, which he did.

Then the man turned to me and said: "Take off my clothes and lay down in the back seat; or I'm going to cut you up." Suddenly, I jumped out of the van and ran down the dark highway. I flagged down an approaching car and was driven back to the restaurant where two policemen were sitting. The hitchhikers were never found.

When I was 21, sitting on a city bus in San Diego, a black man turned to me and said; "I ought to cut you up for what your people did to my people." I tried to explain that I had stood up for his people, but his mind was made up. Thankfully, he didn't act on his threat.

While waiting for a bus downtown Phoenix, a black man walked by me and mumbled something I couldn't quite hear. Then, he turned around and said; "When a black man speaks to you, you better speak back, bitch" and flashed a knife under his jacket. I reported what had happened to the station security guard, but he did nothing.

I've been slapped by black women at a disco for no reason, and my 10-year-old daughter has been beaten up by black girls on the school bus. Again, no one did anything to find the bullies or protect us. Today, I understand what it feels like to be hated because of one's skin color.

Today, I have no sympathy for BLM or KKK. Both are as bad as the other. Both contribute to the race wars exploding in our streets, malls, and cinemas. Despite the call for love, peace, and understanding, racial hatred existed in the hippie era and still exists today.

J Laurence: Saturday in the Park

When I was barely 20, my new-found friend, Smitty, and housemate, Danny, took off for Griffith Park with joints rolled and Frisbees ready. On this warm sunny Saturday in Southern California, we anchored a picnic table and fired up, while keeping lookout for "da man."

With our long hair, beards, prayer beads, and tie-dyed shirts, we blended in with the others at the park, except for a BBQ group from East LA. As a musician, I appreciated the songs blasting from their cassette players, "Soul Man," "My Girl," and "Hot Pants" among them. Wearing Afros and dashikis, the group was having a great time; while the aroma of grilled chicken rose from a grill.

As I started to join them, Danny, originally from Ohio, attempted to hold me back, something I hadn't expected. "Hey man, they're just people like you and me," I told him. "What happened to love one another?"

The experience flashed me back to my high school days where 50 percent of the students were black, many of whom were close friends. Rejecting Danny's racist remarks, I introduced myself to the group, bopping to the music, living in the moment. In a few minutes, several more brothers showed up with drums, guitars and rhythm instruments. Checking for cops, joints of weed unlike any I'd ever smoked were passed, followed by laughter soon after. Smitty joined me and was introduced around the group, while Danny remained stuck to his old-world upbringing. James, one of the brothers, elbowed me and asked: "What's his trip?' looking Danny's way. Shrugging, I replied, "Different strokes, man ... different strokes."

As would be imagined, things changed when I returned later to the house I shared with Danny and his girlfriend. When I told him about my experience that day, he grew increasingly upset and decided that I should live elsewhere. Days later, with only a few bucks to my name, I couch-surfed anywhere I could and ended up staying with Mexicans, American Indians and Tibetan Buddhists, to name a few. Later, I embarked on a year-long ashram experience. To say it was life-changing is a vast understatement. The Buddhist teachings were simple, clear, and grounded in truth, the embodiment of the "hippie way" that I carry to this day.

I find the current political administration's fostering of "separatism" rather than unity to be very upsetting, bringing back memories of the days of Martin Luther King. The rise in today's youth-driven civil rights movements is reminiscent of the "hippie days" with today's crowd numbers equal if not greater. The opportunity to move past separatism requires open minds, much like the approach hippies took years ago. Fortunately, grass roots organizations have formed that focus attention on racism and immigration issues, many of them founded by ex-hippies or children born into hippie families.

As disturbing as they may be, additional lessons about the hidden ideologies of friends, similar to those I learned in the park years ago, can still be gained if we pay attention. While "each to his own" is important, we ex-hippies have an opportunity to cause a shift, one that will foster togetherness rather than today's separatism. Let's get together for a Saturday in the park and revel in our diversity.

Marty Skiles: Respect

I was born in 1957, the last of five kids. Marijuana was almost nonexistent in the small farming town I grew up in. Beer was big. Cigarettes and muscle cars with fat tires were in. Smoking weed was not.

The '60s were a time of peace and love to many people. Those people were called hippies. Marijuana and psychedelic drugs were not uncommon to people older than me. Black lights and posters were on people's walls. "Make love not war" was a big saying at the time. There were protests. There were a lot of protests. I remember seeing them on the evening news. I remember when kids were killed at Kent State. The government was still drafting people into the military. Vietnam was in full force.

In the '60s and early '70s, I liked my hair long and would grow it to shoulder length until I was forced to cut it by my Dad. He would always say "You're lookin' like one of them damn hippies again" which was exactly the look I was going for. I loved wearing those newfangled bell bottom jeans with an un-buttoned shirt exposing my chest. I thought I looked cool, and to some kids my age, I did. I loved the flower child era.

I caught a little grief from the hardcore redneck farm boys that just wanted to drink and fight, but it was worth it. I was living in the make-love-not-war era and believe me, there was plenty to go around. The farther I got away from my hometown, the more the hippie movement I noticed. It was a great time to be alive. I saw Elvis Presley, The Beatles, and The Rolling Stones on *The Ed Sullivan Show*. The Monkees came shortly after with their own show. They were all influences on me, not only because they had long hair, but also because their music was different too. The hippie values of peace and love have stuck with me ever since.

Growing up, I remember segregation and racism: Martin Luther King, Malcolm X, the Black Panthers, and Governor George Wallace standing in the schoolhouse door, I admit I was taught racism. Raised in the '60s in a small, all white, agricultural/farming country town with a racist dad who had racist friends, you can probably understand how that happened. It was only after finishing high school and joining the Army that I learned love, tolerance, acceptance, and respect for others. I'm still learning things and want to thank my Texican wife of 33 years for sticking by my side.

Jean T: You Don't Own Me

My maternal grandmother graduated from university in 1919. My grandfather saw in her the Christian values he sought for the raising of his four young daughters from a previous marriage, carelessly overlooking her intellect. She prayed about it; and supposedly, God told her to proceed to the altar. Later, she claimed God might have been mistaken. Better educated than he, she gave piano lessons and kept a low profile.

My paternal grandmother taught school on the Kiowa Reservation in Oklahoma in the early 1900s, elocution being her forte. Every inch of her 4'10" frame was a force to be reckoned with. When she married my grandfather, a minister, she was careful not to outshine him in the pulpit.

My mother studied piano in college with dreams of going professional. She was president of every campus organization she joined. When my father came on the scene, like her stepmother, she asked God for guidance and was married before graduation 1940. My father didn't want her to work, since he felt it reflected poorly on his ability to support a family. She ran our family like the corporation she should have headed and struggled to empower herself beyond her own generation's expectations.

I was a senior in high school when females were allowed to wear pants for the first time. I recall a male student commenting that "No girlfriend of his was going to wear pants to school." Thankfully, my mother believed no boy should tell me what I could and could not wear. But even in 1970, parents jokingly insinuated that girls went to university to obtain an "M.R.S" degree.

When I enrolled, it didn't seem like much was expected of me. Sex, drugs and rock 'n' roll is what I found. Quitting my studies, I went off to "liberate" myself with some long-haired potters building a kiln in the country. I let no man call me their "old lady" and lifted fifty-pound bags of mortar right alongside the guys. I didn't march for women's rights. But I stood for them, asking for the respect I thought I deserved. Yet there seemed so much to prove, and proving it felt precarious at best.

I lived to regret not finishing my education. As a wife and mother, the fact that I had fewer options for finding employment or for leaving an unhappy relationship became clear. After all I had experienced, I found myself exerting little power over important life decisions. Going back to school when my kids were older, I ventured into a workforce still wrought with sexism, both subtle and overt.

Yet, I enjoyed my work and encouraged another generation of females in my family to expand the boundaries of their own self-worth. Last year, 48 years after I wore my first pants to school, I joined a local Women's March. I did it for myself, for my own mother, and for my grandmothers, women who dared not do it for themselves.

Tara B: Bra Burning

"I just can't stand it anymore!"

My roommate Laurie handed me the hash pipe, jumped up and ran to her room. A few minutes later she reappeared, carrying all of her bras.

"How can I get a good hit if I can't even breathe? I can't take a real breath of air wearing these things. I'm getting rid of them all." She threw her bras on the floor. Then she grabbed the pipe and took the hugest hit you ever saw. She exhaled an ecstatic "Aaahh! Yeah!"

By this time, I was laughing so hard I fell over. I thought this was all utterly brilliant and decided to do the same thing.

"So now I want to burn them," she announced when I returned with my bras. Soon we were carrying our brassieres out to a burn barrel in the backyard. We threw our offending garments inside it and set them on fire.

Soon we heard someone yelling: "What the hell are you doing?! Why do I smell smoke?" It was James, the sociology professor from San Francisco State, who lived in the upstairs apartment. Unmistakable in his giant red beard, he was leaning out his window, freaking out.

"We're burning our bras" we said matter-of-factly.

For a moment, he didn't move. Then he started laughing. "Oh wow! Well, I always thought you girls must be women's libbers; but I never met a bra burner before."

We burst into laughter. "No, no! That's not the reason we're burning them. It's because we can't get really high. We don't want to wear something that cuts off our breathing. We can't get a good hit!"

He started laughing hysterically, then sank down behind his window, still laughing. James was also a great sign painter. In a little while, when we had just about cleaned up our crime scene, James reappeared at his window laughing. "Okay, girls, this is for you." He unfurled a long paper banner out his window which read: "FOR A BETTER HIGH." Beside the words, he had painted a huge burning bra, blazing red and orange.

We fell down laughing so hard we were crying. "Oh my god!" Laurie shrieked, "Flaming tits!"

Then we went inside to get ready to go to the Garuda Tea House where there was going to be live Indian music. We got really gussied up, hippie style, with our newly liberated underpinnings, and set off for Haight Street.

As we were leaving James came out and handed us a joint. "Here. Burn this instead of your underwear." Then he said, "I'm so glad you were born!"

All evening long, Laurie was laughing and telling everyone she was celebrating True Women's Liberation.

I still love hashish, still smoke the sacred herb on a regular basis, still hate bras, still laugh a lot, and continue to work ceaselessly for liberating women from all kinds of restrictions.

Mari S: Civil Rights

As one of the oldest of the baby boomers (1948), I was brought up in a hopeful world where everyone and everything American seemed to be on an upward path. The only thing that gave me nightmares was the threat of nuclear war. The civil defense warnings shown on television were very frightening. Photographs of buildings being blown up and shaken by nuclear tests. Little stick figure animations of people carrying stretchers of injured people to civil defense shelters. We also had the "duck and cover" drills in grade school.

Feminism and women's rights were nowhere in my consciousness. In my world, women had the traditional roles of housekeeping, cooking, and childcare. Women who worked outside the home were not very common.

I would say my family was lower middle class. My Father was able to support our family by making relatively good union wages at a steel mill, and then later as a short-haul truck driver. My mother got up early every morning of his working life, made his coffee and breakfast, and packed his lunch. On cold winter days, she would sometimes even go out and start the car, so it could warm up while he ate.

We were living in the Pacific Northwest where there was (and still is) relatively little ethnic diversity in the population. My parents were from the South, however, so we would visit family in several Southern states every year for our vacation. I became aware and interested in race relations when I was about 14 and the Civil Rights Act was passed in 1964. I saw so many things on TV that I could not understand and that seemed so wrong like average looking white people of all ages screaming at children trying to go to school and civil rights marchers being beaten by police and hit with water from fire hoses.

I remember asking my mother why we never saw any black people when we went south. "They are not allowed to go anywhere you go," she answered. The Civil Rights Era was an eye-opener for me; and a few years later, it was easy to see that women did not have equal rights either. Nurse, teacher, secretary or airplane stewardess were the apparent choices if a young woman wanted to work.

I got married at 18, had a baby at 20 and tried to fulfill the traditional wifely role. But when the "Summer of Love" started appearing everywhere in the media, it was not long before I knew I could not stay married to my husband. He was and is still a nice man, but I was not cut out for a life like my Mom's. In order to be able to leave the marriage, I had to find a job. This was late 1970, and I remember one of the issues being widely discussed in the media was: "Should women be 'allowed' to wear pantsuits to work"? I bought the very first issue of *MS.* magazine in December of 1971 and still have it. The title "Ms." seemed pretty strange at first; but even today if I have to check a box, "Ms." is the one I will check.

It is almost impossible to remember how much pressure there was not to get divorced in 1970. It was still very much looked down upon. I was soon living with someone without being married which, at that time, was labeled "shacking up" or "living in sin." Unfortunately for me, I turned out to be in the vanguard of both the major divorce and living together movements. I took a lot of flak from my family, some friends, and the court system regarding child custody.

For a few years in the '70s, I worked in a factory which employed about 1,000 people. We were paid group bonus based on production rates set by the company. It was not long before I realized that the departments which had the best rates, and where you could make the most money, were staffed primarily by men; and the lower paying departments were staffed primarily by women.

I attended my first anti-war march in 1970. In the mid–70s, I worked with a group which successfully kept Washington State from becoming the dumping ground for the entire Nation's nuclear waste. I've marched, attended rally's, donated to campaigns, wrote letters to my legislators, and supported various liberal/environmental/social causes throughout the years. Within the past two years, my friends and I have taken time out at parties to write postcards to our local, state and national legislators.

I bought my first house in 1982. I was purchasing it on a contract from a young couple who had been purchasing it on a private contract from an older man. When this man found out that I was a single woman, he did not want them to sell it to me because "What would she do if there are plumbing or electrical or other maintenance problems?" It took a little talking, but we finally convinced him that I could handle home ownership.

In my opinion, the invention of the birth control pill is one of the most important enabling women to choose how they want to live their lives. I do think it is unfortunate that the business community and the government have maintained policies which keep wages so low that most women cannot stay home and raise their family if they choose, because most families can't make it on a one earner's wages.

Cathy Matters: Laughing Out Loud

Born in 1932, my mother believed that females were "homemakers" and that males were wage earners and family rulers. In her view, females were expected to wear dresses everywhere, supported underneath by uncomfortably tight girdles with garter belts and bras resembling traffic cones.

Women were urged to finish high school and immediately locate a male to pay the bills and support as many children as the union could produce. The wife was destined to do all of the household chores, including, but not limited to, cooking. cleaning. grocery shopping, child rearing, and husband pleasing.

Growing up, my two brothers had their own bedroom. My two sisters and I shared the other bedroom with my mother. Let me tell you how much fun I had as a teenager sharing a room with my mother.

In the '60s and '70s, women earned far less than men (still do) for the same job, had far fewer legal rights, and were continually exposed to sexual harassment. They were not allowed to own a credit card, serve on a jury, receive an Ivy League education, or even talk openly about sex. We were oppressed.

My home consisted of a single mother with five children. My mother had mental health issues and was an alcohol abuser. She was determined that all of her children should be exactly like her in every way. She wanted us to be good Christians, so she sent us to church & Sunday school at least twice a week. Yet, she never went with us.

When I became sexually active at the age of 16 (after being the victim of rape), I thought it best that I should quickly place myself on birth control pills. At that time, adolescences were not allowed to obtain birth control without consent from a parent. Whoever thought of that idea was definitely a man.

When my mother found the birth control pills I had secretly been able to obtain, she tossed them down the toilet without conversation or direction. If she didn't want me to have sex, this was definitely the wrong way to go about it. All she did was make sure I couldn't protect myself. I was pregnant within a year. Years later, when I asked her why she put me in that situation, she said she didn't know I was sexually active!! Um, birth control pills were not hint enough?

If I were a teenager today, I wouldn't have to confer with my mother about getting on the pill. I'd just go to a clinic and pick them up. The sexual revolution of the '60s and '70s saved millions of women from unwanted pregnancies and death from botched abortions. Those years marked the starting point for women being treated equally to men; although there are still many men who think that women are subservient human beings, placed on earth to please them.

As I raise my closed fist into the air to salute all of the women folk who survived this era and retained their hippie spirit, it makes me want to laugh out loud!

Wanda H: Beyond Feminism

In my hippie days, I didn't think much about my "rights" or the need for another Feminist revolution. As a white female from an ordinary family, I was certain I was protected from boys, criminals, and Communists by laws and my community's mores. My foremothers had secured my rights to vote and to pursue a higher education. My Constitutional rights enabled me to address the bigger concerns of our time: racial discrimination and the Vietnam War. In the USA, being a girl wasn't a big problem (except near construction sites).

We hippies had a great run. We passed Equal Opportunity laws. We ended the War. We did good! But the War had left widows and depleted the supply of marriageable men. Based, in part, on our accomplishments, the greater society was evolving in an unanticipated direction: The Sexual Revolution. More unmarried women were having babies alone, and marriages were imploding. The entire male—female landscape was in flux. Many women suddenly had to support themselves and their families whether they liked it or not. They needed good incomes. I totally embraced "equal pay for equal work" and "equal employment opportunities for women," which the Feminists pushed into law.

I have benefited enormously from the Feminist agenda. Theoretically, American women now get paid by their levels of contribution, not their gender. We also have won important legal battles concerning rights to control our own bodies, share in the economic fruits of a dissolving marriage, and receive protection from abusive mates. Eventually, we will conquer workplace harassment and abuse too.

However, there have been costs to our gender-blending. In the '70s, one regular paycheck enabled a household to buy a home, provide good food, educate kids, and take a yearly vacation. One spouse at home allowed families to supervise their own children and run an efficient independent entity. With the tremendous rise in two-earner households, our economic system has forced a higher cost of living for everyone. Today, most families *need* two working adults just to afford the necessities, never mind to buy a house.

We cherish "CHOICE," but the option for one spouse to contribute at home full-time has been all but obliterated. Rearing kids and maintaining the home are now flourishing businesses for outsiders. Everyone is always exhausted.

I now recognize the important evolutionary reasons why early mankind separated tasks into "male" and "female." Yes, one's physique helps define appropriate roles; but science is discovering the subtler cognitive differences that make one sex better than the other at certain societal functions. For example, recent research showed the onset of specific nurturing instincts in female mammalian brains during the process of pregnancy, birth, and nursing. Males simply do not possess all the neural paths that make childcare "natural" to them.

We need a do-over. Let's go back to square one and take an objective, factual, common-sense view of human nature and how successful modern Western societies should work. Everything should be on the table: capitalism, defense, distribution, rewards, talents, differences, shortcomings, basic needs and responsibilities, inclusion, nature, nurture, and learning. No politicians allowed! If it's done right, the result will be fair. That's all we old hippie chicks really want.

Carol Seaton: Earth Goddess

In the early '60s, I was married with a baby and living in a large affordable house in Nye Beach, Oregon. Young and foolish at the time, we didn't realize that the whole neighborhood was slowly eroding into the sea. My husband and his Coast Guard buddy, Corky, were commercial fisherman; and I could see the ships coming and going from my home. I was so busy decorating the nursery for our son that I didn't realize the house next door was a gathering place for hippies. But my younger sister, who had left our parents' home in California and moved in with us, immediately fell in with the hippie group and introduced me to the movement.

The sense of social justice and creativity was not that far from the values I had learned as a child. In hindsight, my sister has pointed out that "loose morals" were a problem; but I held to my 1950 family values. When I explained being a hippie to my mother, she said she thought she had always been a hippie. Think about it. She had lived through the Great Depression and sung for USO shows during the Second World War. Her generation grew up helping each other and gathering to lift everyone's morale when times were hard. They could not depend on corporations for the good life. They were furiously independent with a strong sense of integrity. I did not see hippieness as new or different. The colors were just brighter.

But the Oregon lifestyle was different. I grew up in LA where my divorced, working mother fed us city food like white Wonder Bread and canned vegetables. Oregon was behind the times and rural. People actually chopped wood to heat their homes! When I first moved there, I was horrified by how primitive it was; but the hippie thing turned the primitive reality into a good thing. Every good woman knew how to split wood, knead bread, cook with natural ingredients, and suckle our babies with our bare breast. There, I was a wife and mother, following in the path of the Earth Mother, using my domestic skills to fulfill my life purpose as a woman.

A wonderful thing about the hippie movement is that, suddenly, the Mother Earth Goddess entered our consciousness. We started using the word "she" where only the pronoun "he" had been used. We were young and believed we could achieve whatever we wanted to achieve with love. Women were no longer the invisible members of society.

Strong families are essential to a strong democracy. We need to remember our past and how important the wife and mother are to our country and to humanity! In hindsight, we haven't given women equal rights but made it taboo to be feminine, which might be good for war, but not for humanity.

I love men; but unfortunately, they tend to be about hierarchy and autocracy, not so much about family and democracy. Femininity is a necessary counterbalance. We need to think of our humanness, not just corporate power, money, and status. I think the hippie movement turned the lights on and the corporate establishment turned them back off. We need to get back to the goddess and the creativity and joy we had. We need love, compassion, and each other. The homemaker does more than clean house. She takes care of our human needs and from this, a civilization is built.

Beth Richards: I Am Woman

I was raised in the 1950s in a relatively typical middle-class family. My dad went to work every day; and my mom stayed home, cleaning, cooking, ironing, and raising her girls. Thoroughly indoctrinated into cultural expectations, we sisters were expected to go to college so we could find a high-performing husband and educate our offspring. Granted, Mom often wistfully told us about her friends who had become professionals—a woman doctor, teacher, nurse, office manager—hoping, I suppose, that we would choose to pursue some field other than housewife.

In those days, the deck was definitely stacked against professional fulfillment for all of us of the female persuasion. Women were not allowed credit in their own name. Domestic violence was hidden and widespread. Wives were expected to bring slippers and a martini to their husband when he got home from work. Birth control methods were marginal, at best.

The dramatic societal shift that happened so suddenly in the '60s, just as I was coming of age, took everyone by surprise. All bets were off. Betty Friedan's book, *The Feminine Mystique*, came out in 1963 and quickly became a bestseller, providing a spark for women to question their sanctioned role in our culture. In 1965, the Supreme Court allowed married people to use the birth control pills that had been approved for human use in 1960. The dialog about what was possible for women began changing in some very fundamental ways.

Along with other dramatic changes in our culture at that time— protests leading to the Civil Rights Act passage in 1964, opposition to the Vietnam War becoming widespread, and the upheaval in rock music beginning with The Beatles—issues about what was not only possible, but socially acceptable, began to change, including women's roles. It was a confusing time to be a teenage girl! Should we? Or shouldn't we? Could we? Or couldn't we?

Looking back from 2018, life is still in some state of upheaval. Women are encouraged to follow career paths and pursue their dreams, even while roadblocks, albeit much lowered since the 1960s, are still present. Families now almost require women to work full-time jobs to maintain familial financial solvency, but little provision is made societally for childcare and household duties. It seems to me that we, in our zeal to make the world a better place for everyone, have only just begun to inch ahead towards a fairer, more just society that works for everyone. The intense cultural transformation that swept through the Western World fifty years ago left a chaos that is still unresolved. The metamorphosis towards greater personal freedom and fulfillment is not yet resolved.

CeliaSue Hecht: We Are Family

In the '50s and '60s, I grew up in the suburbs of New York City where the moms I knew stayed at home doing housework and taking care of the kids. While they were reading and discussing the myths of the happy homemaker via *The Feminine Mystique* by Betty Friedan, we girls in the court were singing "You Don't Own Me," by Lesley Gore. By my senior year of high school, most of the moms were working outside the home in order to receive their own paycheck, credit cards, and a feeling of respect and self-worth. They also wanted husbands who would share the housework and childcare.

I was inspired by the "Mary Tyler Moore" TV show, *Free to Be Me* by Marlo Thomas, and "I Am Woman, Hear Me Roar" by Helen Reddy. I always wanted to do my own thing. I worked as a secretary but found office work boring. I wanted to be a writer but did not know how to get published. Then in 1970, seeking more independence, I moved to Los Angeles and worked for the city. Four years later, I quit.

Looking for my true career, I worked for a brief time at an abortion clinic and volunteered as a hotline counselor for suicide prevention. Finally, in 1975, I met an amazing woman who helped me to change my life. She taught me how to lead seminars, gave me opportunities to be published in her Success newspaper, encouraged me to complete college, and challenged me to travel around the world.

Even though I never burned my bra or protested in the street, I did consider myself a liberated woman when I asked a man out for the first time in my 20s. I attended radical feminist therapy groups and learned that the oppression that I thought of as personal was, in fact, political. It was an exciting time!

As a kid, I had wanted to be the first girl Mickey Mantle; but Little League was just for boys. We girls were not even allowed to wear pants to elementary school. In defiance, we joined together on one winter day and wore the forbidden items to school. Even though we were sent home, our parents agreed that we should not be forced to endure frozen legs.

I was taught that boys and girls had different roles, something that I viewed as unfair. We girls were admonished to beware of peeping Toms, perverts on the bike path and weirdoes on the subways and busses. When boys and men did something wrong, people shook their heads and said "Boys will be boys." But we girls were punished for our own wrongdoings and sometimes theirs. When boys and men whistled, catcalled, and screamed obscenities at us (nowadays called street harassment), we were told that we should not have walked down that street or that we wore the "wrong clothes."

Feminism starts with the premise that all women are real people, aka human beings. With this conviction, women of all ages began joining NOW (National Organization for Women) and challenging the status quo by working at jobs once considered male professions; e.g., doctors, lawyers, religious leaders, welders, truck drivers, accountants, TV news anchors and more. We also ran for public office and joined the Army, Navy, Marines and Air Force. Women took control of their lives with new access to birth control and the Supreme Court's Roe vs. Wade decision allowing women to have legal, safe abortions as opposed to unsafe, illegal back-alley abortions that kill both mother and fetus, the *real choice*. Unfortunately, two-thirds of the States did not pass the ERA (Equal Rights Amendment) which would have ensured that women would be treated equally in all ways including equal pay for equal work.

Today, with a raging and raving misogynist in the White House, women are once again taking to the streets. More than two million women marched on Washington, D.C., after his inauguration, just one of 673 marches in all 50 states and 30 countries. Women rallied in solidarity, speaking truth to power and demanding that Congress take steps to end violence against women, protect reproductive rights, and guarantee equal protection for all women under the law.

The Me Too movement has also brought women together by calling out rapists, sexual abusers, and sexual harassers including powerful men who got away with hurting women for far too long and escaped punishment for their actions.

Women are gearing up for the fight of their lives if/when Brett Kavanaugh is sent to the Supreme court. Some fear that the book *The Handmaid's Tale* by Margaret Atwood is coming to life. I have a different opinion. In my view, the Goddess (Divine Female) is coming back, although she never really left. Numerous books including *When God Was a Woman* by Merlin Stone outline this hidden ancient story when people around the world worshipped the Goddess long before patriarchal Judeo-Christian religions came into existence.

Although women of different ages have diverse views about feminism and what it means to each of us individually and collectively, I feel wonderful about being part of the Sisterhood of Women.

Judah Freed: Be a Man

A lone cowboy riding off into the sunset. Tarzan the ape man swinging on a jungle vine. The brave soldier in war dying for his country. I absorbed such popular "manly man" images of manhood from television and the movies growing up the 1950s and 1960s.

After a long-life journey, I now see manhood quite differently. Today I am a "new man" or a "liberated man," a male who finds strength in kindness and courage in vulnerability. I envision ending male dominance worldwide, especially by white males like me. I advocate equal rights for women and men of all natures. I promote the innate natural equality of all life in creation.

Born and raised in Denver, Colorado, my earliest notions of masculinity came from my father, my hometown and mass media. I grew up to believe that a "real man" is tough and aggressive, never afraid of anything or anyone. A real man never gives up or gives in. He stands on his own two feet, protects himself and his family. He fights off all enemies, even unto heroic death. A real man must be a winner at any cost. I adopted these values among most other American boys of my generation.

Among other boys at school and in my neighborhood, I despaired about ever becoming such a real man. I always was a sickly child, a skinny kid, the weakling that bullies loved to kick around. I was tripped in the hallways at school, taunted on the playground, ridiculed in the boy's locker room, beaten up regularly. I was "jumped" by boys on bikes if they caught me riding my own bike alone. I was the target of bullies who constantly put me down to make themselves feel big.

Life was not much better at home. The third and youngest child with two older sisters, my father had sacrificed his own youthful dreams of being an artist and teacher to marry and have a son, as every true man was expected to do. He projected his buried frustrations onto me through yelling and beatings. I thought father knows best. His rage must be my fault.

Insecurity and self-loathing saturated the cells of my mind and body. I shut down emotionally to protect myself from pain.

In response to violence, as an adolescent inspired by Gandhi and King, I decided to be a pacifist. Despite my conviction, I finally stood up to a school bully in the 8th grade, slamming him against a wall in front of the whole cafeteria. This did stop the bullying, but inside I hated myself more than ever for the horrible moral failure of becoming violent.

Entering high school in 1966, I let go of being a straight-arrow Boy Scout. The Beatles going to India had inspired me to explore eastern philosophy beyond my upbringing in Reformed Judaism. On the news, I saw Vietnamese monks lighting themselves on fire. I saw antiwar protests in the streets of America. Despite what society was telling me about a real man being a violent man, the hippie peace movement made more sense to me.

I wanted to make love, not war; and try as I might to find a girl willing to "make me a man," I stayed a virgin until senior year. That was the year I turned on, the time when inner peace and love finally made sense. Music helped redefine my ideas of manhood. The Beatles' love songs shaped me; so did tunes like "I'm a Man" (two songs with the same title by Jeff Beck in The Yardbirds, and by Chicago).

In the mid–1970s, after three years in a father-figure cult and a year of loose living in Chicago, I was living in LA on Venice Beach, intermittently homeless. My few real friends included a feminist who gave me a button that read, "Any man claiming to be a feminist is just trying to get laid!" One day, she took me to a "men's conscious-raising" session.

It was a life-changing event. I no longer could mindlessly look at women as sex objects or as inferiors. For a good woman to welcome me as the object of her affection, I must see her as whole person, as an equal. ("Viva la difference!") This means I first must love myself as a whole person, equal to any man or woman.

Manhood for me no longer could be defined by superiority, inferiority or victimhood.

I moved home to Denver in 1976 and began my journalism career. I started reading the feminist writings of Bette Friedan and Gloria Steinem and others. Next, I began reading books by men for men. I read *The New Male and The Hazards of Being Male* by Herb Goldberg, PhD. I loved the gender role-reversals of Warren Farrell and his books, *The Liberated Man* and *Why Men Are the Way They Are.* I began talking to other men about how to be a male who treats women as equals. In 1979, I wrote what may be Denver's first newspaper article on workplace sexual harassment.

I began attending men's support groups. The worst ones, prone to intellectualizing and griping about women, soon dissolved. The best men's "circles" have given me a safe place to drop my masks and practice being genuine with myself and others, to feel my feelings, to safely voice my anger, fear, sadness, pain, and joy. One group lasted for years. We men struggle to redefine the meaning of manhood in our relationships with ourselves, with other men and with women. I've found that male rule harms men with shorter lifespans and emotional castration, which is no life at all.

In the early Eighties, I co-founded a Colorado men's network. This gave way to more energetic circles of men following Robert Bly's mythopoetic book, *Iron John*. Such work invited us men to liberate our inner Wild Man in a safe way; so that, instead of being raging beasts, we can become powerful human beings, balancing passion and compassion with honesty and integrity.

In 2005, I was introduced by a friend to the ManKind Project (MKP), which since 1985 had been offering the New Warrior Training Adventure (NWTA) manhood initiation weekends in various countries. The MKP vision calls for men helping men awaken into a mature "male mode of feeling," so good men create healthy and abundant lives without the old male need to dominate. MKP circles in Colorado had been gathering near me for years. I must not have been ready to hear about them, until my gut and heart gave me a resonant and clear "Yes!"

By then, I'd already done a lot of personal growth groups, workshops and trainings. I'd received extensive instruction in "personal growth process facilitation." I was rather smug, frankly, when I went through the "NWTA." During the spring weekend, I made deeper lasting breakthroughs in my relationship with my father and with myself than I had in years of counseling. I still had to find my own inner catalyst for change, and the NWTA was my perfect venue for transformation.

In the years since, I have staffed many warrior weekends and sat in MKP "integration groups" (igroups) from New York to California, including the current open MKP circle near my home in Hawaii. I was founding editor of the "MKP Journal." Lately, I'm serving on the steering committee of the Equitable Communities Initiative in MKP, promoting more equality in sexual orientation and race and ability, intersecting with the national and international gender rights movement.

I stay involved, mainly, because of fellowship with men dedicated to being real. I love that each meeting or gathering opens with a "check in" when we can drop pretenses and be fully present. The work serves me as a husband with plans to do better and as an elder with no plans to retire.

These days I can relate to songs like Billy Joel's "Keeping the Faith" (bridge and third verse).

Now I've nearly finished writing a new book that, among other ideas, calls for the end of patriarchal "alpha male rule" in favor of responsible "personal democracy"; i.e., liberty ruled by self-restraint arising from the inner awareness that everyone on earth is created equally valuable, what I call "global sense."

I see realistic hope in the Me Too movement and in women declaring that #TimesUp for male dominance. We see evidence of the shift in voting booths. Enough is enough. I rejoice at seeing the push for gender equality, but it's not yet sufficient to change our world. How can women and LGBTQ folks be fully liberated, until we straight men are liberated and willing to be their true equals?

I see a steadily growing world movement of enlightened "new men" who are becoming an antidote to the misogyny and bullying so rampant in the government of America today and in other increasingly authoritarian nations. We men are letting go of force to prove our manhood. We're finding our natural power within, without having to dominate anyone.

Grounding my hope, I see websites like GoodMenProject.com, MenStuff.org and XYonline.net. Sites like these confirm that among seven billion humans on earth, millions of "new men" within thousands of organizations worldwide are helping other men mature into the raised awareness of a new man. We are an emerging cultural force. We are the men who join women at the marches.

I believe the pivotal fate of humanity now hinges upon more of us—men and women and all varieties of us—outgrowing the ancient, childish "old male" mentality for organizing society.

If by any chance you are not yet already involved in the uplifting work of changing yourself and the world at the same time, would you be willing to join us?

Raina Greenwood: Let It Be

The Gruens, our next-door neighbors, were selling their house and moving to a retirement community, probably one of the Del Webbs that were springing up. They were an elderly couple, trim and active, controlled and formidable who cast a gimlet eye on our unruly, loud, dysfunctional family. I didn't like to think that my parents' nightly rages and our family fights, which could be heard all over the neighborhood, had driven them from their home; but I can't ask them now.

Their home was immaculate and beautiful, inside and out. It was shaped like a little castle, with rounded sides, mullioned windows, and a vast and highly manicured expanse of lawn. That lawn and its bordering rose bushes were impeccable. It could have been the lawn of an English aristocrat.

Contact between the Gruens, my sisters, and I had tended to occur in the early a.m. and at sunset, when we might see Mrs. Gruen methodically reconnoitering her lawn, pausing to pluck an insolent bit of crabgrass. She had built-in radar and would appear at her window to look down on us if we strayed too close to the rosebushes bordering her lawn. Occasionally, we would exchange greetings, but her expression with me was always a knowing one. I avoided her. I wasn't entirely sure she wasn't a witch, a very town-and-country witch to be sure. I was relieved when they moved out about a year after we moved into our sprawling house on Hillside Lane.

We had some anticipation over who our new neighbor would be. Eventually, we learned that a single man, a bachelor, possibly a divorced man, had bought the house. Hmm. Our family puzzled over this. Divorced? That was bad. Catholics didn't hold with divorce, although we had a divorced relative or two. In the decades to come, there would be more, along with wrinkles and stiff joints. A bachelor? What did that mean, someone like Rock Hudson or Cary Grant? A bachelor for that big house? Was he planning on marrying and having a family, then? Ahh, no.

The bachelor moved in. He seemed to be a perfectly nice, friendly forty-something man, with a full head of silver hair and a matching moustache, exhibiting the same impeccable bearing and grooming that the Gruens had displayed. They were probably kindred spirits. The Gruens had shaded their turrets with beautiful cadet blue awnings, lending a festive, less severe look to the house and offering some relief from the miserable summer heat of inland Whittier.

That was the first crack in the façade. New awnings went up. They were purple. A very beautiful mid-range purple, maybe more magenta. They might as well have been a red lamp and Blue Parrot sign (in the sixties, gay bars tended to advertise themselves by combining a color and an animal in their name). The neighborhood instantly felt that a battle standard had been raised, and those chichi purple awnings had released the poodles of war.

Initially, my dad was just puzzled. "What the hell are those?" My mother responded, "So what." Amazingly, she was actually tolerant, live and let live, on the homosexual issue. Maybe an extended family of bachelor Irish uncles and cousins had informed her subconscious.

My dad was a crackerjack salesman, could talk to anyone, even a now-suspect unmarried male neighbor who had violated an unspoken manly decorating rule. A machine gun in the window would have been more reassuring. We had in fact moved from a neighbor in the San Fernando Valley, who, rifle at the window, had threatened to shoot our dog, Pepper. Just on general principles.

So one weekend, Dad ambled over to chat with the new neighbor, probably prefacing his remarks with a genial "Say, that's some awning you put up." I think it went downhill from there, probably along lines of property rights and maybe some class distinctions. My dad wore gardening clothes that "no self-respecting Mexican would be caught dead in."

After a while, he returned from next door in a puzzled, "What just happened?" mood. Given that he was nothing if not a firm believer in property rights, he parsed this conundrum by saying: "A man's home is his castle, goddammit." He kept a shotgun in the hall closet ready to enforce this belief.

The only time I actually saw him pick it the weapon was the time when my sister Nancy's classmates toilet-papered our house and threw colored miniature marshmallows and toothpicks all over our front lawn. My sisters and I spent four hours picking that shit off our lawn, since we were all teenagers and were guilty by association. Nancy, preening over the elevated status that such lawn terrorism implied, refused to rat her friends out.

Eventually, the different strands of the enigma that was our neighbor came together. Forty-ish. A bachelor. Purple awning. Like one of those 1950s melodramas with the lurid pinwheel turning and the hero clutching his head, Dad finally figured it out. It was possible—hell, unavoidable—to conclude that our new neighbor was a homosexual and that the purple awning was a beacon pulsing in our neighborhood to let other homosexuals know that one of their own had block-busted our straight Whittier neighborhood.

My dad was not the only concerned citizen in our area. Somehow, word got around; and that house became an attraction of sorts. We started seeing lines of cars pacing up our block, slowing down, even stopping, to view the purple awnings. Looking with the eyes of today, it seems impossible to believe. But I remember clearly, it was real. No graffiti or trash was ever thrown; but it was clear that the symbolism of the purple awning in the heart of conservative Whittier, home of Richard Nixon, was not confined to Hillside Lane.

Eventually, a consortium of male envoys made a series of visits to our neighbor. I'm reasonably certain that words were not minced and that ultimatums were issued. I'm sure our new neighbor, who had several decorous all-male parties, had not anticipated the response. After a few months, the purple awnings were replaced by the approved blue ones; and my neighbor put the house up for sale. He had lived in it under a year. I don't even remember who bought it next.

My own experience of gays broadened when I moved to San Francisco. As a campaigner for women's rights on my UCLA campus, I had flirted with same sex relationships, coming close on several occasions. Things began to ease up in the eighties, despite Anita Bryant's campaign. Madonna and her sexual adventurism were a real kick in the pants. So, I felt my own outlook broadening, helped by the gay and trans people I encountered whose friendship meant so much to me and from whom I was learning values of empathy and respect.

Apparently, this tolerant culture of San Francisco was making its way into the most unlikely places. I had a real epiphany about how far and how comprehensively American attitudes were evolving when I approached my mother, then in her nineties and settled into a comfortable assisted living facility in Orange County. The archetypal strict Irish Catholic had matured into a much more humanistic woman. I asked her, "Mom, you know the gay marriage referendum is coming up. Are you going to vote for it?"

"Oh, sure," she said, easily. "If they pay taxes, they *should* be able to get married."

Edwin Thomasson: While My Guitar Gently Weeps

In order to walk the path of the healer best, I became a male nurse back when it was NOT a cool or acceptable thing to be a male nurse.

I have heard many times: "You are a male nurse. All male nurses are gay. All gays have HIV. You will give me HIV. Get out of my room."

I've also heard: "You are by far the most qualified and experience candidate for the job we have ever had, but we only hire female nurses."

Many times, I have heard threats on my life for being different, but there are many here now on the planet that would not have been here if I had not been who and where I was. When the first standards for certifying Critical Care Nurses for Pediatrics and Neonatal were established. I helped write the tests.

Although retired from medicine professionally, I still hope to end my days overseas helping those most in need. Forever more, I only work for free.

Ray York: Let's Live for Today

I am at the ranch, my commune, shoeing Ruby, my horse, a dun-colored half–Arab, half–Quarter Horse with a dark mane. I am strong, athletic, and tan. The sun is setting, and the moon is coming up soon. Ruby feeds on oats, while I brush and blanket him. Then, I leave him tethered, go into my house, and put on a shirt. The day has cooled.

Now the moon is full. I'm riding bareback in the meadow without a blanket or saddle, bathed in moonlight, a dreamy aura that makes the massive bank of blackberry bushes look like they're covered with snow. Ruby and I come to a log fallen across a path. Horse and rider are one being. We leap, up and up.

That's when I wake up. It's all been a dream.

Half asleep, I struggle to get out of bed, no longer strong or athletic. My dream really happened once, but those days are gone.

Today, it takes five minutes to unbutton my pajama tops, and another five to put on my socks. When you have Parkinson's, your life is considerably slowed down. When I walk into the bathroom, with that peculiar Parkinson's shuffle (called a "festinating gait"), I stumble, bracing myself on one of the grab bars placed around the house. Falling is the number one cause of death among Parkinson's people.

When I was 30 at the ranch, falling was out of the question. We never thought about it. Why would we? But now, it's always on my mind. I have fallen many times, each time different, all of them painful—head gashed, teeth broken, ribs fractured. The sound of crashing down is awful too. Think of a 200-pound sack of potatoes hitting the ground, ba–BOOM, a loud dull thud.

Of course, come to think of it, I did fall years ago at the ranch, a spectacular fall as I recall. I was walking Ruby on a very narrow trail 200 feet above the Eel River, when suddenly the trail disappeared, Ruby shied away, and there was nowhere for me to go but down. I managed to keep my heels from catching on the rocks and my arms over my head as I went down, landing on my feet in front of two friends watching my descent with their mouths open. I dusted myself off, gave a little "ta-daa!" and we celebrated the fact that I was still live with my audience.

I still celebrate being alive, even though I can't talk now and can barely walk. We were a healthy lot back on the ranch, except when we were living on zucchinis and government commodities. We lived one day at a time, and I live that way now. It's essential.

The difference is that I don't feel invincible anymore. But I've had the chance to realize that people are kind, and eager to help me. It's a good feeling.

My Sweet Lord

I grew up in the largest and wealthiest Presbyterian church in town. The sanctuary was awe-inspiring with carved wooden pews for hundreds. Huge chandeliers hung from the towering cathedral ceiling, spilling subdued light onto the faithful. But the most impressive feature of the sanctuary was a huge stained-glass window filling most of the front wall. Every Sunday, vibrant blues and reds bathed the worshipers in warm color. If God ever came into that building, he/she probably streamed in through that incredible window.

I was a good boy. I went to Sunday services, memorized the stories, recited the liturgy, and sang all the songs. I was so enthusiastic about being righteous that I seriously considered becoming a minister. (Sorry, Mom.)

In 1968, as a high school senior, I was elected the president of the church's "youth fellowship" and introduced to our new youth minister, a red-haired, straight-talking, middle-aged refuge from Scotland. I liked him immediately.

He preached the evils of money to a wealthy congregation and the wisdom of youth to the vanguard old. Finally, after a tumultuous six months, he was fired for telling young people what their parents already knew: blacks were being secretly excluded from church membership.

For some reason, the elders allowed my minister friend to preach one last sermon before the full congregation. I'll never forget it. The Sunday morning service started at 11:00 a.m. with a full house. We recited our beliefs and paid our dues.

Then, the great hall fell silent; and my friend rose to the podium. For a few long seconds, he said nothing. Everybody was nervous. Then suddenly, a blast of music filled the ceremony. It was The Beatles, singing "Nowhere Man." The rebellious pastor had planted huge speakers in the back.

147

As the music blared, extolling the misery of a meaningless life, the faithful got restless. The sanctimonious squirmed in their seats, and a few walked out.

Then when the tension and the music seemed to have reached an unbearable pitch, the cathedral fell suddenly quiet. Like John the Baptist, my redheaded hero let 'em have it. I can tell you that a mighty sermon was delivered to the heathen on that day. Fingers were pointed. Hypocrites were exposed. In the longest 15 minutes in recorded church history, this man of God railed against the holy men and women who failed to open their hearts. The next day, his office was empty. I left too, never to return.

These days, I keep an open mind about a "higher power," as they say in my Narcotics Anonymous meetings. Who lit the fuse for the big bang? Do departed souls really live in paradise, or does our energy simply dissipate into the air when we die? About these and hundreds of other esoteric questions, I can only say: I don't know, and I don't care. What I do care about is how people treat each other every day.

I'm OK with religion as long as it's not organized and doesn't hurt anybody else. We're all free to believe what we want, but do the believers really have to build majestic stone monuments as a testament to their faith? Wouldn't those millions spent on "houses of worship" be better spent on the needs of real people? And what about religious wars that are still raging today? If there's a "god," does he/she really favor one set of believers over another or command the "righteous" to destroy the non-believers? I doubt it.

On the cover of its August 1966 issue, Time *magazine asked a simple question: "Is God dead?" The faithful answered in furious denials. For non-believers, it was no big deal. God couldn't have died. He/she/it wasn't alive to start with.*

I certainly believe that many things, in fact, an inconceivable number of things, are beyond my comprehension. If the definition of "god" is something so great and so powerful that it defies our frail understanding, then I believe. If the definition of god is some Zeus on a mountaintop, hearing prayers, dispensing miracles, dispatching crusades, and picking our pockets to build fancy cathedrals, then count me out. I'd prefer to think that God is sleeping, not dead; while a bunch of God-wanna-be's are running the store.

I like to think that God is love, the essence of kindness, a simple soul like Jesus who washed the feet of his followers, preached hope, healed the sick, and even forgave his enemies as they killed him. Anyone who gives that much love must be filled with god. And so, it is with us. As goodness flows through our veins, so god flows. Where there is love, there is god.—S.L.R.

Rick Denney: I'm a Believer

It was 1967. I was out of high school with the whole world before me. I could hardly wait. Finding where I might fit in was the furthest thought from my mind. I just wanted to spread my wings and explore everything I could.

So, I moved into a big house with four friends who shared my enthusiasm. I was able to do whatever I wanted, with no parents telling me to be home at a certain time. I could sleep all day and party all night. Wow, life was great! I started doing drugs and hanging around others who did the same. Our house became the place to be every night.

Suddenly, one of my roommates stopped doing drugs and decided he would move out, a decision that mystified me. The day before he left, he explained why he was leaving. He said he had been to a peace rally in downtown Portland and someone had given him a flyer. He pulled it out of his pocket and showed it to me. In big red letters across the top, the paper asked, "DO YOU KNOW JESUS?"

What? I started laughing, thinking that he was trying to pull a joke on me. He wasn't. He told me he never gave God much thought, not many of us did in my circle. He said he had been to a couple of meetings with the Jesus freaks, (as they were known) and had given his life to Jesus.

"Are you kidding me," was my response. "Nope, I am dead serious," he answered. I tried to reason with him, but he was determined and off he went. I thought he was crazy. How could he be so stupid!

A few months later, I ran into him at a local park where we used to buy drugs. He recognized me, and we began talking. He told me that his life had been completely changed, that Jesus is the answer, and if you don't know it now, you will. He said he was praying for me. "What? Don't bother," was my response, and I hurried to get as far away from him as I could. The nerve of that guy praying for me.

As time went by, I often wondered what happened to Dave. I heard he went into the service and was sent to Vietnam. Meanwhile, my life became filled with adventures, mostly leading to dead ends. Feeling disillusioned, I began to understand what my friend was talking about. I realized that I was searching for answers, but not ready to turn to religion. I had gone to church a few times growing up, and I knew that route was not for me.

One night, I found myself at that same park trying to score some drugs. There was loud music coming from somewhere. Unsure where, I followed the sound for two blocks where I came upon a large tent in the middle of a big field. The music was unusual, so I ventured forward and into the tent. Standing on a platform surrounded by chairs, a rather heavy-set lady was signing. I listened from the back row.

The place was packed. A few minutes later, the music stopped. A man popped up to the stage and asked the crowd: "How many of you know Jesus?"

"What! Are you kidding me?" I thought. Not wanting to be noticed, I slithered down in my seat. He asked people to come forward to receive Jesus as their savior. The whole thing seemed funny to me. People were crying and carrying on. It was quite a site. When the lady returned to the stage, I saw my opening, jumped up, and left.

The experience of that night made an impression on me. Years later, I came to understand God orchestrated that evening. For years, I had fought God tooth and nail. But the seed was planted; and eventually, I understood that my friend Dave was right. Today, I have received Jesus as my personal savior. Time has a funny way of working things out. The search for me is over, but the journey continues.

Wayne Lee: Hello, I Love You

I've just read Michael Pollan's fascinating *How to Change Your Mind: What the New Science of Psychedelics Teaches Us About Consciousness, Dying, Addiction, Depression, and Transcendence.* It gave me a kind of flashback to Independence Day, 1980.

I didn't know it at the time, but this would prove to be the last of the 150 or so times I'd dropped LSD, mescaline or psilocybin over a 13-year span. A dozen of us commune members ate acid that day. When we started to get off, a few brothers picked up their guitars and started strumming some of our Family anthems: "I Shall be Released," "Into the Mystic," and "Truckin."

Needing to be alone, I wandered down to the meadow, pulled off my clothes, and sat in the tall grass. At first, I tried to meditate; but my brain was racing faster than Fritz the Cat on fast forward. Then, just as I was about to give up and go explore the river, I heard a voice say:

"Sit down. I want to tell you a few things." I recognized it immediately. It was God. "Truth is more beautiful than the loveliest song," it said. "The first man across the field leaves a trail that others may follow," it said.

For the next several hours, I sat there, receiving each nugget of cosmic wisdom as it fell from the cloudless sky and scribbling it in my notebook. God gave me advice, recited poetry, made me laugh.

"Of course, I make jokes. Just look at you!"

This was the funny, familiar voice—and palpable presence—of a jolly uncle, not a punitive, unapproachable Almighty.

"Every day is the day of decision until you decide," it said.

That one made me think. What, pray tell, did I need to decide? Then it hit me: I had learned all I needed to learn from chemicals. From now on, I would open those doors of perception through nature, prayer and meditation. It made me think of the Firesign Theater zinger, "No false drugs for me—I'm high on life!"

I've been meditating more-or-less daily ever since. Once in a while through the years, I would be fortunate to experience the same kind of universal oneness and wonderment I did on drugs; but I was frustrated that I couldn't do it on demand. Then in January 2015, I was gifted by Spirit with a new way to meditate. In time, I came to call it Open Gate Meditation, because it showed me how me to open all the "gates" of my being to let myself out and the universe in. As I've developed the technique over time, I began to transcend almost every day. Besides being relaxing and blissful, the experience still gifts me with the kind of insights I used to get on hallucinogens.

Like the final entry I wrote in my notebook that Independence Day in 1980: If your voyage is to God, you will arrive.

Larry M: Dancing in the Street

The movement that produced the hippies heralded in a political protest crusade for the record books, a music bonanza that will probably never happen again, and a little discussed new age religious revival. Those who already had religious inclinations, went to church, and followed the rules of Christianity said: "Show us something new."

When it came to spiritual options, there was a lot to choose from: revival of Eastern religions, most notably Maharishi, yoga, renewed interest in the occult, Jewish Kabballah, return to nature ala Thoreau, Scientology (some would say this is not a religion), and even the psychedelic experience such as Carlos Castaneda's search for a shaman.

Ashrams became a popular destination for some seeking enlightenment. Even George Harrison of The Beatles was there taking sitar lessons from Ravi Shankar. In his writings, Timothy Leary extolled the religious virtues of LSD. Along with Richard Alpert, his cohort at Harvard and later know as Baba Ram Das, Leary wrote about the transitional states between death and rebirth requiring a guru guide.

I was raised a Catholic and educated for eight years by the Jesuits, an order founded by Ignanius Loyola in the 16th century to counter the Lutheran threat to the church's authority. The Jesuits are a curious mix of storm troopers and left-wing intellectuals, frequently at odds with the Vatican and incredible educators. But for me, they didn't cut it. I was more influenced by Alan Watts, a popularizer of Eastern religions. I read many of his books, listened to his talks on FM Pacifica radio, and loved his concept of "the religion of non-religion."

Today, I would say that I'm either an agnostic or a Neo-Paganist. Don't laugh. Paganism is the only religion that has true integrity. After all, Christianity is simply a pagan religion with a new name, essentially copied from the ancient Persian religion of Mithra, a popular religion during the Roman era. No matter what they claim, Christianity doesn't answer the question: "What's it all about." At least the pagans were honest enough to admit that they don't have the answers and that everything is a mystery.

We need the old hippie's loud and colorful celebration of life, dancing in the streets, not the Christian "You are born in shame and sin and need a redeemer sent from the sky god who is pissed off."

Linda R: Jesus Freaks

While going to a concert in the summer of 1971, I met two teens from a religious group referred to as the "storm troopers of the Jesus Revolution," according to *Time* magazine. Prior to our meeting, I had become disillusioned and dissatisfied with conventional Christian church doctrines. So, when I met these non-traditional "Jesus Freaks" who spoke of Jesus as a revolutionary and God's only law is "Love," I immediately gave up my car, my family, and my scholarship to a Christian college to pick up the cross and follow.

The teens took me to a commune of about 100 people living together where we shared what little we had to "go into all the world and preach the gospel," not unlike joining Mother Teresa. Each member served according to his/her ability. When, at 18, my high school career assessment test revealed that I was best suited to be an elementary school teacher, I knew this was my calling and soon became my main job in the group.

After many years, the group evolved and changed names. Their so-called schools separated the children from their parents and indoctrinated them with teachings by the group's leader. Most of the teens/children completed 8th grade with a phony diploma, because according to the leader, Jesus was coming in 1993.

As a member, I moved to France, then later to Japan, Thailand, Philippines, and eventually China. All the while, we were strongly discouraged from reading the news. It wasn't until several years later that I learned the top leaders were engaging in child abuse and sexual abuse with underage children. I had heard stories before from teens who left the group saying they were abused, but the group's leaders warned us that these accusations were false. So for a long time, it was hard to know who was telling the truth. It wasn't until a group representative told bold-faced lies directly into the camera while being interviewed on International TV that I soon left the group. Thankfully, my husband and three grown children were already gone by then.

When I think back about how innocently the group began and remember the intelligent, productive people with families who became good missionaries, I shiver knowing that the group is still promoting lies and deceit. But there's one thing the leaders didn't count on: They couldn't take away our genuine faith in Jesus/God and our determination to keep going despite their corruption.

Barry Sommer: I Can See for Miles and Miles

At 22, having been raised Jewish yet never really embracing the heritage provided, I felt there was something more but had no idea where to go to find it. As fate would have it, I was given the opportunity to go to Thailand.

One year after the end of the Vietnam War, I found myself standing in front of a 500-year-old Buddhist temple watching monks in saffron and white robes make their way up the steps towards a giant reclining Buddha. Flowers, incense and prayers wafted towards the heavens; and I felt as if I was supposed to be there. I had never experienced this feeling, not even during my Bar Mitzvah. To suddenly have what some would call a spiritual experience left me dazed and confused.

As we travelled around the country, I saw not only the physical ravages of war that Thailand had suffered. But I also saw how a simple people survived and thrived even under the greatest threat to their safety. I experienced a culture where peace and non-violence are familiar struggles but despised to their core. I saw the profound effect that turning to internal spirituality has on the human psyche, a lesson I've tried to take to heart.

I was fascinated by the number of temples, statues of the Buddha and worship fetishes that fill the country. Spiritual symbolism in Thailand is rampant, a trait that we in the West have abdicated to the gods of inclusiveness. I was not alone in my reverie. Many hippies like myself were in the country, experiencing similar revelations and connecting with like-minded souls as we tried to escape the modern world and gain an understanding of our place in the universe.

It wasn't until I returned home that the lessons I had gained in Thailand began to manifest themselves. After visiting so many temples, I began to understand the relevance of individual piety. Having been raised in a monotheistic house, I was taught that there is one true God. Yet Buddha was not a god, nor is he revered as one. Internal conflicts formed, and I had to figure out what was true for me.

Today, I know that the exposure to a very different culture, coupled with a need to find my place in the world, has opened my eyes and my heart to the wider world of being a true human. I've come to see how I can make a difference in my world and to understand that a life lived fully is what truly matters.

Robert O: Won't Be Fooled Again

In early 1972, I proposed to my friends that we should have church services at The Farm where we partied most of the time. I wanted to be the one to organize and lead those services. I wasn't interested in being affiliated with any one religion. I just wanted to gather, touch on wisdom from various teachers, and share spiritual insights.

I hoped the drugs we were doing would help us grow as spiritual beings. I especially looked for mind expansion in psychedelics. Our non-church church services lasted one Sunday. Lack of general interest and my own attention on getting high the easy way doomed the lofty idea to failure.

The craving for altered states soon dominated my life. I found myself increasingly frustrated with the partying and with the drugs in particular. I wanted to be writing and truly practicing my spiritual life. I couldn't seem to pass up the drugs or alcohol, and I was looking for a way out.

I had been planning a year-long trip around the United States for 1973. Before leaving, I was introduced to Dianetics and Scientology. I completed the introductory Communications Course intensively in one week and really liked it. The Scientologists prohibited the use of drugs while taking part in their services. For me, it was a way to get off the party merry-go-round and learn about a new way of life that might help me realize my potential as a spiritual being.

Despite my curiosity, I immediately left on that trip around the country according to plan. My drug-free lifestyle didn't hold at that point. I hitched with a friend, a dog, a guitar and a backpack most of the way. We fasted for spiritual vision, while accepting drugs and alcohol from the fun people giving us rides. We took jobs at times to fund the travel. We partied hard, burned in the desert, and hopped a freight train. I panned for gold in the mountains of Colorado, sang for food, communed with nature and then circled back to Scientology. It was there that I settled.

What followed was a 35-year involvement with a religion that was in fact a corporation. I spent some money and lots of time trying to buy spiritual enlightenment. I would probably still be trying if it weren't for a special person who pulled the veil aside and revealed the church for what it really was.

After a year of heavy resistance, I was finally ready to tear myself loose from the grip Scientology had on me. I stepped away and opened myself to a relationship with God as I never had before. Returning to detachment from any one religion, I reached to the Divine Intelligence of which we are all a part.

The hippie movement helped bring that awareness to me. My search for truth and connection that I started in the '60s is alive and well. Obscured at times, it was never lost.

Steve Gifford: I Say a Little Prayer

As a young hippie, I learned that being into praise-and-blame is unwise; but I didn't understand. I tried with all my might to be good but got criticized by other hippies when I failed to meet their expectations. I got angry and masochistic, hit bottom, and lost my job and the home where I lived with my hippie friends. The trauma of all that precipitated my getting bipolar disorder.

In the beginning of my mental illness, I continued to try to be a vegan, as I had become one in my hippie community and thought that was where it was at. Then one day, I got violently ill when I ate vegan, then got ill when I tried to eat meat, or indeed, anything. I was unable to eat and fasted for three weeks until I attended a Christian church service, got saved, got prayed for, and got healed. I was no longer vegan, not out of preference, but from necessity. The Lord had persuaded me He wanted a relationship, not a good boy. In the Bible, it talks about becoming free from the Law, i.e., in my case, my rule that I had to be vegan in order to be spiritual.

Among my hippie friends and I, prayer was something you did looking in each other's eyes. Later, I discovered that writing prayer-poems can be a very effective form of spiritual practice and great therapy. Sharing my poems with others has been very rewarding.

I now both meditate in silence and pray with words, while maintaining my hippie interfaith beliefs. These days, I'm disciplining myself by listening to online sermons by a very famous Southern Baptist preacher; although I skip the sermons that don't look to be enlightened. I also follow the Pope, the Dalai Lama, the teachings of Hazrat Inayat Khan, and political commentary on the Internet. I am in a long-term relationship with a wonderful lady and much more at peace these days. "Whatever you may do, be kind to others, kind ta *you!*"

Larry Roszkowiak: Magic Carpet Ride

The hippie culture sprang out of the accelerating materialism of the 1950s during which Americans slipped into a reverent worship of consumer goods. A sub-plot of this period was that this growing materialism had begun to reduce the role of religion in our society. Families still went to church, but it had no more spiritual significance than a trip to Sears. Religion had become more of a thoughtless, social pageant, more useful for showing off your new car or mink than anything spiritual.

The newspapers were alive with science news. "Barriers" were being broken. The realms and secrets of sound, speed, gravity, light and space were being explored and explained to all. Americans were beginning to worship knowledge. When we hippies discarded what we considered to be the gross commercial materialism of American society, some of us threw out science. We condemned entire industries and, with that, came an implied condemnation of the knowledge that made their foul deeds possible.

Out of a desire to find new ways of progressing society, we chose to "open our minds" to alternative ways of understanding life, existence, universe, etc. The average hippie day could be counted on to include at least some exposure to the rhetoric and symbols of astrology, tarot, I Ching, Ying/Yang, and yoga. Slipping in the mail slot with this blizzard of beliefs was Christianity, or to be more specific, American Christianity.

Before long, it seemed like somebody would always interrupt a good party by asking, "Have you heard of the Jesus People?" or slipping the word "Lord" into their conversations. Short-lived, semi-impromptu, groups would form giving themselves pious sounding names like "Brothers" and "Disciples." My favorite group was composed of guys who lived in the woods and called themselves "The Brides of Christ."

Now, several steps in the 21st century, we have a significant portion of the U.S. citizenry who believe that water can be walked upon, that they are chosen ones, that death is temporary, and that someday all the good people will be wealthy.

As hippies, we worked to soften and sweeten the world. We gave life to some wonderful human qualities that had lain dormant. Unfortunately, we undermined our own goal of a progressive and inclusive society by incorporating religion, along with its regressive and exclusive values, into the movement.

J Laurence: Take It Easy

For decades, many of our parents sought out psychiatrists to solve their problems. Unable to afford the price, others were left to their own devices, sometimes with disastrous results. Still others turned to religion, hoping their prayers would be heard.

As an observant yet spiritual child, I found the structure of organized religion distasteful, the ideologies illogical, and the memes senseless. As I matured, my grandparents' relentless criticisms of others, devotion to ritual, and victim-mindset gnawed at my soul. I sought change and challenged their beliefs for which I was made an outcast.

Those of us in the hippie generation challenged the politics and economic policies of the time, using music and protests as tools. The rise of East meets West spirituality stirred the pot further, drawing me in like a moth to a flame. This new "personal growth" therapy skirted the usual psycho route in favor of self-help books by astute authors, followed by workshops merging Eastern spirituality with personal growth. Traditionalists labeled them as cults; although concepts like "finding truth" and "remaining present" were, in fact, foundations taken from Buddhism. As these workshops proliferated and enlightened, emotionally charged graduates took on the world with vigor.

Coming from a highly dysfunctional family from which I first attempted escape at age 5, my need for growth was critical. Obviously, I wasn't alone.

Every workshop I attended was packed with people of all ages, backgrounds, economic differences and challenges. The one thing we shared was the knowledge that life could *and would* be better.

Today, I am confident that we can heal ourselves. Those who are willing will grow. Those who resist will remain where they are, continually padding a proverbial row boat, round and round, with one oar.

Patricia Lapidus: excerpt from *The Farm That Tried to Feed the World*

"At our core, we were a spiritual people inclined toward mutual helpfulness. We looked to invisible levels of being for guidance with the visible. This was the glue that held us together and foretold our future as we intended to create it."

Nancy Pruitt: God Is Love

As a pre-teen, watching or reading great love stories intrigued me. Maybe it's a female thing to be obsessed with finding "real love." I thought that if I could just be smart enough, sexy enough, fit enough and talented enough, my prince and best friend would ride in, find me and whisk me off into a life of security and true love. I've come to realize that such delusions are normal.

My mother preferred to call her religion: "God is love." A hand-painted china tablet with those words inscribed on it sat on our side table. This belief allowed her to answer most questions about religion in her own simple, yet exquisite, way. But I was confused. If "God is love," why do I need a man to feel loved? The question wasn't fully answered until my sixth decade.

With the sexual tumult during our youth in the 1960s, finding real love in which one person was devoted to another challenged both young men and women. Our beloved singers gave us timeless advice about love for each other and our neighbors. They told us to "live and let live." R&B, Rock, Blues, Folk, Broadway and popular hits encouraged social acceptance for everyone. "All you need is love," we were told. Sadly, we later awoke to the reality of political deception, greed, injustice, betrayal, and frustration.

Today, I see more hate than love. Political correctness and exploding gender names have added to the mix. But even if the world fell to pieces, I would still look for ways to express love to those around me. For without love, we perish like untouched newborns. God is love, and understanding his love allows us to transform.

I think my Mom figured it out. God is love. It's a message I've passed onto my only son. Love's circle is unending.

Teach Your Children Well

When I was 20, the thought of having children never entered my drug-addled brain. I was too busy taking care of myself, more or less, to be responsible for another human being. And yet to my eternal surprise, nothing has brought me more happiness in life than my two sons, one who was born when I was only 25.

I love those boys (grown men now) through and through, top to bottom. I consider myself extraordinarily lucky, not only because my sons are such marvelous human beings; but also because I love being a father so much. Some dads don't.

I feel sad for parents who seem to love their children, but don't seem to like them. They feed their offspring, clothe them, perhaps even treat them to everything that money can buy; but you sense that they're not really connected, heart to heart, with them. Somehow, in the deepest, most vulnerable spot of their being, children sense this distance; and it hurts deeply and permanently.

Dick Gregory was a black comedian who championed civil rights from the 1960s until his death in 2017. As a performer, speaker, organizer, writer, and entrepreneur, he was constantly traveling. His wife and ten children rarely saw him. When asked about his absence as a parent, Gregory said, "It was never in my psyche that I'm going to be a great father. Mine was: I'm going to be a great fighter for the liberation, whatever it takes."

I think he missed the point. Of what value is the struggle for a better world if we abandon the most important creatures on this planet—our children? Loving them, supporting them financially and emotionally, is our first responsibility. Nothing else, no matter how noble, is more important both to the children themselves and to our mission of transforming this crazy world into a kinder, more peaceful place.

The term "generation gap" originated in the 1960s to describe the grow-ing chasm between parents and their kids. Undoubtedly, generational dif-ferences have always existed. Perhaps, we had more time to think about them in the '60s or perhaps the media was quicker than usual in condensing these differences into a catchy phrase.

My father and I had no generation gap during my younger years. We were too busy doing things together, like fishing and hunting. But when I reached 14 or 15, we began to do less and less. By the time I married at 23, we were hardly speaking, except for brief explosive moments filled with criticism about my hair length and career choices.

The year my first child was born (his only grandson), my Father learned that he would die soon from cancer. Neither one of us reached out to the other in those final months. Now it's too late for both of us.

Frequently, I find myself talking with strangers about their relation-ships with their parents. Maybe I'm trying to justify my own dysfunction, or maybe I'm just curious. It's always an unexpected delight when someone's face lights up talking about his/her Mom and Dad.

Unlike the relationship I had with my Father, I'm amazingly close to my sons. Knowing them and sharing in their lives is my greatest joy. I feel profoundly lucky that the generation gap passed us by.—S.L.R.

Nancy Pruitt: Another Mother for Peace

From the start of my marriage in 1972, my husband and I ran on the beach and joined a health club in Santa Monica. This shared passion devel-oped into a career in health and fitness for me after returning to college in the early 1980s where I graduated with a degree in Physical Education, emphasizing Dance with Nutrition. I felt my true calling was teaching exercise and better nutrition. My two jobs at the Golden Door Resort in Escondido and Director of Aerobics in Encinitas were my happiest times before motherhood. I felt I was making a difference in people's lives. The feedback I received made it even more gratifying.

When I became pregnant with my son in 1987, I realized that now my most important job was to be the best mother I could be to him. As a single parent, I always worked to support us. I showered him with love and supported his interests in sports, music and travel. At the age of 31, he has become an accomplished nurse anesthetist, graduating with honors and a special award for using humor in a medical setting.

Raising him with the ideals learned in my youth during the hippie revolution enabled me to give him the love and attention needed for a successful life. I wanted him to find his own voice politically and he has. I hoped he would find real love, and he has. I gave him the freedom to choose his career path, and he has surprised and delighted me in his accomplishments every day. I showed him about a cause greater than our own. He definitely learned that too. I imbued the need to give of ourselves to those less fortunate, and he does. His tenderness toward animals was easily nurtured. He enjoys his wonderful dog adopted from a shelter. He understands responsibility.

Once on a Mother's Day project in grammar school, he wrote: "I love my mother, because she chose to have me." He called me his Rock, and I have been steadfast in being his biggest fan. He has compassion, humility, and perfect comedic timing.

No matter how many photographs I sell or paintings I create in my years to come, the greatest contribution I actually did make was being a devoted mother, one who gave her son his wings to seek his own wonderful life adventures and make a difference in our world.

Kahish: Consciousness Raising

We had just moved into this old Victorian mansion that mom rented for $75 a month. Across the street, several houses brimmed with colorful people. My mother, who lived outside the box and studied metaphysical books, became friends with one of the ladies across the street, a young mom with a couple of young children whose house was full of various adults wearing fringed vests and leather hats outcropped with long wily hair. She and the other women wore flowing colorful dresses and beaded headbands. Everyone spoke softly, pooled their resources, and ate meals together.

Within our neighbor's shared house, rooms were divided by floral Indian tapestries, giving each couple or family their own space. Occasionally, I'd catch bits of free expression wisdom and philosophy hinting at the common thread hidden within their existence. It was the life of a true hippie community within the city, a community brewing outside the confines of convention. The year, 1967, was the crest of a new era. I had roadside seats.

I came away from the experience with a true definition of a hippie, an image that I folded neatly in my brain and to which I compared myself. I was always building on my own philosophies in life. While I felt I understood the purity of the hippie philosophy, I thought I would never measure up to it. I never called myself a hippie; yet my lifestyle of nonconformity, questioning authority, and being anti-war places me in the counterculture category.

The basic philosophy of living simply in peace and harmony stayed in my heart through all these years. To respect the land, nature, and each other has always seemed a no-brainer to me. Taboos are broken to prove we have control over outside authority. For many, breaking off establishment controls by replacing them with other controls changed the course of our lives.

J Laurence: Heart of Gold

Hippies were often subjected to "old world" traditions of child rearing; some involving both physical and verbal discipline, a technique that rarely resulted in family closeness and often led the punished child to seek escape. I suspect this contributed to the copious number of "missing children" in those times who ended up in communes or on the streets. As a middle child, I was subjected to this sort of child rearing; until after high school, I finally escaped, never to return.

While frowned upon by some, communes offered community, compassion and structure, much of which lacked in the dysfunctional family. In addition, typical family responsibilities for chores, work, spiritual practice, skill development, and creativity were "eye opening" experiences filled with joy, love and opportunity for change. Organic sustainable living, laughter, pot-smoking conversations that mattered, helping others, learning to listen, thinking clearly ... everything was done without judgment.

Later, living in Sonoma County with a hippie couple, I never dreamed life could be so grounded. Disagreements were handled calmly, growth being the goal. Filled with morning meditations, vegetarian lifestyle and summers spent at the nude beach, we lived a life of simplicity. Working with a family that owned an organic apple orchard, I learned the art of cider making, hard work that it was. Augmented by selling "lids," our pantry was stocked, smiles on our faces. This was life unlike the one my parents had taught, one whose essence would be carried for years. With never a word of gossip, judgment or vicious anger, peace was all that mattered.

Observing others, whether family, friends or strangers, we have the opportunity to grow, to learn new perspectives, and most importantly, to experience and share joy. Family members willing to open up to other views have the prospect of becoming closer. Had hippies not challenged the status quo, the family unit may have remained stuck in the mud like mine which is still so dysfunctional that siblings never speak, celebrate or interact in any way. Perhaps, one day, we will realize that joy exists in every moment waiting to be found.

Henrietta B: Free to Be You and Me

The fabulous '60s and '70s, what wonderful times they were; and what sad, heartbreaking times they were. I very much considered myself a hippie and loved what defined me as a young adult. I was raised with an amazing work ethic that never left me or failed me. I loved to read and write, and still do.

I remember sitting around a campfire, listening to someone play the guitar or harmonica, talking, laughing, and passing the occasional "joint" around. Other times, my friends and I would sit by a creek reading our poetry to each other. With flowers in our hair and patches on our jeans, we sang and danced to The Beatles, protested the Vietnam War, and did sit-ins at Rocky Flats, a nuclear weapons facility northwest of Denver. I wore a copper bracelet with a POW's name on it and scoured the papers daily to see if he made it back home. He did!

My one regret was never making it to Woodstock. Maybe it was good that I didn't, as I was definitely going through a rebellious stage at the time. I lived in small-town USA and could not wait to "get out" and see the world. I graduated in 1968 and thought the Peace Corps was going to be one of my next steps in life. Not to be.

Fast forward, I became a mother in 1970, shortly after turning 20. My little girl learned to be a free spirit and an independent soul by osmosis, I think! Raising a child as a single parent and working full time (thank goodness for that work ethic) was challenging. But the other single mothers and I worked out arrangements that gave us opportunities to have our own freedoms, too. In many ways, I feel I "grew up" alongside my daughter.

Today, looking back, I would not trade those times for all the world. I developed a love for music, an open mindedness for the life choices of others, a desire for peace, and a faith in humanity. I often think that if we could return to those times, we would all be the better for it. I've developed a strong determination to be my own definition of self and to continue to cut through the inculcated beliefs/programming that would define me otherwise.

My daughter is a successful entrepreneur, and we have a beautiful relationship to this day. We laugh over the fact that I knew she was gay long before she had the courage to "come out" to me. I have nothing but love and admiration for her! I have a strong passion and compassion for human and animal rights. I find today's times are challenging. My hope is that, by being the person I have become, I can make a positive contribution to a better world.

Patricia Lapidus: excerpt from *The Farm That Tried to Feed the World*

I decided that, when I had children, I would show that children could be raised without frowns and spanking. This early purpose was in full expression by the time I lived on The New York Farm with my three little boys.

I remember that sunny afternoon when we first arrived, the rolling hills, maple, birch, hornbeam, and wild cherry trees on the ridges above the fields, raspberries and blackberries decorating the paths through the woods. I was happy. Our future stretched out before us.

By a combination of love, attention, and miracle, we brought the boys safely to this green valley community of "aunts and uncles and cousins" where we were our own family and, at the same time, part of a peaceful, trusted extended family. Having grown up in one, I loved the chatter and clatter of a large household.

Having waited until the age of thirty to have my first child, I was as invested in my three small boys as a parent could be, with all the closeness of nursing and nurturing. Some days, their soft cheeks and sweet voices 'bout took my breath away. These children were my visionary activity. What could be more revolutionary than raising strong, competent, loving children? It would prove to be a bond strong enough to weather later hardships.

In this new place, home schooling was easy when shared among the dozen or more families. With talk of windmills and solar panels, the men ran a construction company; and the women helped each other with house and garden chores. Even in comparative poverty, we mothers were able to stay home with our little ones. I sure didn't want to go to work. Part of freedom for women is letting them raise their own children.

In the long run, I was unable to continue raising my children in an extended family, whether chosen or inherited. But with their experiences on The Farm for a foundation, my boys were able to handle public school from an outside perspective. They knew when others were genuine and when they were posturing. Facing problems, they learned to advocate for themselves. I won't pretend that they didn't suffer from growing up in an insular family and a decadent culture. But they have kept their boats afloat and are now doing well as parents.

Ray York: One Love

I was at my wit's end about what to do next in life, so I decided to give one year in service in the hopes that my path might get straightened out in the process. I joined VISTA (Volunteers-In-Service-To-America) and went to work at a food bank. As I suspected, the experience was good for me; and after a year, it set me straight on the road I was looking for.

But that was a minor effort. The real thing I've done to make this world a better place is have four children. One son works at a great newspaper in New York. One daughter, now a widow, is putting her two girls through college. She works for a TV network in LA and has shown an incredible amount of spunk. I have another daughter, a legendary softball player and coach, who's raising three children in Colorado and has gone back to school to be a nutritionist. I have a son in Oakland who started his own business online and has guided it to the top in its field. All my children are successful, but that's not the point. More importantly, they're good people, kind and generous.

When I think about the future and what I'll leave behind me when I go, I don't think of food banks or politicians or America achieving its ends in the world. I think of my kids, and their kids, and how every one of them has turned out just right, not a piker among them. I know that I'm leaving the world in good hands.

Carol Seaton: Today Is the First Day of the Rest of Your Life

I have protested war and written letters to the editor of the *Register Guard*, a daily local newspaper, about matters of social justice. I joined a march on the State Capital to support school funding and a fast started by Peg Morton to maintain spending for the needy. I helped Mary Regreth create Grandparents for Family Justice and devoted my time to organizational work, stunts to get media attention, and testimony at a public hearing in the State Legislature on behalf of the group, resulting in fundamental changes in the Children's Services Department's policy regarding working with grandparents. Results like that are real spirit boosters.

I included my very young granddaughter in my homeless advocacy work, and she also grew up to be an advocate for social justice. That was not my intention. Fighting for social justice has taken a toll on me, especially my efforts to call attention to the homelessness problem. I had to quit a volunteer position for St. Vincent de Paul; because I just could not take calls from frightened mothers needing housing immediately, knowing we had nothing to give them. Thank heavens, things have improved since then; but so much more needs to be done. Now my granddaughter is on the battle lines. Her son stayed with me after she was brutalized by the police.

I am fortunate that my circumstances have almost always allowed me to volunteer. Perhaps having a career that took advantage of my college education would have been better; but for me, the family had to come first. I stayed at home to care for my children; then I cared for my Grandmother with Alzheimer's and my mother with ALS, followed by caring for my grandchildren and now my great-grandchildren.

My family knows I start every day on the Internet with the intent of making the world a better place. That's what long-lived people should be doing, because we are history, and our perspective has value.

The Devil's Bargain

Named after a 15th century English group who envisioned a world without private property, the Diggers were an acting troupe that used guerrilla theater to promote a freer America. Between 1967–68, they flourished in San Francisco, performing original political plays in the streets, promoting free clinics and free food distribution, and writing prolifically about the evils of materialism. They coined the sayings: "Do your own thing" and "Today is the first day of the rest of your life."

The Diggers weren't interested in making the capitalist system fairer. They wanted to eliminate it all together. They called money and credit "stupid ideas." They wanted to create "Free Cities" full of "Free Families" with free food, free medical care, and even free money. To finance these ideals, the Diggers offered excellent suggestions such as barter, volunteerism, and re-distribution of surplus to those in need. Unfortunately, we still needed cash.

My dad called it "The Almighty Dollar." I call it a maniac that's been kicking my butt for as long as I can remember. Truthfully, I don't hate money per se. After all, it's just paper—or more accurately, ones and zeros. What I hate is people attributing some kind of symbolic meaning to money, giving it value above and beyond what it can buy.

We all know the rap: people "with" are better than people "without." Higher incomes, bigger houses, fancier cars, and more elegant clothes define success. Renting an apartment, driving a used pick-up, and earning minimum wage are sure signs of failure.

I hate good people doing bad things to get more. I hate the rich wasting millions, while so many have so little. I hate parents devoting all of their waking time to earning more for families they ignore. And I hate honest, hardworking people feeling bad about themselves for not being more "successful."

And yet, despite my best efforts, which have been numerous, I cannot escape the need for cash. I used to say that, some day, I would walk away from this capitalist bullshit and live on a mountaintop without property, without money. Unfortunately, all the mountaintops are owned by somebody. There's no free land and no free lunch. In order to survive, I've been forced to accept the fact that I have to pay the landlord, in one way or another.

Other hippies faced the same reality. Eventually, we all had to pay for a place to stay, food, electricity, gasoline, medicine, fees, taxes, and all the rest. In fact, I think the lack of cash did more to dismantle the Hippie Nation than LSD and the FBI put together.

We all needed cash; and so, we were forced to dance with the Devil. Necessity demanded that we enter the world of private property, the world of buying and selling, the world of living paycheck to paycheck. We had to support ourselves, and we had to support the families we soon attained. In the end, we were innocents who sold our bodies to survive.

In the last 50-plus years, some brothers and sisters have danced a little; and some have danced a lot. Some are selling their pottery to tourists. Some are running Wall Street. Either way, the real world took our innocence; and we will never get it back.

In my opinion, the only practical defense against materialism is to personally own as little as possible. In this regard, I'm succeeding.

Once I owned a beautiful new home, which I could not afford. I tried, night and day, to earn enough money to pay the mortgage, pay the insurance, pay the plumber, pay the utilities, pay for new furniture—and still pay for food. I was carrying those 2500 square feet on my back. Eventually, the most beautiful object I had ever owned flattened me; and the Man took it back. Today, my material assets include an old car, an old computer, and a bunch of old clothes. That's enough.

I've heard that everything you own, owns you. I agree. The more you own, the more time you must devote each day to acquiring, maintaining, and protecting your things. Accordingly, there is less time and energy for other priorities like your family, your fellow human beings, and yourself.

A Princeton University study found that having more money makes you happier, but only up to a point ... that point being an annual income of $75,000. The less you earn below that number, the unhappier you are. Earn more than this magic number, and your happiness quotation levels out. (Of course, that's in America. Imagine how rich you'd be with $75K a year in most parts of the world!)

Whatever the magic number, we have to ask ourselves: When is enough enough? And what's the kind thing to do with all that extra money that's really not making us happier?

I look at million-dollar houses and think: who really needs this kind of monstrosity? Do they have 25 children? Have they adopted a tribe from East Africa or a boatload of Syrian refugees? I doubt it. Rich people certainly have a right to be extravagant, but why? Are they really happier? I doubt it.

Distinguishing between "want" and "need" can be tough sometimes, and I'm not suggesting that we completely stop buying things we want but don't need. But I am saying that spending money is a drug. It produces an immediate high that wears off quickly.

I'm reminded of Christmas toys that Santa brought to my two young boys. Based on confidential conversations with the old elf, I know how hard it was to pay for those shiny new treasures placed under the tree. Looking back, I remember how surprised I was when the kids abandoned their trinkets after a few days, preferring to play with the boxes the toys came in.

When I was 20, I heard about an economic maxim championed by Karl Marx, although not originated with him: "From each according to his abilities, to each according to his needs." I liked the sound of it and still do.

Back in the day, I invested a considerable effort researching how to compassionately design a governmental system in which each person contributed according to his/her ability and received according to his/her needs. Theoretically, I thought, fair distribution of wealth was merely a logistical problem, solvable with the right set of rules.

I eventually realized that, while government has a legitimate role in deciding who gets what, no one is smart enough to anticipate and balance all the variables that real human beings bring to the marketplace; and that, even if such an impossibility became possible, the resulting system and its necessary regulatory apparatus would rob its "beneficiaries" of any chance to live freely. Just look at Russia and China for proof of that.

I still believe in "from each/to each," but I don't think we need a corps of regulators to make us do it. Instead, let's just do more of what we're already doing; i.e., sharing what we have on a voluntary basis. As a contributor to this book simply says: "There's plenty for everyone if we share."

As hippies, we've always believed in sharing our food, our homes, and our love. Millions of "non-hippies" do the same every day. Giving is an essential part of human nature, a part that testifies again and again that the world is full of good if we will only see it.

At the same time, I think it's safe to say that hippies, like most people, expect others to be responsible, to pull their own weight and contribute according to their ability. It's only fair. While I imagine that each of us has given less than we should have, or could have, from time to time, I reject the stereotype that hippies were/are lazy freeloaders. Based on my own experiences and those who contributed to this book, it's clear that we've worked and earned our way, even when we would have preferred to be chasing rainbows.

In 1971, anti-war activist Abbie Hoffman published a book titled Steal This Book *as a guide for counterculture activism. His ideas included strategies for obtaining "free" items necessary for survival such as food, housing, transportation, education, medical care, and drugs. Among those strategies was to steal from the capitalist "pigs" including actually stealing his book. Ironically, over a quarter million copies were sold that year. No one knows how many were stolen.*

From what I can tell, Abbie had a good heart and keen instincts, except in this case. Stealing won't build a better world. Only fairness and kindness can do that. Regardless of what political philosophy you espouse, replacing one selfish, greedy system with another selfish, greedy system, even in the name of revolution, is no change at all.

I believe that those who can work should and that the able should support the unable. I believe that each of us has a right to private property that shouldn't be "reallocated" without the owner's permission. These aren't capitalistic values or communist values. They don't belong to any "ism." Pulling your own weight and sharing are simply the right things to do.

For many years, I thought of myself as a failure, at least in the work department. Today, I realize I didn't fail. I just did what I wanted to do. As it turns out, I was only interested in new ideas, not money. I was great at creating a variety of businesses but lousy at maintaining them. As it turns out, I was relatively successful as an inventor but an utter failure as an entrepreneur. Sorry, Dad. Today, I see myself as an artist of sorts; and I'm OK with that.

I have college buds who have become very successful in their careers. One is a celebrated professor at a prestigious university. The other is a big-time lawyer. They've spent the last 50 years mastering their crafts and achieving an admirable degree of recognition and praise. I'm happy for them and hope they are happy with themselves.

I used to compare myself to these guys and wonder "What have I done with my life? Why don't I have a big career like they do?" But I know now that we all did what we wanted, and that was the point all along.

My father was raised in a small, red clay town in Georgia. His father ran a service station by day and, apparently, drank and gambled by night. My grandmother stayed at home with the children when she wasn't fighting "demon rum" with the Temperance League.

My father was so poor that he never told us how poor he was. Occasionally, he would mention eating meatloaf without meat and sleeping five to a bed; but he carefully avoided any other details about the bad old days.

In 1954, my father started his own tire business. Financed by a small loan from a friend and his weekend gambling winnings from golf and gin rummy, Dad's three-person enterprise grew into an upper middle-class moneymaker.

The secret was my father's personality. He was a charmer. This handsome poor-kid-made-good was loved by all. His friends and customers were dazzled by his warm demeanor and clever conversation. He could flirt with the ladies with one breath and talk sports with the guys in the next.

After 20 years in business, my father realized his American Dream: a successful company, a beautiful house in an exclusive neighborhood, expensive cars, classy clothes, plenty of friends, and the key to the country club.

The only thing missing was happiness. As the oldest child, I was often the only sane voice in a home drowning in alcohol. It was my job to referee more drunken fights than I can remember, protecting my sisters from the vulgarity and utter cruelty that two frightened, frustrated alcoholics can inflict upon each other. For the children, our white house on the hill was a nightmare, clean and respectable on the outside, ugly and terrifying on the inside. I couldn't understand why everybody was so unhappy if having money was so great.

Growing up, I never heard my parents use racial or ethnic slurs. They didn't tell stories about Jews, or Poles, or black folks. But they did hate "white trash," vaguely defined as no-good ignorant white people. (I realized later that they actually meant anyone in a blue-collar life.)

My parents had the delusion, as many do, that people with more are better than people with less. Having grown up poor, they had probably experienced that kind of ridicule at the bottom of the ladder looking up. Unfortunately, when it came their turn to be on top, they chose to look down.

I was, as they say, "estranged" from my parents when they died. Looking back, my father must have wondered why I didn't love him more after all he had done for me. Of course, I did love him. I just didn't like him particularly. After all the sacrifices he made to keep me safe and secure, he probably expected much more appreciation than he got, particularly on his deathbed. I wasn't there. Ironically, it was his mistaken belief that money buys love that pushed me away.

One day in 1973, I returned from work, climbed the skinny stairs to my apartment, and found my friends smoking the most excellent hash, while "Stairway to Heaven" blasted in the background. Within 60 seconds, I was climbing with them, higher and higher, into a seriously fine buzz.

Today, when I see rich donors affixing their names to buildings, charities, and other "good deeds," I have to wonder. Do these people really think they can buy their way into heaven? Are they so insecure here on earth that they need to build monuments to themselves?

The Millionaire was a TV show from 1950–60 in which a fabulously wealthy man, named John Beresford Tipton, gave million-dollar cashier's checks to unsuspecting individuals. Delivered by his Executive Secretary, Michael Anthony, the show focused on how the recipients reacted to becoming suddenly rich. While individual reactions varied, the "lucky" beneficiaries were always thrilled to have the money, at least initially. The show was based on the widely held assumption that everyone wants to be rich. Personally, I'll pass.

Maybe it's like coconut. Somewhere in my childhood, I got sick eating coconut cake. The thought of eating it again makes me nauseous just like the memories of my parents' drunken money delusions and my ex-wife's constant howling for cash make me nauseous. Maybe it's like cocaine. I'm afraid to go anywhere near it. Maybe it's a hippie thing, or a spoiled rich kid thing, or some other thing that's hidden under the next layer of my awareness. Whatever the reason, if Michael Anthony calls, tell him I'm not at home.—S.L.R.

Rose V: She's Leaving Home

Looking to escape my parents and start a new life on my own terms, I moved to Austin, Texas in the early 70s. It was one wild and crazy place. My first night there happened to be my 21st birthday. I sat alone on the hood of my car eating sardines out of a can with the beginnings of panic. I needed a new hippie family, and I needed it fast. I was discovering that for all the protests against the Man and his money, being poor alone just didn't have the same ring to it.

Eventually, I met a few gypsy souls like myself; and when we weren't working, we spent all of our time together trying to live that hippie dream. We went to every be-in, love-in, Eeyore's Birthday Party, and anything else we could find that was free. They were some of the kindest people I have ever met.

Slowly but surely, as the rents got higher and the food got pricier, each one of my friends drifted away to have babies or to stick their big toes in the corporate world where we all swore we would never go. I reluctantly realized that, if I were going to survive, I would have to go there too. But as usual, I decided to do it hippie style.

Instead of *being* the Man, I would plant plants for the Man. Then, at least, I could remain the Earth Mama I thought myself to be. So when I finally got clients, I showed up with big hippie hair, small shirts, and patched jeans doing the watering, planting, and weeding that nobody else wanted to do in the 100-degree heat of Texas summer.

Over the years, my company has grown; and at least on the surface, I've slowly become the Man I railed against, complete with a corporation, real estate, and nice cars. My dad would have been shocked at how his hippie chick daughter turned into an entrepreneur with actual assets on a balance sheet. There are, however, significant differences between the Man with the heart of greed who was the corporate villain of my younger days and the corporate team captain I try to be now.

The main one being that money has taken a back seat to creativity and the people who work with me. Today, I have a family of the most artistic and creative craftsman I have ever known. They are free thinkers that push every creative envelope to help build walls, rivers and gardens, not only connecting buildings to the ground but, more importantly, connecting the people inside those buildings to the earth. My team understands the importance of art for art's sake and works every day to create peaceful, inspiring spaces that bring all of us together.

Ashley Kent Carrithers: The Past Is Just a Goodbye

Like most of us, I was brought up in a pretty conditioned manner with homogenized templates presented rather ponderously. All involved fitting in with societal and industrial norms, studying hard, going to college, incurring some "friendly" student debt, sowing those pesky wild seeds for a moment, and then getting my nose to the grindstone of production and competitive consumption.

It all sounded fine, especially with the dangling cavorting carrots of wealth: country clubs, cruises, starter castles, etc., were presented as goals, goals worthy of sacrificing everything else until infirmity, obesity, and desperation delivered the ghastly promises of the gold watch, Tupperware parties, retirement to Arizona, and shuffleboard excitement with other wrinkled wrecks. Check please.

So, I was a good boy, subscribing to normality through prep school and during college. Got a bunch of A's. Was captain of the tennis team, a National Merit finalist, things like that. Married the cutest, most intelligent, and most socially connected debutante. Had a tented wedding on her estate—swans, an orchestra, and the mayor of Cleveland.

Today, many years later, as I pass the night under the stars in a mountain meadow, my mind transcends the throngs of mindless automatons who, in their vast and unrelenting multiplicity, are murdering the actual Earth I am cuddled upon. Away from schools, jobs, churches, and all the rest, I find some essential happiness cloaked in endless mystery that echoes in the infinite space stretching out in all directions.

Barry Sommer: Get Back

I'll willingly admit that by the late '70s I was married and on the path to a corporate existence. Well, if you can call working in Hollywood a "corporate" job, I was in the middle of it. My wife was a producer, and I was a local DJ doing voice-overs for radio and TV commercials. I quickly lost those hippie ideals I thought would be my driving force during adulthood, because the pressure and requirement to always be better tomorrow allowed no time for me to forward my hippie ideals or live them out, except for the six weeks a year when the wife and I vacationed in the desert east of LA.

It wasn't until I retired a few years ago that I saw my days as more than a time clock. Now that I can decide where, when and how I could be of the most help, I want to give back to those who need it, my community and the world around me. Now I volunteer at my local nonprofit community radio station and the local museum. I help with our annual Oregon Dunes City Triathlon, and I'm a local city planning commissioner. All this is very satisfying and humbling at the same time. Volunteer work, when one can see results from their dedication almost immediately, cannot be beat.

My selfishness turned to service for my fellow humans, and I feel so much better knowing I have the time to give back expressing the morals and ethics learned through my hippie family.

Dan T: Working for the Man

Immediately after high school in 1974, I left home for San Francisco. The '60s I was looking for were most definitely over. I landed with a bunch of guys who painted houses. A few jobs a month plus easily gotten food stamps was more than enough to buy food, weed, beer and pay the rent.

In the spring of 1975, Stephen Gaskin and some of his people came through San Francisco. These were the people I was looking for, and I fell in with them immediately. I ended up moving to the New York branch of The Farm where I continued in the house painting trade; but all the money went into the pot. In New York, we had fewer people than the Mothership in Tennessee; and we ate better. When I moved to Tennessee in 1978 and got married, things in the main commune had loosened to the point where people were allowed to have "Saturday money" that they could use for whatever. I used it to fix up an old VW bus that we left in, never to return.

We ended up back in SF in 1979 where I immediately returned to house painting, old Victorians this time that always needed paint. I put together a crew of guys and tried to keep up the camaraderie that I had come to savor on The Farm. A toke in the morning to bond, and off we went.

I had acquired another old VW and found I liked fixing cars, so I started a small side-business doing so on the street. Moonlight Motors was born. At first, I tried to give everyone a break by charging cost for parts. That lasted about a month as I had rent to pay etc. After our second daughter was born, I realized I needed a real job and got one doing the same kind of work. As it turned out, I wasn't hired for my experience but because I'd lived on The Farm. Hippies from there had a reputation as honest and hard working.

We moved east in 1983, and I am still fixing cars 38 years later. Six years ago, I started a business called Moonlight Marine, building and repairing kayaks and canoes. My business has grown organically. Word of mouth has done it all.

Compared to working with hippie folks on The Farm, I don't think of my later work experiences as "working for the Man." But I have missed being part of a crew of like-minded people, working hard, sharing a common goal, enjoying good vibes, and trying to do something positive for the planet.

I still get some satisfaction from fixing things; but as the role of fossil fuels in global warming becomes more obvious, the more conflicted I feel. Now more than ever, I'm eager to transition full-time from fixing cars into my boat-building trade. Within the kayak community and the nonprofit groups with which I associate here in the Hudson Valley, I find the same common spirit that I first encountered at The Farm.

For 26 years, I served on our community association board trying to keep the community spirit alive—with no pay, of course. My wife is a library director and is focused on community service.

Ray York: Does Anybody Really Know What Time It Is?

In 1973, our commune signed a bill of sale for 670 acres of land on a mountainside that sloped down to a jade-green river. For that glorious piece of real estate, we paid $100,000, a paltry sum now, but enormous then. We agreed to pay $10,000 a year for ten years. True to our lineage as twinkle-eyed hippies, we had no idea at all how we would pay for it. But we were already in love with the land.

We had no income-producing skills. We could cook and cut firewood, ride horses and herd cattle (the land came with a small herd), grow zucchinis in a garden, and even build a small dam to water that garden and to provide drinking water for our kitchen. But how to come up with 10 grand a year was almost beyond our imagination. Sell pot? That was more complicated than it seemed, and dangerous. We had no desire to break the law. Sell cattle? Our cattle were skin and bones. The first payment loomed.

Then we heard through the grapevine that the 10,000-acre horse ranch just north of us needed hay for their horses. Lots of it. We did a little arithmetic on our fingers and saw that, if we succeeded at this, we would have our money, and signed on to supply the hay.

The job was enormous. We rented a flatbed truck, bought hay hooks, learned trucker's knots to secure the loads, and began. We'd make the trip to the valley, 20 miles below, load the truck with bales of hay, drive it back up to the horse ranch, and deposit it in their barn. Over and over. With two crews, men and women in each, we made two trips a day. It was exhausting, grueling work, most of it under a hot sun; but we persisted. In a month, we had made our $10,000 and more, with days to spare. Skinny men grew muscles, and the women were a revelation. They couldn't always hoist the larger bales; but they could do everything else, including driving the truck.

I remember driving to a remote field in the valley at dawn with mist rising from the earth like a scene from a Millet painting, with Chicago playing on our boom box: "Does anybody really know what time it is?" I felt blessed doing this work. It was primal; it was ennobling; and for some, it was redeeming.

We repeated the process every summer for ten years, until the mortgage was paid off. It was great to be able to work really hard for one month and play for eleven. And every year since, 46 so far, we have celebrated our feat.

Looking back, I see that our hard work gained the respect of our non-hippie neighbors, many of whom must have assumed we would fail. We had disproved the myth of the lazy hippie.

J Laurence: Love Animals. Don't Eat Them.

In a small community in Southern California, the early '70s launched an array of new directions, one that forever changed my life. A food co-op, called "Love Animals Don't Eat Them," offered local produce, organic bulk foods and health remedies along with spiritual educational resources. The co-op was staffed by members, a new concept for me at the time.

Here, members received credits for hours worked which could be applied to purchases or shared with other members. When educational programs were available, credits could be applied towards the cost.

The social aspect was not only unique, but in ways, similar to the "social networking" we have today. Memories of laughter, intellectual and spiritual discussions, sharing of nutrition knowledge and, on occasion, interacting with spiritual masters that wandered in created a center of "nourishment" for mind, body and soul. Already vegetarian, as well as experienced in the kitchen, I found myself involved in various capacities, learning constantly. One of the more important "breakthroughs" was learning how people can "cooperate" in an environment that supports open dialog and non-violent communication.

In addition, the mastery of being responsible, conscious and present, concepts I was aware of but had not yet embraced, enhanced my life in many ways. Associated with the coop was a "family commune" where I was also a member. Looking back, were it not for my learning the communal system of living, I might have suffered drastically during the many months of couch-surfing that followed.

Jean T: Moondance

At four years old, I remember sprawling on our lawn, pondering life, death, and reality as I understood them. As a schoolgirl, I believed every word Jesus taught, while recognizing that church doctrine and behaviors considered moral by society fell short of the Love Jesus was talking about. My father, a minister, had an image to uphold in the community. My life seemed a prison within a goldfish bowl with God, my parents, and the congregation watching my every move.

Once, after a rain, my teenaged friends and I, having thrown off our shoes with abandon, splashed through water that gushed along the curb of a local park. I'd felt happy for once, empowered and free. Instead of rejoicing with me, my parents chastised me, saying what if I'd been seen in my jeans and no shoes? Why, people might think I was a hippie! Stunned, I determined right then to become one. I stopped listening to my parents or my religion.

Later on, from the round, open door of a tipi in central New Mexico, watching Venus move across an early sky, I felt the magic of dawn, the earth beneath me, and the power of the natural world. Each morning, I pulled fifty buckets of water from an old hand-dug well on our property, looking out to the mountains beyond. Now and again other hippies stopped by. Sometimes we threw together a sweat lodge out of willows, blankets or tarps and danced bare breasted under the moon, flames from our fire bouncing shadows upon the trees. It felt sacred and connected me in ways I hadn't fathomed to the spirit that lives in all things.

But one can't stay in Neverland forever. I left New Mexico for Montana. Those were hard times for hippies who were aging into their thirties, choosing parenthood, and getting real jobs. Boys cut off their hair on their way to becoming businessmen. Reluctantly, some put on suits and ties. My husband earned an engineering degree, and we moved to Seattle to work for "the man." I was a soccer mom. We took out loans from a bank.

Still, we raised our children differently, determined to hold true to our belief in a brotherhood of love, peace, and freedom. We upheld these ideals, while finding it difficult to achieve them within ourselves, our workplaces, our relationships. As my marriage fell apart, I began again to explore various spiritual and indigenous traditions and recommitted to my own personal growth.

Today, my kids are young professionals in the city. But they talk about taking Ayahuasca with a shaman in South America and of their deep respect for nature—our vision of a kinder, more compassionate world passed on to a new generation. Having come full circle, I'm in New Mexico, caretaking a large adobe in a small quirky town. From a nearby lava flow, I watch the moon rise over Carrizo Peak, just west of where the tipi sat and we danced under a darkened sky.

Kahish: Do You Believe in Magic?

My mother did not become a hippie. She always was one. When the hippie movement started, my mom fit right in. She was in her late thirties, which was older than many embracing peace and freedom, and also different in the sense that she had her own philosophies about her role in this world and society.

I remember getting evicted from the last house we were living in. We had always rented a place, but my mom just didn't pay bills, thinking God would always provide. With no food, possessions, or a real plan, we wandered around the park to catch a place to crash, which was ironic. In the preceding two years, we had been taking in transients ourselves. After asking a few people, someone referred us to another person who invited us up to his small apartment. He said all five of us could spend one night, including my two other sisters, my mom, a homeless acquaintance, and me.

While we were there, I recall my mother delivering her typical monologue about reincarnation, the 144,000 chosen people and the psychic abilities in these end times. Our host countered everything she said by bringing out the I Ching book and cards, presenting a reading, and declaring that this was the only real manifestation of truth.

Today, I give space to people embroiled in their own belief systems. There is never any way to present alternatives that they may embrace. I believe that each person has his/her own path and that they learn and grow at their own pace. While each person's contributions may affect others, the intended target rarely gets the message.

Wanda H: Money

I've been rich, and I've been poor. Rich is better, mostly.

I grew up in genteel poverty. Despite the tight budget, my parents instilled in their large brood a traditional sense of propriety—respectful behavior, honesty, modesty, hard work and achievement. One of their canons was that well-bred people *never* discuss money; so, we kids grew up without a clue about our financial status and with only a vague awareness that we were a little bit poor.

When my generation came out as hippies in college, we all dressed down in solidarity with the less fortunate. We rarely knew each other's financial standing. We hitchhiked, shared food and class notes, and traded skills. Being penniless was a common bond, and no one gave it much thought.

When we graduated or otherwise faced self-support, we suddenly had to redefine our relationships with money. We needed clothes for work and a place to live. Reliable transportation became essential, as did grocery money. As we married and started families, we became responsible for the welfare of others. The wide world functioned differently than had our sharing economy. We had to acknowledge *money* as the necessary medium of exchange in the adult world, and we had to concern ourselves with acquiring it.

I was hired into a well-paid position upon earning my degree. After a short period of confusion and over-spending, I learned how to manage my money. I lived comfortably but within my means, purchasing my first house a few years after graduation. Realizing early that I would be old someday, I stayed at that first job long enough to earn a vested pension, a lifesaver today in my retirement.

In mid-life, bad times arrived in the form of a debilitating illness that ousted me from the workforce years before my anticipated retirement date. Fortunately, the proceeds from selling my mortgage-free home and my well-honed "making do" skills enabled me to weather the temporary storm. Eventually, I recovered sufficiently to buy another home. I rebuilt an equity cushion that, sadly, was wiped out during the financial crisis, when I used it to bail out my son and his family. We have survived 2008, but we are not thriving. I've been poorer, but I've certainly been richer too.

These days, my attitude toward money is "$10 short at month's end = extreme stress; $10 over = a good night's sleep." I prioritize my needs and wants. I live in a quiet, safe zip code and maintain an adequate "emergency" fund; but I no longer try to afford travel and restaurant meals. I'm glad for my early experiences with frugal living, both as an unspoiled child and as a flower child. I've never felt "entitled" to material wealth or envious of those who have earned a lifestyle more comfortable than mine, although I deeply resent those who've cheated their way into "the 1 percent." I am content in my elder years; because I have "enough," and have always played fairly with others, including financially. Sure, more mad money would be fun, but a clear conscience born of hippie ethics and that surplus $10 per month are all the wealth I really need.

Sal Polcino: Sex, Drugs and Rock and Roll

You are 16, and you go to work in a factory that paints bombshells headed to Vietnam. It doesn't matter what you think about the war. Even as your friends are headed to fight in that god-forsaken jungle, you are nearsighted, with but only one goal: to buy a Fender Stratocaster electric guitar like Jimi Hendrix's.

You drop out of school. Seek out sex, drugs and rock 'n' roll. Grow your hair out. Go to Woodstock with your brother. Fight your way through the rain and the muck and the horrible hippies for a spot on the hill where you can see the performers. Fall asleep and miss most of the show while bearded, naked, slovenly dropouts trip over you and call you names. Walk through human feces back to your brother's brand-new cherry red Camaro and leave on the second day of the festival. You go home, cut your hair, and learn to play soul music. Pick a new hero—James Brown. Start experimenting with drugs. Discover cocaine, the miracle brain food.

You spend your twenties getting laid, playing Top Forty and tending bar in pick-up joints in Seattle. Hear electric jazz for the first time and aspire to a new goal, a new hero—Miles Davis. Practice for ten more years.

You work through your thirties managing a jazz club where you meet all your heroes, including Miles, while putting tens of thousands of dollars up your nose. Move 1,200 miles away to try your hand at the big time in Hollywood. Meet some of the best players in town and become part of the hippest set before meeting a Seattle girl who takes you back to the misty mountains of Washington state.

You get married, buy a house, and take a job running a warehouse. Feel empty and stagnated. Do more drugs. Come home to find your wife has cleaned out the bank account and run off with a crack dealer. Get clean and move back to LA.

You discover your friends have all moved on or become incredibly successful. Falter around looking for work. Work as a background actor for four years barely paying the bills, yet having fun and working with celebrities. Hit bottom financially.

You form your own band with weekend warrior musicians that have day jobs now. Make a record that hits number one on the college jazz charts, but receive royalty payments of twelve cents a quarter. Give up.

You suddenly remember that, according to Mr. Jeffries, your high school English teacher, you have a talent for writing. Blog for your band. Get noticed. Blog for some famous bands. Sink lower into financial oblivion. Have a family member suggest that you go back to school and get grants and loans, while honing your skills. Go back to school.

You fall in love with journalism and write for the school paper. Become editor-in-chief then production manager. Get noticed again and write freelance for the *Times Community Newspapers*. Keep playing jazz around town.

You learn the lesson here. Have a backup plan and stay in school.

What Now?

Is the Hippie Nation still alive? And more importantly, is there still a chance for a worldwide Aquarian Age of love, peace, and understanding? Some contributors to this book are profoundly discouraged about the fate of the hippie ideals and the future of the world. Others believe the heart of the Nation still beats. This last chapter reflects their divergent perspectives.

For many years after my hippie conversion, I tortured myself for failing to live up to my ideals and failing to change the world in some "great" way. A Golden Age hadn't descended from heaven. Wars still raged. The greedy were still greedy; the violent, still violent; the suffering, still suffering. Nothing seemed to work, no matter how hard I tried.

Finally, I realized I had misinterpreted this whole Age of Aquarius thing. As it turns out, my purpose in life is not to change the world in some "great" way but in many small ways. I'm not here to be rich or famous, but to be humble and anonymous. My assignment is not to build skyscrapers, discover the cure for cancer, or sit in the Oval Office. My job is to help old ladies cross the street, feed my family, and leave this place a bit happier than I found it.

But what about the Aquarian utopia my generation was supposed to bring, the one full of harmony, understanding, and so on? As it turns out, maybe we over-promised. Maybe our mission isn't to make a perfect world but to make a better one. Maybe my generation isn't superior to any other but the latest incarnation of a human spirit longing to be happy and free. Maybe we're all doing the best we can. And that's enough.

At a time in our history when pessimism about the human condition seems epidemic, perhaps we have underestimated the power of ideals. As Victor Hugo said: "Nothing is stronger than an idea whose time has come."

Maybe hippies are "naïve dreamers" as some critics have said, but that's a good thing. Those who see light in the distance, when others see only darkness, are the ones that keep us moving forward, the ones that give us hope when all seems lost. Hippies didn't originate the concepts of love, peace, and freedom; but they had the audacity (as Barack would say) to believe such things are still possible.

I believe the world is getting better all the time. We are evolving into kinder, more peaceful human beings despite what we witness on the evening news. No amount of pessimism or regressive national policy can reverse the natural evolution of people becoming their better selves.

When I look around, I see the everyday folks living peacefully with each other regardless of gender, color, nationality, religion, sexual orientation, age, or disability. I see sincere smiles and polite respect. I see tolerance and kindness. I see acceptance, if not totally in heart, then in deed. I see what makes America great ... its people.

Of course, there are exceptions. Murderers, rapists, thieves, and abusers of every kind still vomit their evil onto the world. Of course, good people must do what they can to oppose them and heal the damage they have caused. But I think it's important to remember that the bad actors are the exception. People who practice peace and love in their own small ways are the rule. We are the calm sea, peaceful and powerful, that appears after the storm and cannot be destroyed.

At this particular moment in history, we have a president who seems to distain every value that America represents. To some, The Donald is the antichrist who will destroy the country. I disagree, not because I support him in any way; but because, in the long term, he's done us a favor.

His pied-piper rhetoric has encouraged the haters and hurters to crawl out from under their rocks into the light where we can clearly see them. This is not to say that all of Trump's supporters are "deplorables" as Hillary once said. Absolutely not! I'm totally convinced that the vast majority of those folks, like the vast majority of all voters, are good people doing what they think is best for the country. No, I'm talking about the neo–Nazis, women abusers, pedophiles, homophobes, bigots, and warmongers who are increasingly showing their real intentions.

As the 1960s and early '70s taught us, seeing evil is the first step in stopping it. When the general public clearly saw villains like Birmingham Police Chief Bull Conner directing attack dogs and fire hoses against civil rights demonstrators, long-time FBI Director J Edgar Hoover breaking every law to stop Dr. King's crusade for equal rights, Chicago Mayor Daley sending local police and National Guard units with "orders to kill" against anti-

war demonstrators at the 1968 Democratic Convention, Georgia Governor Lester Maddox enforcing segregation at his restaurant with a baseball bat, VP Spiro Agnew taking bribes in the White House, and Nixon orchestrating dirty tricks against his "enemies," things changed.

Civil rights legislation was passed. Crooks were forced out of office. Many folks began questioning authority as never before. Soldiers returned from Vietnam. Minds and hearts became more open.

The Donald is inadvertently giving us the same opportunity to see evil for what it is and do something about it. By bringing ugliness into the light, he's awakened kind, quiet, previously silent people to the fact that, despite the passage of laws and the passing of decades, bigotry still exists in America. Discrimination still exists. Abuse still exists. It's not an illusion or a product of somebody's "fake news." It's real; and it's here in America, not everywhere, of course, or even in most places, but it's here.

The Prez has forced us to make a choice. Do we want his version of America built on self-interest, division, greed, and fear? Or do we want an America that guarantees liberty and justice for all? Do we want an America that builds walls or one that echoes the words on the Statue of Liberty: "Give me your tired, your poor, your huddled masses yearning to breathe free?"—S.L.R.

Jack Jacobi Verde: Magical Mystery Tour

A person enters a reality of time when love was surrounded by the light of God; so beautiful HIS presence, so wonderful His song. How wonderful to have been part of this family of love, at that holy time when people sought peace in infinite love, forming a light of that shone outward from their faces into a crystal of flowers and feathers all those voices that sang in the open air of the '60s.

I was there in all its magnitude of wonder and light that came from within the stream of the tree of life. It was nothing less than a miracle, a collective conscious in action, a peace and a love that came from within unto a world of pain and war.

Within the hearts and souls of all those that chose to enter inside a grand spirit of love that showed itself in those days, we can say that we conveyed the image of God, transcending time and space unto a realm of wonder and infinite adventure. Within the very soul of all that is and will ever be good in humanity, there I saw it shining in the faces of freed souls as I looked into their eyes, those hippies of the '60s now gone.

Today, we have lost our way from that inner circle into a diseased realm. I miss those days! I miss the spiritual life, I miss myself lost into a mad world of things and greed. What happened to us? What is this disease that plagues us now?

We have died and don't see them anymore! We are victims of a nightmare someone thought of, and through their great hate, made a dark hole for us to be buried in. I feel a great loss. I feel that we have been murdered for and by things, for trinkets, for rags that we hang on our corpses. I mourn our passing! It is so sad, so very sad!

Barry Sommer: The Needs of Many

In the late '60s as I quickly approached draft age, I wanted to believe that global peace would break out any moment. I desperately wanted the peace movement to take hold, yet there was a bit of self-preservation and ego involved. I didn't want to die in a far-off land for a cause I had little interest in, and my dad didn't want to lose me either.

I felt that the more we all believed in the same goals, which us hippies laid out as a manifesto of sorts (through music, poetry, protests, etc.), the more the world could be healed of its bigotry, hatred and xenophobia. It appeared to work for a short while, until man once again decided he as an individual was more important than society as a whole.

The strides made through the 80's evaporated by the mid 90's, done in by the greed that became rampant, the ugliness of class warfare, and the beginning of the end of the middle class, all precipitated with the abandonment of social mores and the rise of the "Me" ideals. We have progressed; yet in many aspects, that progress has been backwards.

I had high hopes for a sea change in thinking, but it seems everyone has ignored the Star Trek rule which states "The needs of the many outweigh the needs of the few ... or the one." Today we have identity/tribal politics and a chasm instead of a community. Our hippie belief in the oneness of humankind has been relegated to the dustbin of history like a small exhibit at some museum.

Lew Jones: Hey Jude

Fifty years ago, I was a 17-year-old high school student who didn't drink or smoke. By the time I was 19, I was drinking beer and smoking pot. That year, a friend took me to Gresham, Oregon, to see the Grateful Dead. All the Bay area bands would play there, because it was a safe place to get high. I thought the Dead were really bad for destroying the song "Good Lovin'" by The Young Rascals; while their fans, wearing giant smoky hair mops and colorful clothes, danced in sweaty circles, arm in arm, ripped on the acid in the wine being passed around.

In Gresham, Oregon, there was a place called Springers Ballroom out in the country. All the San Fran bands would play there, because it was safe place to get high. When I saw Canned Heat, I was shocked to see how way-out the Bay area hippies really were.

Today, I remember the feeling that other social realities exist. The concept of diversity was central to how hippies lived their lives. Because I was a hippie, I can easily integrate with other cultures. I maintain my values by living clean, eating vegetarian and prayer. I remember the leader of The Rainbow Family telling me once that when people are cruel and intolerant, "you have to out-love them."

I think of life as "we" rather than "I." I play music that still leans on a surreal creative sound. My heroes are still John Lennon, Jimmy Page, Jim Morrison, and The Beatles. I follow the words to Hey Jude: "Don't you know it's a fool who plays it cool by making his world a little colder."

Even though I haven't smoked any in 35 years, I still think pot is a young way to be happy and that no one should go to prison because of it. While nobody liked to work back then, today, I relish a solid day that pays my bills.

Today, our society sells hippie culture on info commercials as a fad rather than a revolution. It's weird to watch commercials selling compilation CDs of our precious time of freedom. The good do die young, as we can see by the bloated, facelifted nostalgia singers jerking at our purse strings. I still value peace and love and incorporate these values in my dealings with others, but to render the hippie movement as an antique roadshow is disheartening. It's hard to see emotional monistic voices lauded as mega-hit makers, violence treated as a means of entertainment, and love stories used to neutralize the magic of sex.

As hippies long ago, we were like lost souls, too young to grasp the hardships our World War II parents endured. Vietnam and Iraq were both reminders that chanting has no power to stop war. Today, it's all bought and sold with no delusions that butterflies will stop tanks. Hippie values might have been our last attempt to be human beings. I still embrace the core values.

Susan Hawke: Tell It Like It Is

I watched the harmonious, healthy ideals of the hippies in the 1960s downward spiral into belligerence and addiction in the 1970s. Turned out freedom wasn't free. I also navigated the nuances of mass self-exploration that "devolved" into nihilism in the 1980s. Violent Arnold Schwarzenegger movies and spectacular Michael Jackson records made millions in pop icon Madonna's "material world." But so did the "We Are the World" records and "Live Aid" concerts that raised funds for famine relief in Africa. Americans embraced altruism on a global scale.

I found sweet relief in the "anti-ethos" of the 1990s. I'd joined with those who rejected popular hype and instead reveled in new sub-genres of art. This included the rise of grunge music, the advent of hip-hop, the resurrection of spoken word, and creative expression for its own sake. A decade later, I was stunned to see flannel shirts and hiking boots adorn storefront mannequins in New York City! Again, I felt the queasy swing of our pop culture pendulum to another, over-exposed extreme.

I listened to the dramatic drumbeat of the media that accompanied these cultural transformations. At times, I participated in media missions to trigger emotions myself. Accuracy somehow became secondary, a real concern as we consume more information in larger amounts at higher speeds.

Today, the line between "news" and "entertainment" is blurred. In the 21st Century, the perennial chicken-and-egg question remains: Does mass media simply give the audience what it wants, or does it actually "create" our conversations? Who are "the media" now, anyway? Why, it's you and me!

To make the world a better place, I am simply slowing down. I try to reserve judgment until I know the facts. I try not to overreact to the sound bites I hear and the news segments I see. I place a high premium on accuracy. Truth is power. Truth is *everything.*

I now know it's *not* necessary to ride each swing of our popular culture pendulum to its farthest end. To make a positive change, I try to be patient, compassionate, and calm. I try to stop long enough to *listen* to the views of those in my vicinity: People like you and me.

Risha Linda Mateos: Space Oddity

I honestly feel I was born on the wrong planet—war, rampant consumerism, environmental degradation and species destruction are all so repulsive to me. I often find myself glad to be getting old and nearer to my jumping off point, since I cannot bear to witness the end result of our infinite growth on this finite planet. I believe that the current administration in government is the final nail in the coffin and only a new generation of "hippies" might be able to pull us back from the brink.

Rick Denney: My Generation

Growing up in the '60s, living values associated with the term "hippie" was a wonderful and unique experience. The power of that experience lingers fifty years later. As the saying goes, "It was the best of times. It was the worst of times." Early on, it was a time of peace and love, a time of care and compassion toward our fellow man.

Believing we could really make a difference, our ideals were focused on changing the world. Our values were not measured by the length of our hair or our unorthodox clothes. They revolved around a mindset. We searched for new ways to achieve a better world, using social discourse to question the status quo and challenge people to think outside the box. We used drugs like LSD to heighten our awareness and sometimes to deaden the thought that we were being unsuccessful in our attempts.

I don't know exactly when or where; but somehow, the movement began to break down. Looking back, it might have been destined for failure from the beginning. Each faction of the movement had its own agenda, philosophy, and mission. Many became infiltrated with people more interested in themselves than the original purpose, although some remain true to their cause today.

I would like to believe that '60s values can be carried on into future generations, that the dream has not died, that it can reinvent itself with the same compassion it had in the '60s. But looking around, I can't seem to locate anyone to pass the torch to. Can you?

Linda R: Eve of Destruction

In 1968, I was 15 years old, growing up on Main St. in a small, obscure town where there were no blacks, Hispanics, or Asians, only white families whose farms were passed on from one generation to the next. Sometimes, I still long for those long walks in the woods behind our house, the fact that we never locked our doors, and how neighbors looked out for one another in America.

At 18, I learned to play the guitar and often took it to school, playing Bob Dylan songs in the hallways. I went from wearing penny loafers, plaid skirts and turtle neck sweaters to wearing blue jeans to school for which I was given a three-day suspension. Thankfully, my friends started a successful campaign to have me reinstated.

During my senior year, I began questioning why my 18-year-old male friends were being sent to Vietnam to die on the battlefield but weren't allowed to vote. Why were university students protesting the War and four shot on campus for no reason? The times were ripe for cultural revolution. One of those changes that happened was a return to Christian values. Love One Another and the Jesus Revolution exploded.

Up to then, my biggest teen struggle was breaking away from my parents' demand to join "Rainbow Girls," an exclusive group for daughters of Masons/Shriners designed to turn young women into virgins and homemakers. This was the late '60s when "Make Love Not War" was our philosophy. My father was devastated as he told my family how my friend and I were sitting in the town square like "hippies." "How does a hippie sit?" I asked. That was about all I could take. The older generation simply could not grasp why us hippies were rejecting their cold materialistic society, why we wore ragged blue jeans and tie-dye T shirts, why we let our hair grow, why we longed to "get back to the Garden," as Joni Mitchell would say.

Those days of "All You Need Is Love" are now long gone. Since that time of natural childbirth, the joys of being a parent, and strong family ties, 60 million human lives have been wiped out through abortion, robbing our faith, our babies, our families, and our love, replacing them with AI, humanoids, and robots. Sometimes, I hear "The Star-Spangled Banner" and weep. When I go to Fourth of July events, tears roll down my cheeks when the crowd's cheers roar at the exploding fireworks. I weep for what was, and now is not, for the rose that is out of bloom, for the flicker of the flame slowly fading. In one short generation, a society whose democratic values was once emanated around the world has become one of the most materialistic, debt-ridden, war-mongering, violent societies the world has ever witnessed.

Tom S: Groovin'

In October of 1967, a funeral march was held in San Francisco for "the hippie," said to have been killed by too much fame when the Haight-

Asbury district was overrun by tourists, hippie wanna-be's, and parasitic hangers-oners who saw an opportunity to fleece the lost and vulnerable.

Or maybe the hippie era ended in 1969, after Charlie Manson and the tragic disaster at Altamont. The mainstream media, which had eagerly reported on a small group of free and joyous people taking something called LSD and listening to the Grateful Dead, now just as eagerly proclaimed the dark side of those supposedly "innocent" hippies.

No wonder so many true hippies had already headed for the safe anonymity of the hills. Those back-to-the-land communes came and went. A few survived, evolving into something long term, like Twin Oaks and East Wind. The mainstream press, of course, wanted to emphasize those that failed to show conservative Middle America that their materialistic world still ruled.

To me, the end of "hippiedom" felt like it came in 1980. Dylan was going through his born-again phase, becoming mostly irrelevant. John Lennon was assassinated on December 8, 1980, a sucker punch that told us The Magical Mystery Tour had ended.

But what really changed the course of time was the election of Ronald Reagan as president, taking the country in a direction it has never gotten over. Reagan despised the counterculture and everything it stood for. He sold the country a fantasy of Horatio Alger hucksterism and John Wayne bravado. "Trickle-down economics" that wiped out the middle class, "ketchup is a vegetable," and "If you've seen one tree, you've seen them all" summarized his politics.

The '80s seemed like a black hole in a lot of people's lives. Punk rock was ascendant, mocking every value for which hippies stood. Plus, too many hippies went from smoking a joint to alcohol and cocaine. "Greed is good!" replaced "far out man!" as the country's motto. Society moved on, and the hippie counterculture seemed more and more like a distant memory.

But if you're willing to look a little closer, beyond The Fame Machine, you'll find that values like love, peace, and freedom still live. The Rainbow Tribe still gathers every summer around the country to share their "good vibes." If you check out YouTube videos from that the hippie era, you'll find teenagers commenting on their wish to have lived in that time. Psychedelics are becoming a legitimate area of medical research.

"What a long strange trip it's been," sang The Dead. I can't deny mistakes were made; but if I had a chance to do it all over again, I'd be there.

Beth Richards: If I Had a Hammer

All we wanted was peace on earth, love and respect for all beings, fair sharing of the resources of our planet, and caring for the least of us. Was that too much to ask?

In the 1960s era, our songs instructed us on how we had to think to establish a better planet. We thought we could end war. "The Universal Soldier" would lay down his arms and embrace all enemies, would refuse to fight wars that benefit a few people who wanted to control everyone. "Peace Train" told us we could do this. We thought we would end racism. "Southern Man" would change his ways and embrace his brother humans of all skin colors; "We Shall Overcome" told us that it was possible to change the basic way our species thought and operated. We thought peace and love would reign on earth if we just believed in it enough. "Imagine" how we could all work together to change the world.

We were going to "Break on Through" to another side, to learn to live in love. "Teach Your Children" told us how to instill our ideals in the next generation. Bob Dylan told us in "Blowin' In the Wind" that this ideal might be nebulous, giving a warning that it might not work out so well, but reminding us to keep the vision. I maintain hope that we can pull ourselves together, that we can, indeed, overcome our fears and doubts and choose love and harmony as standards.

We have come a long way towards acceptance of differences, but we still have a long way to go. I pray that the ideals expressed in the timeless songs of the hippie era will stay on our radar and help future generations to keep working towards the message conveyed in "If I Had a Hammer!"

Janice L: Flashing the Peace Sign

The sixties were about peace and love ... or so we thought. The Vietnam War was raging and our boys were dying, and killing Vietnamese, even children. We were horrified. Why did the Establishment perpetrate this slaughter? Why were people of other races treated terribly? We were all children of God, children of the Earth.

My friends and I envisioned a world where people (and animals) could coexist harmoniously. Many of us became vegetarians, myself included, appalled at the way cows and chickens were raised. We saw a world in which money was not the ultimate goal. Sharing and having peak experiences were. We pooled our resources and opened free stores. Free clinics were established for the poor; and in San Francisco, the Diggers formed to help other hippies and runaways with food, clothing and other essentials.

We wanted children and adults to live free and unfettered on the land. We believed in Truth and Beauty, with capitals. We believed in the power of self-expression and the glory of the natural world. Organic gardening became very popular, and natural foods stores proliferated. Yoga began to be a common practice; and Eastern religions, with their transcendental practices, were introduced to the West.

I saw a world where people respected the planet and all of its inhabitants were living without poverty or oppression. Having made a visit to Peru, my birth country, at fifteen, I had seen the sad results of that oppression. I was fortunate enough to live in an upper middle-class neighborhood. My family lived in comfort, yet I observed that affluence did not always bring happiness. I rejected the status quo and the "straight" definition of success.

More than fifty years later, I am saddened to see that many of our dreams have not come to fruition. Poverty and racism are rampant. Violence is far beyond anything that we knew in those halcyon days. Economic injustice is more pronounced than ever and an obsession with the superficial has reached new heights.

However, I see hope in the youth. My grandson, four years old, plays with children of all races and nationalities, not noticing the differences. Some teenagers that I have talked to cherish the same ideals that we did back in the day, even in these harsh and cynical times. Transparency has become the order of the day, and all types of cultures are celebrated.

As a hippie mother who gave birth in 1973, I am proud to say that my son, and his children, are people who contribute to the well-being of the Earth and its inhabitants. I still flash the peace sign.

Noa Daniels: Across the Universe

The '60s and the '70s reflected the voices of a collective soul. It was a time when a spirit swept through a nation. It was a magic awakening of millions of young people inhaling life with one breath and exhaling a consciousness of that life with the next. It was a time to explore and celebrate, including all that lived and breathed. We embraced the reality that we were part of a much larger creation and creator. We not only celebrated the love within humanity, but also united under its banner. With one voice, we stood together as brothers and sisters, pushing back against the confinement that told us we could not. In defiance, we said, "Oh, but we can! There is no limitation in love and life, and you will not dictate to me. We will show you the way."

We rejected the lies that were told. No longer willing to accept the status quo, we embarked into the new land of the soul, freely expressing ourselves, accepting our bodies, connecting with others, and celebrating our music. We became one voice, one person. We took care of each other, because we were not strangers. We were family. When one voice spoke, we all listened; and voices were free to speak. We were encouraged to question. We listened to one another without sanctions, and we moved as one body.

So, what happened to this collective spirit? Like Adam and Eve, in our naivety, we went astray. We began to put ourselves first. Those of us who excelled greedily grabbed the power and, to this day, refuse to give it up. We saw younger generations emerge on our heels who did not understand the spirit, replacing it with something new but less pure.

We have become shallow. We admire ourselves, and the power we wield. Our children have been taught that comfort is their right, and there is no reason. They silence any voice of free expression, any voice that may question or debate or cause the uncomfortable. All are silenced as politically incorrect. There is no free speech, no dialogue, no appreciation of the mind or thought or of each other anymore. There is only a contrived stereotype of what should be and what should be made to be.

So where is that beautiful spirit once so wild and free? It lies quietly listening, watching, and waiting. It speaks quietly, but it still speaks. Like still waters, it exists in beauty. It is a voice that appreciates peace, values inclusion, encourages art, music and love. It mourns the loss of free speech and healthy debate, but it is not lost. It is real. It remains.

Do not be fooled. It is not weak. It remains deeply embedded in the collective soul and DNA of a creation born to be free. It is the spirit of humanity, and it will never be suppressed for long.

Beth Richards: We Can Work It Out

The message was strong: Love, not war, is the answer. The Vietnam War was raging, and so were the protests against it. The civil rights movement was alternately simmering in nonviolent marches and boiling over in ghetto riots. When the Summer of Love began in the Haight-Ashbury district of San Francisco in 1967, it was a reaction to the negativity and anger that permeated the news. We envisioned a more positive view of human potential and wanted to fill the earth with love, sharing and acceptance. We believed we could create peace and cooperation, certain that the old ways would fall away and everyone would support one another.

The drugs that were popular then, such as LSD, showed many users that they were connected with all beings, that we are truly all one. That realization led to widespread thinking that we can change the world by choosing to love and respect one another. Some of our cultural icons began exploring Eastern religions such as Buddhism and Hinduism, the tenets of which reminded us of how connected we are to the universe. The Beatles learned Transcendental Meditation from the Maharishi, The Who extolled the teachings of Meher Baba, and numerous gurus from India and Tibet made their way West to teach their version of peace and love. It all seemed so *possible!*

Many of us joined or started communes with the idea that we could share our lives. We tried hard to create this new and upbeat world that we all envisioned. I have lived in several communal situations, including the Farm in Tennessee with 1800 people following a vision of strong families rooted in awareness of the earth; the Love Family in Seattle that recreated a Medieval social structure of strong households tuned into serving God; and the Great Lakes Life Communities in Michigan, dedicated to ending nuclear buildup and war. All these new communities sought to embody love as the central driving force for changing how the world works.

Unfortunately, most of these attempts at intentional communal living eventually came apart. Human emotional tendencies like greed, envy, jealousy, and laziness made it difficult for people to tolerate one another and maintain the emotional stability essential for the long term.

Perhaps we humans are too emotionally complicated to be able to keep love central in our lives. Perhaps competition for resources and the desire for things, fed by masterful marketing, pulled us away from the dream. Today, many who experienced that era of hope back in the 1960s and '70s have become jaded, realizing that changing the world with the gospel of love is more difficult than it seemed and that dreams, thoughts, and prayers are not quite enough to transform a society. Even so, we are still working on ourselves and the world around us to make our dreams a reality!

Ocean M: Return of the Jedi

My parents where the original hippies. Actually, they weren't even hippies. They were "beatniks," as my mom corrects me—those poets and outcasts that thrived in New York and San Francisco during the 1950s, creating what has been quite accurately called "America's first counter-culture."

The beatniks were the seeds from which the hippie movement took root, blossomed and eventually transformed American mainstream culture. Don't believe me? Just ask The Beatles, or my ma.

I grew up in a house where "love is all we needed" and "peace will save the day." I went to a hippie school where we sang songs in a circle every morning, ate our organic lunches in the garden and went camping together several times a year. My parents were involved in civil rights movements, the anti-war movement, and the budding environmental movement—including things like "urban ecology."

The beats and the hippies opened the American psyche to Buddhism, psychedelics and a return to Native American style values, including a renewed respect for Mother Earth. They were going to change the world. I remember feeling that a new age was dawning. The force had awakened.

But then the eighties hit, featuring Reagan, the war on drugs, mass incarcerations, and conflicts around the globe, especially in the Middle East. The pressure was on to get a good job, make lots of money and buy big houses, cars and television sets. My hippie upbringing began to feel irrelevant—worse, it felt like a liability.

Extreme capitalism and materialism became the new standard. The Empire had struck back. The hippies faded away into places like upstate New York, Vermont, Oregon and Humboldt County, California, where my ma eventually ended up.

The 1990s saw the hippies pretty much dip completely off the radar. But the seed that they had sown began to bear fruit. Yoga and meditation became normal American pastimes. The environmental movement became mainstream. Organic food and natural healthcare became part of the daily life of millions.

I became a writer, escaping the so-called "land of the free" to live in less complicated places like Guatemala, Peru, and other hippie havens. Eventually though, my writing began to turn back towards many of those original hippie themes.

While living with natives in the Amazon, I learned about Ayahuasca, a potent psychedelic brew that has the power to change perspectives. I began writing about the environment, eventually getting my own environmental column in a widely distributed music magazine. I started writing about sustainable food production, socially conscious travel, solution-based environmentalism, and the power of plant medicines. Full hippie, full circle.

And now, the USA is in the grips of a crisis like it has never experienced before, one that will define its future and probably the future of life on earth. War, greed and environmental destruction are only checked by those lasting values of the hippie movement that still remain. It's a face-off that will determine the destiny of humanity, and it's looking grim, folks.

But don't forget, this is a trilogy after all. Now it's time for the Return of the Jedi. It's time for those hippie values, having congealed into a new relationship with the earth and each other, to overcome. And they will.

Don't believe me? Just ask my ma.

Stuart Glascock: Howl

I was a teenager in the early 1970s, but old enough to be deeply, deeply steeped in hippie philosophy. I was staunchly anti-war, pro–McGovern, anti–Nixon, pro-women's rights and pro-civil rights. I experimented with psychedelic drugs, smoked weed and hash. I saw Frank Zappa live in concert when I was 14. He was a trip.

I was younger than most hippies—in fact, too young to participate in the iconic marches, demonstrations and music festivals of the 1960s. But I was deeply influenced by them. I studied and emulated the culture of those folks who were just a few years ahead of me. I wanted to be like them. I wanted to *be* Abbie Hoffman. In the late '70s, when I met Abbie Hoffman, I knew for sure.

Years later, I saw Abbie again, speaking at the Naropa Institute in Boulder, Colo., at a writer's conference focused on Beat Generation writers. I sat in the front row, mesmerized. Abbie had reached middle age, but fire still raged in his belly. He talked about "How the '50s, '60s, and '70s led to the '80s."

He was on fire, in his element, unfiltered and surrounded by a thousand friends, probably all hippies. I'll never forget that night or that speech. Abbie was wearing a T-shirt that said "Howl Forever." It's become my unofficial mantra.

I'm approaching 60 and I still want to be like Abbie Hoffman, the Chicago 7, Mario Savio of the Free Speech Movement, the Students for a

Democratic Society (SDS), and the beat generation writers. They taught me to always stand up for what you believe and never turn your back on a social problem over which you might have some influence. My idols taught me about the right to free speech and the right to peacefully protest against your own government.

I believe the hippies forged great progress toward Democracy in this country. Hippie activists fought for and won many, many battles: freedom of expression, voting rights, student rights, sexual freedom rights, civil rights, anti-war demonstration rights, and more.

I was a newspaper journalist. Over my career, I've written for the *Los Angeles Times*, *USA Today*, *Asia Times*, and *United Press International*, among many other newspapers and magazines. I tried to elevate just causes and have the clips to prove it.

Now retired and unencumbered by the mainstream media nuance of objectivity, I'm a little more politically active again. What I learned from activism of the hippies is still useful today. Indeed, a new era of activism may be coming. Abbie Hoffman, Allen Ginsberg, Ken Kesey, Jack Kerouac, Tom Hayden, and Timothy Leary would approve.

Stack K: What the World Needs Now Is Love

I stumbled on a path in the dusk and unexpectedly came upon a clearing in the woods. I was hungry, and I had to move. A muffled chorus of Creedence Clearwater Revival faded behind me and then exploded in a roar from the crowd on the hillside. After a day and a half of overwhelming excitement, I needed a quiet space. Night plunged into the pines. Somewhere across the clearing, my little tent lay burrowed beneath the trees. I kept going. Waist high grasses waved silently in the mysterious, shaded glen. I rubbed my eyes and tried to focus. On the far edge of the field, a crackling fire under-lit a small village of painted school buses, tepees and tents. Forty hours earlier, the same spot had been empty, quiet and unknowing.

I walked the perimeter up against the woods and stopped by just short of the new camp. A dozen or so people moved in and around the site. On one school bus roof, a bearded man sat under a large, floppy leather cowboy hat, fingering a wooden flute. Beside him, a little girl wearing a flower print dress leaned against his leg, tapping her bare foot to the music he played. A band of young children spilled from the bus below and began running and laughing around the fire. I pinched a piece of tall wheat grass, put it to my lips, and let my eyes wander. A streak of red sky shot from the treetops and out to a fabric of dark purple beyond. Wisps of thin clouds threatened rain in the distance. I had to decide whether to venture through or circle around the encampment. I inched a little closer and veiled myself in the early evening shadow of a giant Scotch pine.

At the fire, a woman suddenly stood and adjusted a large black pot hanging above the flames. She poured liquid into the cauldron and emptied a bowl of cut vegetables into the pot. A startling scent floated across to my hiding place. I moved closer. The woman was beautiful; her movements, quiet and direct. I watched the slow, intent pace of her actions and absorbed the confidence of her presence, the grace and care of someone comfortable and intuitive with her gifts. The brew came to a gentle boil, and she dropped several handfuls of noodles into the concoction. She called to one of the children and whispered in his ear.

"Dinner's ready!" he shouted and ran around the campsite like a new age town crier.

The woman leaned to stir her creation. A long, dark braid rolled from her shoulder and over her breast. Slowly lifting her head, she looked up to me and smiled. I froze in her discovery. Her family slowly gathered around the fire, and she ladled the steaming noodles into an assortment of ceramic bowls. One by one, they were passed around the circle until each person was served. Fragmented energy became one. A quiet hush filled the woods, and I heard the low sound of the wind in the trees. She filled two more bowls, set one down in front of herself and held the other out to me. Only ten feet away, I still couldn't move. She whispered again to a child beside her, and the little girl stood up, walked over and took my hand.

"Come on. It's time for dinner," she stated in a tiny matter-of-fact voice and brought me to my place beside the cook. A sweet unfamiliar smell drifted up from the bowl in my lap. It led my eyes to a haphazard design of red pepper and green scallion strips swimming in a maze of thick, wide noodles. Bright green broccoli flowers next to shiny mushrooms. A coarse fresh herb and a handful of chopped peanuts rested on top. The bowl throbbed like an optical illusion, like the double image of a tropical plant. I lifted my spoon to begin eating, but the man next to me suddenly reached for my hand. I paused for a second, slightly confused; and the cook gently seized my other hand. Soon, I sensed every hand touching around the fire.

Two children giggled. "Stop it! You're tickling me, cut it out!"

The man with the flute spoke quietly.

"We want to thank the great Earth Mother for the food we are about to eat and the joy she gives to us each and every day."

The touch lingered. We held hands in silence, and I smiled at the woman who had just created this focus with her energy. She returned the smile, squeezed my hand, and let it go. This broke the chain and started the humble feast. People talked quietly and joked as they ate. No one spoke to me or asked my name. It didn't matter. A moment became fixed forever in time, a connection cemented by the magic of the senses fusing to the essence of my deeper soul.

Bowls were passed back for second helpings. I held them for the Earth Mother. She refilled them patiently, taking time to make sure each dish felt whole, adding a piece of broccoli or pepper, a little additional liquid, just enough noodles to every bowl. She finished each creation with the fresh herbs and peanuts. I devoured my second helping, while she watched me.

"Do you like it?" she asked.

"Yes, very much. But what is it, exactly?"

She smiled. "Noodles," she answered.

"But what is this flavor? I never tasted this flavor before."

"Do you mean the fresh ginger, or the sesame oil and cilantro?"

I didn't know what these things were. Her words flew right by me. I had another bowl and stayed a little longer by the fire. People slowly stood and moved away. Those remaining sat in silence, absorbed by the flames dancing through the fire. The Earth Mother disappeared into a teepee. I never saw her again.

Later that night, under warm light drizzle, I headed back toward the stage. I never did make it to my tent. There was no reason to. I knew something in me had changed, something had been made more aware. I sensed a true meaning in the continuity of life held together by shared experience. I understood for the first time the need for ritual. I was seventeen, sheltered and unaware. But now I was in love with ginger, sesame oil and cilantro. I was in love with Earth Mother. I was in love with life.

Early the next morning, when the rain stopped, I sat on a hill shared by half a million people. At dawn, Jimi Hendrix played a revolutionary version of the Star-Spangled Banner. I must admit, I was a little confused by the music. But somewhere deep inside, I knew what he was trying to say.

At Woodstock, there was very little fresh water access for the huge number of people. They didn't count on a half million of us. Long lines snaked from the few water spigots. You waited for an hour or more to fill your bottles, partying with the people on line around you. There was this one guy, with a long, strawberry colored braided beard who would wait and fill two big jugs and then walk around offering people drinks, especially new people coming in from the road. When his bottles were empty, he'd go back and stand on line. I saw this guy for five days on my way to and from the stage. It didn't even feel strange. We owned a new world. We moved to communes. The Water Man inspired us to share what we had.

I formed the essence of who I am by living through the sixties and seventies. But it's almost impossible to still carry all those beautiful feelings and hopes from that era, those precious ideals that blossomed for so many of us who came of age right inside the center of the hippie days. It's all there still in my heart: the love of freedom, of nature, of equity, of justice. It's just that there's a lot less people to share these beliefs and experiences with.

Obviously, the true concepts of the love revolution didn't last too long. People smelled money. Soon after Woodstock they were checking backpacks at festivals, not for drugs or weapons, but for food and beverages, all available at upscale prices inside. It was all over, over for the true meaning of the hippie movement, the rejection of the dull, non-creative, homogenized, restricted, complacent, neo-materialistic generation that preceded us and on into a new world of a group sharing lifestyle, filled with music, empathy and excitement. Music everywhere was the soundtrack for our shared lives together. But eventually even the music was co-opted. The communes came and went. We learned about trees and water sources and gardening. We learned up close how hard it is to share in freedom and equity.

We had kids, bought houses and put Caribbean vacations on credit cards. We tried to keep the ideals, or at least some of them, and project the image of freedom in our lives. As life moved further from 1969, materialism crept in and the struggle to maintain it grew every year. As a culture, our need to pay attention to the world began drifting away.

Friends started talking about investing extra money with "my guy." "You can double your money!" they said. You wonder if you should do it. What extra money? The '80s and '90s grew dark under the weight of capitalism. The hippies fell asleep.

Bush, Cheney and the invasion of Iraq shook the slumber. A little. Then Obama put the old hippies back to sleep. They thought everything was all right. It was time to protect their lifestyle for old age. They could feel good about being a hippie and still keep their stuff.

And then suddenly, Trump appeared. Are we really surprised to find ourselves living under Trump? And throughout the entire process, the digitalization of the planet has taken over and created zillions of individualisms on phones and computers, oblivious and counter to the very core of Woodstock values, ignoring the richness of one-on-one personal exchanges possible outside their doors. Preserving the ideals of hippiedom seems less possible than ever.

So, is there a chance to bring back the great days of the late sixties and early seventies? Can we see the light of future generations looking to return to the message of the hippies? Tune in, turn on, drop out! Be here now!

The same dire circumstances that we faced then seem ever present today. We can only hope that a more open and less materialistic generation will embrace and expand our hippie values. If time holds out, if we can keep the truth alive, if some of us hold on to the beliefs of a long, gone era; maybe someday, we'll see the return of the Water Man.

Hippie History

Year	Event
1960	Black students stage first sit-in for civil rights.
	The FDA approves the world's first commercially produced birth-control pill.
1961	Amnesty International is founded.
	Freedom Riders begin traveling to the South in buses to protest segregation.
	John F. Kennedy becomes president.
	The Peace Corps is established.
	Bay of Pigs invasion of Cuba ends in disaster.
	Soviets launch first man in space.
1962	Andy Warhol exhibits his Campbell's Soup Can painting.
	Joan Baez appears on the cover of *Time* magazine.
	John Glenn becomes first American astronaut to orbit the globe.
	Rachel Carson publishes *Silent Spring*.
	Peter Paul and Mary win Grammy for "If I Had a Hammer."
	Rolling Stones make their first public performance.
	Students for Democratic Society draft political manifesto "Port Huron Statement."
	U.S. and Soviet Union begin 6-day crisis over nuclear missiles in Cuba.
	James Meredith enrolls as first black student at Ole Miss.
	Marilyn Monroe dies of overdose.

1963 Betty Friedan publishes *The Feminine Mystique.*

First Nuclear Test Ban Treaty is signed.

Martin Luther King makes his "I Have a Dream" speech.

Pete Seeger performs the "We Shall Overcome" concert at Carnegie Hall.

President John F. Kennedy is assassinated.

The Equal Pay Act becomes law.

Buddhist monks burn themselves alive in Vietnam to protest the war.

Civil rights leader Medgar Evers killed by white supremacist.

Peter Paul & Mary win Grammy for Dylan's song "Blowing in the Wind."

1964 Beatles appear on Ed Sullivan for the first time.

Civil Rights Act prohibiting discrimination in facilities and employment passes.

Free Speech Movement begins at University of California at Berkley.

Gulf of Tonkin Resolution authorizes Vietnam War.

Ken Kesey and the Merry Pranksters transverse country in psychedelically painted bus.

Martin Luther King, Jr., wins Nobel Peace Prize.

Hard Days Night released by The Beatles.

Cassius Clay (a.k.a. Muhammad Ali) becomes world heavyweight boxing champion.

John Lennon's first book, *In His Own Write,* is published.

Lenny Bruce convicted of obscenity for nightclub performance.

Nelson Mandela sentenced to life in prison.

President Johnson declares "War on Poverty."

The Rolling Stones appear on *The Ed Sullivan Show.*

Three civil rights workers are killed in Mississippi.

Warren Report says Oswald acted alone in JFK assassination.

1965 *Help* and *Rubber Soul* released by The Beatles.

"Teach-ins" regarding Vietnam conducted by universities across America.

Bob Dylan booed at Newport Jazz Festival for playing electric guitar.

Cesar Chavez organizes grape boycott for worker rights.

First U.S. combat troops arrive in Vietnam.

Owsley Stanley starts LSD factory, making large quantities of acid available.

Race riots break out in Watts neighborhood of Los Angeles.

Voting Rights Act prohibits discriminatory voting practices.

Ken Kesey and his Merry Pranksters hold first, then second Acid Test.

It's My Life by The Animals is released.

Grateful Dead formed.

"Satisfaction" by The Rolling Stones tops the U.S. charts.

"Do You Believe in Magic" by the Lovin' Spoonful debuts.

Malcolm X assassinated.

Martin Luther King leads voting rights march in Selma, AL.

LA Free Press, first "underground newspaper," begins publication.

U.S. troops in Vietnam number 200,000.

1966 *Human Sexual Response* by Masters and Johnson is published.

Black Panther Party established.

Civil rights pioneer, James Meredith, is shot while marching across Mississippi.

First U.S. sex change operation takes place at Johns Hopkins.

National Organization for Women (NOW) is founded.

The Jimi Hendrix Experience debuts in London.

Crawdaddy, first rock n' roll magazine, debuts.

Students protest Dow Chemical, maker of napalm used in Vietnam.

"Monday Monday" by the Mamas and the Papas reaches #1 on the charts.

Revolver is released by The Beatles.

B-52s begin bombing North Vietnam.

"Good Vibrations' by the Beach Boys is released.

Simon & Garfunkel release album *Sounds of Silence*.

Radio stations ban The Byrd's "Eight Miles High" for "drug" lyrics.

Star Trek premiers.

Stokely Carmichael delivers famous "Black Power" speech.

The movie *Born Free* is released.

1967 "Flower Power Day" is celebrated in NYC.

Beatles release *Sgt. Peppers's Lonely Hearts Club Band* and *Magical Mystery Tour.*

Smothers Brothers Comedy Hour premiers on CBS.

100,000 antiwar protesters demonstrate in Washington, D.C.

First "Human Be-In" happens at Golden Gate Park in San Francisco.

Aretha Franklin wins Grammy for "Respect."

Age Discrimination in Employment Act becomes law.

Abbie Hoffman litters NY Stock Exchange with anti-war leaflets.

Anti-war group Another Mother for Peace is founded.

Arlo Guthrie releases *Alice's Restaurant.*

Groundbreaking film *Guess Who's Coming to Dinner* is released.

U.S. and USSR agree to prohibit nuclear weapons in outer space.

Priests Daniel and Philip Berrigan burn draft records.

"Light My Fire" by The Doors hits #1.

Muhammad Ali refuses military service on religious grounds.

Rolling Stone magazine publishes its first issue.

The Moody Blues release "Nights in White Satin."

The Turtles release "Happy Together."

Wildflowers by Judy Collins debuts.

Thurgood Marshall becomes first African-American on U.S. Supreme Court.

I'm OK. You're OK, a guide to transactional analysis, is published.

Che Guevara killed by Bolivian soldiers.

Youth International Party (Yippies) founded.

Cream releases its second album *Disraeli Gears.*

Jethro Tull is founded.

Otis Redding writes "Sittin' on the Dock of the Bay."

Race riots explode in Detroit.

The Graduate starring Dustin Hoffman is released.

1968 "In-a-Gadda-Da-Vida" by Iron Butterfly enters the charts.

Carlos Castaneda published *The Teachings of Don Juan.*

American troops in Vietnam peak at 536,000.

Back-to-the-land magazine *Whole Earth Catalog* is first published.

Armies of the Night, Norman Mailer's account of anti-war protests, is published.

Police beat protesters outside Democratic National Convention in Chicago.

Jimmy Paige forms Led Zeppelin.

Beatles visit the Maharishi Mahesh Yogi in India.

Joni Mitchell's debut album *Song to a Seagull* is released.

Love-in held at Malibu Canyon.

Lt. William Calley's troops massacre civilians at My Lai, Vietnam.

Martin Luther King, Jr., assassinated.

Police attack antiwar protesters in Chicago outside Democratic National Convention.

Robert F. Kennedy assassinated.

Rock musical *Hair* opens on Broadway.

San Francisco State creates first Black Studies program in U.S.

Shirley Chisholm becomes first Black woman elected to Congress.

Soul on Ice by black activist Eldridge Cleaver is published.

"The White Album" released by The Beatles.

Two Afro-American athletes raise Black Power salute at Olympic awards ceremony.

2001: A Space Odyssey is released.

John and Yoko release their album *Two Virgins.*

Richard Nixon elected president.

Students begin seven-day occupation of Colombia University.

Tet Offensive proves U.S. vulnerability in Vietnam.

The Band releases *Music from Big Pink.*

The movie *Yellow Submarine* premiers.

1969 *Abbey Road* released by The Beatles.

"Age of Aquarius/Let the Sunshine In" wins Grammy's Record of the Year.

Tommy, rock opera album by The Who, debuts in the U.S.

Native Americans seize Alcatraz Island and demand its return.

Beatles make last live appearance atop Apple Records.

Bob Dylan releases *Nashville Skyline.*

Crosby Stills & Nash release eponymous album.

Gays battle police at Stonewall Inn.

Two million protest Vietnam War across the U.S.

John and Yoko release "Give Peace a Chance."

Joni Mitchell releases *Clouds*.

Longest student strike in American history ends at San Francisco State University.

Man killed at Altamont rock concert featuring Rolling Stones.

Neil Armstrong becomes first person to walk on the moon.

Newsweek magazine declares 1969 as "The Year of the Commune."

Oh! Calcutta! an avant-garde theater production featuring full nudity, debuts.

Sly and the Family Stone's "Everyday People" is certified gold.

The movie *Easy Rider* is released in the U.S.

Weather Underground begins violent "Days of Rage."

Woodstock rock festival takes place in upstate New York.

Cream performs its final concert.

John Lennon and Yoko Ono start their "Bed-In" for peace.

1970 Construction workers ("hard hats") attack anti-war protesters in NYC.

Elton John releases "Your Song" in the U.S.

First Earth Day is celebrated.

Four students killed at Kent State during anti-war protest.

George Harrison releases *All Things Must Pass* album.

Dr. Benjamin Spock, famed pediatrician, is arrested for draft opposition.

Janis Joplin and Jimi Hendrix die of drug overdoses.

Environmental Protection Agency (EPA) is created.

Mother Earth News is founded.

National Organization for the Reform of Marijuana Laws (NORML) is founded.

Police kill two at Jackson State during student demonstrations.

Timothy Leary escapes from prison with help from the Weather Underground.

American forces bomb Cambodia as part of escalated Vietnam strategy.

Crosby Stills Nash & Young release *Deja Vue*.

Eric Clapton records his solo debut album.

Paul McCartney announces the break-up of The Beatles.

Santana releases *Abraxas* album.

Gray Panthers formed to protest discrimination against elderly.

1971 "The Farm," one of the earliest and most successful communes, created in Tennessee.

Be Here Now, a spiritual guide by yogi Baba Ram Dass, is published.

Activist environmental group Greenpeace is founded.

Rock opera *Jesus Christ Superstar* debuts on Broadway.

Ms. magazine is founded.

Jim Morrison dies of drug overdose.

Our Bodies Ourselves, women's guide to health and sexuality first published.

Led Zeppelin releases fourth album featuring "Stairway to Heaven."

Pentagon Papers, secret report on the Vietnam War, published in the *New York Times*.

Layla and Other Assorted Love Songs by Derek and the Dominoes released.

Sonny and Cher Comedy Hour debuts.

Tapestry by Carol King is released.

26th Amendment lowers voting age to 18.

Vietnam Veterans Against the War begin demonstration in D.C.

American Pie by Don McLean released.

Classic sitcom satire *All in the Family* debuts on TV.

May Day anti-war protesters try to shut down the Nation's capital.

Police kill prisoners and hostages at Attica Prison riot.

1972 *The Joy of Sex*, an illustrated sex manual, is first published.

Black militant Angela Davis is acquitted of murder and kidnapping charges.

Equal Rights Amendment sent to the States for ratification

Jane Fonda makes radio broadcast from North Vietnam.

Phillip Berrigan and others acquitted of plot to kidnap Henry Kissinger.

J. Edgar Hoover, FBI Director since 1934, dies.

John Lennon's film *Imagine* is broadcast on national TV.

Nixon re-elected as president.

Shirley Chisholm becomes the first black woman to run for president.

Watergate break-in occurs.

James Taylor/Carol King song, "You've Got a Friend," wins Best Song Grammy.

1973 American Indian Movement (AIM) occupies Wounded Knee in protest.

Billy Jean King beats Bobby Riggs in tennis "Battle of the Sexes."

Federal Rehabilitation Act prohibits discrimination based on disability.

Paris Peace Agreement formally ends Vietnam War.

Pink Floyd releases *Dark Side of the Moon*.

Roe vs. Wade decision by Supreme Court legalizes abortion.

Military draft ends.

Last American troops leave Vietnam.

John Lennon releases *Mind Games* album.

Last episode of *Rowan and Martin's Laugh-In* is broadcast.

Vice President Agnew resigns amid bribery charges.

1974 *High Times*, a monthly magazine about marijuana, is first published.

Nixon resigns presidency as a result of Watergate scandal.

Patty Hearst is kidnapped by the Symbionese Liberation Army.

Hippie Quotes

Mass civil disobedience can use rage as a constructive and creative force.
*—*MARTIN LUTHER KING, JR.

Darkness cannot drive out darkness. Only light can do that.
Hate cannot drive out hate. Only love can do that.
*—*MARTIN LUTHER KING, JR.

The struggle of our people for freedom has progressed to the form where
All of us must make a stand either for or against the freedom of our people.
You are either with Your people or against them.
You are either part of the solution or part of the problem.
—"To My Black Brothers in Vietnam," ELDRIDGE CLEAVER

I saw the best minds of my generation destroyed by madness,
Starving hysterical, naked,
Dragging themselves through the Negro streets at dawn
Looking for an angry fix....
—"Howl," ALLEN GINSBERG

The only people for me are the mad ones,
The ones who are mad to live, mad to talk, mad to be saved,
Desirous of everything at the same time....
*—*JACK KEROUAC

His hair has the long jesuschrist look.
He is wearing the costume clothes.
But most of all, he now has a very tolerant and therefore withering attitude

Toward all those who are still struggling in the old activist political ways,
While he, with the help of psychedelic chemicals,
Is exploring the infinite regions of human consciousness.
—The Electric Kool-Aid Acid Test, TOM WOLFE

They always say time changes things.
But you actually have to change them yourself.
—ANDY WARHOL

Burn, baby, burn!
—STOKELY CARMICHAEL

Acid is not for every brain. Only the healthy, happy, wholesome,
hopeful, humorous, high-velocity should seek these experiences.
Unless you are self-confident, self-directed, self-selected, please abstain.
—TIMOTHY LEARY

LSD melts in your mind, not in your hand.
—UNKNOWN

Drop acid, not bombs.
—UNKNOWN

We were very fortunate to have a little time in history
when LSD was still legal
And we were able to experiment with drugs just like we
were doing in music.
—JERRY GARCIA

When you smoke herb, it reveals you to yourself.
—BOB MARLEY

Reality is a crutch for people who can't handle drugs.
—UNKNOWN

Avoid all needle drugs. The only dope worth shooting is Richard Nixon.
—ABBIE HOFFMAN

If you remember the '60s, then you weren't there.
—UNKNOWN

I do my thing, And you do your thing.
I am not in this world to live up to your expectations.
And you are not in this world to live up to mine.
You are you, And I am I, And if by chance we find each other,
It is beautiful.
—Frederick Perl

Most people do not really want freedom.
Freedom involves responsibility
And most people are frightened of responsibility.
—Sigmund Freud

Free at last! Free at last!
Thank God, Almighty,
We're free at last!
—words of an "old Negro spiritual,"
quoted by Martin Luther King, Jr.

We shall overcome.
We shall overcome.
We shall overcome some day.
—Negro spiritual sung by
Civil Rights demonstrators

The New York State Freeway's closed, man.
Far out!
—Arlo Guthrie at Woodstock

Whenever you find yourself on the side of the majority,
It's time to pause and reflect.
—Mark Twain

If a man does not keep pace with his companions,
Perhaps it is because he hears the beat of a different drummer.
—Henry David Thoreau

Until the philosophy that holds one race, superior, And another, inferior,
Is finally and permanently discredited and abandoned,
Everywhere is war.
—"War," Haile Selassie/Bob Marley

Injustice anywhere is a threat to justice everywhere.
—THE REV. MARTIN LUTHER KING, JR.

Love gives naught but itself
And takes naught from itself.
Love possesses not nor would it be possessed.
For love is sufficient unto love.
—The Prophet, KAHLIL GIBRAN

God doesn't call us to be successful.
He calls us to be faithful.
—MOTHER TERESA

This way of "life" is a way of death.
To work for the industries of death is murder.
To know the torments Amerika inflicts on the Third World,
But not to sympathize and identify,
Is to deny our right to love—
And not to love is to die.
—REVOLUTIONARY FORCE 9, 1970

Every brother should have what he needs to do his thing.
—"The Digger Papers," THE DIGGERS

Make war on machines, and in particular,
the sterile machines of corporate death and the robots that guard them.
—Steal This Book, ABBIE HOFFMAN

Soul music taught us how to move our ass.
—ELDRIDGE CLEAVER

No nukes is good nukes!
—UNKNOWN

We will bury you.
—NIKITA KHRUSHCHEV, Soviet Premier

I know not with what weapons World War III will be fought,
But World War IV will be fought with sticks and stones
—ALBERT EINSTEIN

You cannot, simultaneously, prevent and prepare for war.
—ALBERT EINSTEIN

When the rich wage war, it's the poor who die.
—JEAN-PAUL SARTRE

Hell no! We won't go!
—ANTIWAR CHANT

Someday, they'll give a war and nobody will come.
—CARL SANDBURG

The truth is more important than the facts.
—FRANK LLOYD WRIGHT

Tell it like it is!
—HOWARD COSELL, Sportscaster Extraordinaire

All paid jobs absorb and degrade the mind.
—ARISTOTLE (384–322 BC)

Try not to become a man of success, but rather to become a man of value.
—ALBERT EINSTEIN

You're either on the bus or off the bus.
—KEN KESEY, quoted in Paul Perry's On the Bus

My advice to people today is as follows:
If you take the game of life seriously,
If you take your nervous system seriously
If you take your sense organs seriously,
If you take the energy process seriously,
You must
turn on, tune in, drop out!
The Politics of Ecstasy, TIMOTHY LEARY

I am no longer accepting the things I cannot change.
I am changing the things I cannot accept.
—ANGELA DAVIS

We have to talk about liberating minds as well as liberating society.
—ANGELA DAVIS

I am not a hoodlum. I'm a community organizer
—BOBBY SEALE

The task is to transform society; only the people can do that,
not heroes, not celebrities, not stars.
—HUEY NEWTON

We draw our strength from the very despair
in which we have been forced to live.
We shall endure.
—CESAR CHAVEZ

The gift we can offer others is so simple a thing as hope.
—DANIEL BERRIGAN

Lying and war are always associated.
—PHILIP BERRIGAN

Nuclear weapons are the scourge of the earth; to mine for them,
manufacture them, deploy them, use them, is a curse against God,
the human family, and the earth itself.
—PHILIP BERRIGAN

Very few people chose war. They chose selfishness and the result was war.
Each of us, individually and nationally, must choose:
total love or total war.
—DAVID DELLINGER

I never learned hate at home, or shame. I had to go to school for that.
—DICK GREGORY

Without freedom of choice, there is no creativity.
Without creativity, there is no life.
—DR. BENJAMIN SPOCK

It would be easier to pay off the national debt overnight
than to neutralize the long-range effects of our national stupidity.
—FRANK ZAPPA

I finally got it: empower girls and everything changes.
—JANE FONDA

We don't forgive people because they deserve it.
We forgive them because they need it—because we need it. We all need it.
—JANIS JOPLIN

Politics is how you live your life. Not whom you vote for.
—JERRY RUBIN

I have hope in people, in individuals;
because you don't know what's going to rise from the ruins.
—JOAN BAEZ

Instead of getting hard ourselves and trying to compete,
women should try and give their best qualities to men—bring them
softness, teach them how to cry.
—JOAN BAEZ

Peace is not something you wish for, it's something you make,
something you do, something you are, and something you give away.
—JOHN LENNON

The thing that gave me the most pain in life, psychologically, and it gave
me tremendous pain psychologically, is man's disrespect for nature.
—JONI MITCHELL

Love opens all doors, no matter how closed they may be,
no matter how rusty from lack of use.
—MAHARISHI MAHESH YOGI

If you're not ready to die for it,
put the word "freedom" out of your vocabulary.
—MALCOLM X

Having a place in society is far less important than
creating a society in which one would want to have a place.
—MARIO SAVIO

The Pranksters were just so much fun ... such a hoot.
We took time to have fun,
which is really rare in my experience as an American.
—MOUNTAIN GIRL

The self is just not a worthy enough vehicle to worship.
—PETER COYOTE

The human race is challenged more than ever before
to demonstrate our mastery,
not over nature but of ourselves.
—RACHEL CARSON

The more clearly we can focus our attention on the wonders
and realities of the universe,
the less taste we shall have for destruction.
—RACHEL CARSON

We're all just walking each other home.
—RAM DASS

The game is not about becoming somebody, it's about becoming nobody.
—RAM DASS

Brotherhood is an ideal better understood by example than precept!
—RAVI SHANKAR

Some men see things as they are and ask why.
I dream of things that never were and ask why not.
—ROBERT F. KENNEDY (re-quote)

I have learned over the years that when one's mind is made up,
this diminishes fear;
knowing what must be done does away with fear.
—ROSA PARKS

Traditionally, American Indians have always attempted to be the best
people they could. Part of that spiritual process was and is to
give away wealth, to discard wealth in order not to gain.
—RUSSELL MEANS

Service is the rent that you pay for room on this earth.
—SHIRLEY CHISHOLM

Dream the impossible dream and the world will not grind you under,
it will lift you up.
—TERRENCE MCKENNA

Whatever you are doing, love yourself for doing it.
Whatever you are feeling, love yourself for feeling it.
—THADDEUS GOLAS

We ourselves are imbued with urgency,
yet the message of our society is that there
is no viable alternative to the present.
—TOM HAYDEN

The war industry people are very together; they know exactly
what they want; they don't even have to talk to each other.
The peace industry people are just intellectuals who are
very critical of each other. Unless the peace industry is powerful,
we're always going to have war.
It is as simple as that.
—YOKO ONO

You become "hippie" when you realize how to be happy.
—UNKNOWN

Don't let the man keep you down.
—UNKNOWN

Why be rude when you can be nude.
—UNKNOWN

If everyone demanded peace instead of another television set,
then there would be peace.
—JOHN LENNON

All we are saying is give peace a chance.
—JOHN LENNON

Work like you don't need the money.
Love like you've never been hurt. Dance like nobody's watching.
—SATCHEL PAIGE

Never doubt that a small group of thoughtful,
committed individuals can change the world,
indeed, it is the only thing that ever has.
—MARGARET MEAD

*We must be willing to let go of the life we planned
so as to have the life that is waiting for us.*
—JOSEPH CAMPBELL

*Love takes off masks that we fear we cannot live without
and know we cannot live within.*
—JAMES BALDWIN

Your mind is like a parachute. It doesn't work unless it's open.
—JORDAN MAXWELL

*The only way to make sense of change is to plunge into it,
move with it, and join the dance.*
—ALAN WATTS

*When the power of love overcomes the love of power,
the world will know peace.*
—JIMI HENDRIX

And in the end, the love you take is equal to the love you make.
—"The End" by THE BEATLES

Index

221